To Don +
Thanks for your
support

Kirsch
05

MW01242929

To Don + Phyllis
Thanks for your
support

(signature) '05

Who Says I'm Small

By

J. B. Tischendorf

authorHOUSE™

1663 LIBERTY DRIVE, SUITE 200
BLOOMINGTON, INDIANA 47403
(800) 839-8640
WWW.AUTHORHOUSE.COM

© 2005 J. B. Tischendorf. All Rights Reserved.

No part of this book may be reproduced, stored in a retrieval system, or transmitted by any means without the written permission of the author.

First published by AuthorHouse 06/15/05

ISBN: 1-4208-2889-4 (sc)
ISBN: 1-4208-2890-8 (dj)

Library of Congress Control Number: 2005901654

Printed in the United States of America
Bloomington, Indiana

This book is printed on acid-free paper.

THE REVIEW

When Juanita Saxton found out she was pregnant, she was determined to do everything correctly to ensure her child's good health and happiness. She watched her diet, carefully researched the birthing process and quizzed her doctors. She even found a place to live that was more conducive to raising a child. When baby Erik came into her world in April of 1969, Juanita's life filled with light, and Erik was the sun.

However, it was not long before the happy mother noticed some peculiarities. Erik seemed to sleep for very long periods of time, and did not appear to be developing skills on schedule. While told she should be blessed to have a baby that did not fuss constantly, Juanita Saxton (now Tischendorf) was nonetheless concerned. Her unease at numerous doctor visits reached a crescendo when Erik was diagnosed at ten months old as being an achondroplastic dwarf. Bones that lack the cartilage cells that help them grow define this hereditary disorder. Affecting as many as 40,000 babies a year, achondroplasia causes shortened limbs, yet there is normal trunk and head growth. With this diagnosis, the author found herself having to put on a number of hats to complement the one she wore as a mother: she became a sleuth, a student, and a pillar of strength.

As seen through the eyes of his mother, the book chronicles in careful detail Erik?s struggle with achondroplasia, Their mutual journey toward overcoming obstacles in order to gain as much normalcy as possible is presented in a thoughtful and gentle manner. An opening sequence telling of Erik's respiratory troubles while on vacation reflects every mother's nightmare, and prefaces Tischendorf's determination to understand her son's diagnosis.

A family history of size disproportionate ancestors provides some clues, yet cannot change Erik physically. Ultimately, he undergoes surgeries and body braces, extended hospital stays, and the burden of having to learn to walk again following a paralysis. Yet, through his strong faith in those who cared for him and his mother's unwavering support, Erik persevered.

Any parent faced with the challenge of raising a special needs child will benefit from Tischendorf's story. The preparedness and calm of the mother who saw her child through a life-threatening attack pervades this book. She offers hope to those in similar situations with the realization that the belief in a happy ending can overshadow the greatest of difficulties.

Cymbre Foster, Editor
ForeWordreviews.com

DEDICATION

First and foremost this book is dedicated to Erik, but he shares this dedication with the individuals who played major roles in the successful conclusion of the story.

For my family's generous assistance in gathering information; for their patience, love and encouragement, I wish to show my appreciation. To each of you I dedicate this book.

To the doctors and nurses who not only gave Erik excellent medical assistance but also found time to demonstrate love and understanding, please accept my warm appreciation through the dedication of this book to each and every one of you.

ACKNOWLEDGEMENT

I would like to thank my husband Mark Tischendorf for the wonderful job he did in designing the cover background. I love you, Mark.

I would like to also thank Bruce Bearsley for providing advertising support in the wording of the cover and the press kit information.

PROLOGUE

So, I'm doing my quiet time, thinking there must be something more that I can do. I have read passages of the bible in the hope of finding an explanation, or at least a reason, for all of this. "What's the hardest part of being a mom?" someone once asked me, long before my expectations of motherhood had changed so dramatically. I thought about it for a second before responding that the hardest part was letting go.

When I made that statement I had no idea of its truth, at least not to the extent I know it now. There is so much more than I ever expected between birth and letting go. For starters, consider the pain of helplessness when placing the life of your child in the hands of strangers, or coming to terms with life by trying to deal only with the present while selectively forgetting the past and centering the future on no more than whispers from heaven. Those whispers gave me the inspiration to overcome hardships and to seek the love, courage and integrity to make it through yet another day.

FOREWORD

This is a true story—all of it is true—of one little boy's struggle to surmount the obstacles life placed in front of him and to behold the gifts of living.

My son, Erik, continues his trouble-laden climb. His fortitude derives from love, support and the will to survive. What may seem to be insurmountable obstacles are to him only temporary setbacks, slowing but not stopping his progress. Again and again, Erik struggles on.

I will reach out to shelter and protect him, offer him strength for fortification, yet Erik takes no more than he needs of what I am prepared to give. He knows that this is his journey and that there are times when there is little his parents can do to help him on his way. Success can only be achieved from within himself.

Erik is a survivor, an independent soul who will capture your heart.

BEING A MOTHER …

Somebody once said a mother is an unskilled laborer … somebody never gave a squirmy infant a bath.

Somebody once said it takes about six weeks to get back to normal after you've had a baby … somebody doesn't know that once you're a mother, normal is history.

Somebody once said a mother's job consists of wiping noses and changing diapers … somebody doesn't know that a child is much more than the skin he lives in.

Somebody once said you learn how to be a mother by instinct … somebody never took a three-year-old shopping.

Somebody once said being a mother is boring … somebody never rode in a car driven by a teenager with a driver's permit.

Somebody once said teachers, psychologists and pediatricians know more about children than their mothers … somebody hasn't invested her heart in another human being.

Somebody once said if you're a 'good' mother your child will 'turn out' … somebody thinks a child is like a bag of plaster of Paris that comes with directions, a mold and a guarantee.

Somebody once said being a mother is what you do in your spare time … somebody doesn't know that when you're a mother, you're a mother ALL the time.

Somebody once said 'good' mothers never raise their voices … somebody never came out the back door just in time to see her child wind up and hit a golf ball through the neighbor's kitchen window.

Somebody once said you don't need an education to be a mother … somebody never helped a fourth-grader with his math.

Somebody once said you couldn't love the fifth child as much as you love the first … somebody doesn't have five children.

Somebody once said a mother can find all she needs to know about child-rearing in books … somebody never had a child stuff beans up his nose.

Somebody once said the hardest part of being a mother is the labor and delivery … somebody never watched her 'baby' get on the bus for the first day of kindergarten.

Somebody once said a mother can do her job with her eyes closed and one hand tied behind her back … somebody never organized seven giggling Brownies to sell cookies.

Somebody once said a mother can stop worrying after her child gets married … somebody doesn't know that marriage attaches a new son or daughter-in-law to a mother's heartstrings.

Somebody once said a mother's job is done when her last child leaves home … somebody never had grandchildren.

Somebody once said being a mother is a side dish on the plate of life … somebody doesn't know what fills you up.

Somebody once said your mother knows you love her so you don't need to tell her … somebody isn't a mother.

CHAPTER 1
JUNE 27, 1988

I keep asking myself what can be said about a child's life when it appears to be ending before entering the next stage of living. Or, even if I knew what to say, how to say it? How do you translate the 'specialness' of your child so people can truly understand that it goes deeper than parental love; deeper, even, than what can be said of love in words? If I could break it down, separate love into piles, there would be one pile for parental love, one pile for love of friends, and another pile for the love of his relations. If I could extract and separate all the different kinds of love that exist in our universe in such a way, until the role players are bare of any of the physical or mental ornaments that are a part of the 'child bearing package', what would be left? Could it be seen, touched, smelled? Could it be understood without having known the role players before?

What is it? I guess you might say it is a case of having too much time to think. All I do is think. I think about God. He is the Supreme Being and his will will be done. But what could explain his will to take the life of my son? Should I thank him for allowing me to be Erik's mother? Would it be offensive for me to beg for more time? What type of prayer should I pray, or what must I do, to keep Erik with me forever?

What do I know? I don't know anything anymore, apart from the fact I can't take much more. Why can't things be normal?

Normal, ha! Now there's a concept. I don't even know what normal is. I don't think I've ever experienced normal. But I do know reality. Reality brings pain and suffering.

It was the end of June: a month that had been wonderful for us. Erik had graduated from high school with honors and awards, and we were in a position to give him the graduation present that he wanted most—a trip to California for the summer, to visit his Aunt Dorothy. It was to be a happy separation for all of us; there had been no reason to believe otherwise.

Sure, we had gone through more than the average parents in helping our child reach adulthood. But all of that was way behind us now. Little did we know we were about to face a medical crisis, the magnitude of which we had not experienced since 1976, when Erik was all of seven years old. Why now? What had we done, or not done, that we must be forced to relive history? My son had graduated and had been given his first opportunity to really spread his wings before going on to college. We should have been happy, only my world seemed to be falling apart and I didn't know why.

Perhaps the word 'normal' should never have been defined and placed in the dictionary to describe everyday life. Maybe I have been living a normal life without knowing it.

On Sunday June 26, 1988, Erik left for Mission Viejo, California. In Rochester, at 4:00 am EST the next day, I received a call from Erik's Aunt Dot. The conversation began with her asking me to listen to Erik's breathing, as she was worried about him. From three thousand miles away I listened to Erik breath as she held the phone to his mouth. He sounded congested but I told Dot not to worry, that he was probably just having some allergy problems and that if she got him some Teldrin in the morning it would clear up. Why should I have assumed anything else? Erik often had problems with his allergies during the summer months.

Dot relaxed and we continued our conversation. She had called nine hours earlier to let me know that Erik had arrived safely, so now we could talk just to take advantage of the phone call. I remember we were laughing, but I don't remember what had been said that was so funny. I do remember the tightening of my chest, making it hard to breathe, when I heard Dorothy say, "Wait a minute, something is happening."

That was all Dot said but the words cut through me like a knife. Call it a mother's intuition or sensitivity to disaster, but I knew something was happening to Erik. I knew there was cause for alarm.

I gripped the phone, waiting for Dot to say something more—anything. Then all too quickly her voice was back on the line, telling me what I didn't want to hear.

"I think Erik is having some kind of attack!"

The sound of my wildly beating heart resounded in my ears, making it hard to hear what she was saying. Dot tried to describe what was happening to Erik, but my memory banks had already retrieved the data from so long ago and pushed the dreaded information to the forefront. I knew that Erik was convulsing.

What should I do? What should I have her do? The answers were all in my head somewhere; I just had to locate them and verbalize them to Dot. Then, like so many times in the past, I found the strength to be able to take charge.

"Dot, keep calm. Lay down the phone and go to Erik. You have to make sure he doesn't bite his tongue. Try to find something to put in his mouth—something wooden or made of leather is best."

Dot didn't say a word. I heard the sound of the phone as it dropped from her hands and hit a hard surface, perhaps her table. I visualized it hanging from its cord, swinging like a pendulum, while I was in suspended animation, unable to do anything more than wait.

For the rest of that morning, Dot traipsed back and forth to the phone, alternately seeking support from me and tending to Erik when he started convulsing again. Having never faced this type of situation before, Dot was doing amazingly well. Knowing that she was in control of herself and the situation was some comfort to me. All she needed was my support and instructions to keep her going—I could not fail her now.

I thought back to when Eric had last had convulsions—I had taken him to Emergency, only to find his doctor wasn't there to meet us. The situation had been devastating, with Erik being transferred until his doctor finally arrived. I knew Dot had to arrange for Erik to see a doctor straight away—but would it be possible to find one?

This was a defeatist attitude, and it wouldn't help Erik if I continued thinking along that line. Of course the doctors in California would be capable of helping Erik. They had attended medical school, just like the doctors in New York, and would be well-versed in all sorts of illnesses and the complications related to physical handicaps. I just needed to explain Erik's medical history, and they would pick up from there.

When Dot was able to come back on the line again I told her to look in the telephone book for neurosurgeons located in her area. While she did this I pulled out my notes on Erik's medical history and laid them out on the floor. Though I knew most of it by heart, I wasn't willing to risk forgetting to mention something important once the doctor had been contacted. Of course Erik's regular neurosurgeon, Dr. Cotanch, and his pediatrician, Dr. Boettrich, would have to be contacted, to make sure his medical history was forwarded to the attending doctor, but the neurosurgeon would want to know as much as I could tell him straight away.

There was one plus in our favor: Dot worked for the telephone company in California, and therefore had three lines running from the one phone. She could dial on one line while I waited on the other, and then connect the lines for a conference call. Having found the number of a local neurosurgeon, Dr. Peterson, I could hear Dot whispering, "Please, oh please answer", as she waited for the call to connect. When she got through to Dr. Peterson's answering service, she was barely able to talk through the choking sobs building in her throat, but managed to explain to the operator that her nephew was having a seizure. When asked if Erik was a patient of Dr. Peterson, Dot explained that he was visiting from New York, then repeated that he was having a seizure, and that he needed to see a doctor immediately.

In a controlled, authoritative voice, the operator told Dot to remain calm and that the doctor would respond shortly. She advised Dot to watch Erik closely in the mean time and record the details of the seizure. To help her with this, the operator listed a series of things to look for.

I can still remember the questions reeled off by the operator as I eavesdropped over the phone: Was there twitching of the limbs? If so, which ones and on which side? Did the head twist; neck go rigid; eyes turn or roll? Was there drooling or foaming at the mouth? Was there a chewing motion or smacking of the lips? Did he bite the inside of his cheek, his tongue or lips? Was there loss of bladder or bowel control? Did he experience nausea? Was there any vomiting? Was there major movement during the convulsion or seizure? Did he maintain consciousness throughout the seizure? Were there prolonged muscle contractions only, or was there a period of prolonged muscle contraction alternating with relaxation? How long did the seizure last? What other symptoms were present?

Once she had finished talking with the operator, I could hear Dot pacing nervously for a while, and then there was silence. I thought I would go crazy waiting for her to talk with me. What was she doing? Finally I heard her voice.

"Erik seems okay now, but I don't know." She was barely able to control the hysteria that was clearly mounting within her—I could sympathize totally. I tried to calm her; giving her hope by saying that it might have been nothing serious but we had to make sure. I then tried to help her answer the operator's questions by asking questions of my own which, though apparently unrelated, indirectly supplied us with information. I shared what I could remember from Erik's previous convulsion, and together we managed to find an answer for most of the operator's questions. I then told Dot that the danger may have passed but, because of his medical history, we needed to get him checked. Dot agreed.

The other line rang and Dot again put me on conference call. I was relieved when I heard Dr. Peterson identify himself. Without waiting to be asked, Dot breathlessly started describing what had been happening that morning, her words trying to race ahead of each other as if she feared the call would be disconnected before she had painted an accurate picture of the situation. When she could think of nothing else to add, she informed the doctor that Erik was her nephew and had come to visit her. Still breathing heavily, she then mentioned that Erik's mother was on the other line and could fill him in on Erik's history.

Trying to sound calm and in control, so the doctor would feel confident that I knew what I was saying, I introduced myself as Erik's mother. Then, choosing my words carefully, I explained to him first what I knew—that Erik was having convulsions—and that, though he hadn't had any in a very long time, there had been previous episodes. I then went into a detailed description of Erik's medical history, starting at the beginning and working my way forward. Every so often, Dr. Peterson interrupted to ask Dot if there was any change in Erik, and when she responded that he seemed to be resting peacefully, though his breathing was quite raspy, the doctor said, "That's good", before asking me to continue. When he asked if Erik was experiencing convulsions or a seizure, I was at a loss and had to ask him to explain the difference.

"Well," he said, "convulsions are when a person's body shakes rapidly and uncontrollably. During convulsions, the muscles contract and relax repeatedly." All I could say was that I believed he was convulsing but wasn't sure.

Dr. Peterson told me not to worry, and that the term 'convulsion' is often used interchangeably with 'seizure', although there are many types of seizure, some of which have subtle or mild symptoms that differ from convulsions. Seizures of all types are caused by disorganized and sudden electrical activity in the brain. He went on to say that, in any case, neither is a trivial symptom. Whether or not this was the first time Erik had had them, we were right to move so quickly, as when a person experiences any type of convulsion or seizure, they should be attended to immediately or taken to the emergency room if necessary.

I found it soothing to let the doctor take command, as he seemed to have everything under control. He managed to quell the hysteria in Dot's voice, took note of the mounting worry spicing my words, and knew just what to say to keep me going. His questions to me and his orders to Dot were unmistakably those of a professional who knew what needed to be done. When I had exhausted all that I felt needed to be said, the doctor asked Dot to call an ambulance and said that he would meet her and Erik at the Mission Viejo Hospital, Regional Medical Center.

As Dot looked up the number and called an ambulance, the doctor told me to contact the local hospital, as well as Erik's doctors in Rochester, to notify them of what had transpired. "You need to make these calls immediately, Mrs. Saxton. We are going to need as much medical advice as we can get from the doctors so that we don't waste precious time."

Precious time, I thought; yes, time was precious. As I wrote down Dr. Peterson's contact number and that of the Mission Viejo Hospital, Regional Medical Center, I hoped this fancy named institution was ready for a child with Erik's medical problems. But I didn't have time to think about this, as Dr. Peterson continued asking questions. "Tell me, what is the name of the hospital there in Rochester?"

"Genesee Hospital."

"Good, can you get me the phone number?"

"Yes," I said, then read the number to him from my address book.

"Good, Mrs. Saxton. Now the name and numbers of his doctors."

The sound of pages flipping as I looked through my address book was like music to my ears—this, at least, was something I was certain of. It was a lot easier to supply a couple of phone numbers than have to sift through the memories of the past to come up with information about Erik. "Dr. Cotanch is his neurosurgeon and Dr. Boettrich is his pediatrician," I said, then read out their office and emergency phone numbers.

"Any questions?" Dr. Peterson asked.

In unison, Dot and I asked, "Do you think he's going to be all right?"

Without pausing to reflect, Dr. Peterson replied, "I don't see why not. You have both done a wonderful job of filling me in on

7

everything, and we should be able to take it from here. Just keep doing what you're doing to help each other through this until the ambulance gets there."

Then there was silence, and time seemed to freeze. I tried to picture the kind doctor and wondered if he felt as confident as he sounded, or if this was beyond his expertise and there would be nothing he could do to help Erik. I also wondered if Erik was really all right or if Dot was just trying not to worry me. I wondered so much that I was sick to the stomach and had to race to the kitchen.

When I came back to the phone I could hear a doorbell ringing and Dot yelling, "Just a minute", as she hurried to answer it. I gripped the receiver tightly in my hand, as though afraid it might somehow slip out. I could hear the sound of bustling motion in the room as Dot picked up the phone and said, "The ambulance is here."

Dr. Peterson then asked to speak to the paramedics, relaying to them all the information Dot had given him.

"I'm hanging up now, ladies. Everything is under control," Dr. Peterson said once he had finished talking with the paramedics.

"Dot," I said, but she had already left the phone again. The sounds of the activity in her room filled my head. Dot was now taking the paramedics to Erik, and I could hear muffled voices every now and then as they shouted out orders to each other. There seemed to be three others in the room apart from Dot, but I wasn't sure. I tried to imagine what is was they were doing, until Dot came back on the line.

"Try not to worry, Nita; they're just about ready to transport Erik to the hospital. I will follow them in my car and call you when we get there."

I nodded, forgetting she couldn't see me. "Dot, don't forget to take Erik's wallet—his medical card is in it."

"Sure, I will." From the sound of her voice I could tell she was on the verge of tears, as was I. I then heard her say that they were ready to go, and the line disconnected. I slowly pulled the receiver from my ear and stared at it as though I could see beyond it, before finally managing to return it to its cradle. I was alone. I wanted to cry but there was no time—I had calls to make. First, I called the

Genesee Hospital and asked for the records department, explaining the situation to them and why I needed them to share Erik's medical records with the Mission Viejo Hospital and Dr. Duane Peterson. There was red tape involved, of course, which prevented them from giving out this information over the phone.

I didn't have time for stumbling blocks, so I hung up and called Dr. Cotanch's emergency number and left a message with his answering service for him to call me immediately. I then did the same with Dr. Boettrich. All I could do was wait. Dr. Cotanch was the first to call back. I filled him in on all that had happened and told him I would be sitting by the phone all day. Dr. Boettrich called soon after, and I repeated to her all that I had told Dr. Cotanch.

The matter was now in the hands of the professionals. I had done all I could to help my son; all I could do now was make sure I kept the phone line open. Thank goodness we had two phone lines in the house. I used the other line to call my family and Erik's father, who was in New York City, to inform them of what was happening. I was told that my husband was over seven hundred miles away on a job site and couldn't be reached until later that evening, but I was able to leave a message. My son was almost three thousand miles away, in the midst of a crisis, and I wanted to be there with him; only that was not part of my instructions. I had to be the go-between, the central point of contact, until I was told otherwise. I doubt it would have been possible for me to feel more alone.

It felt like my whole world was crashing down around me. What was happening to my life? I wasn't strong enough to face this alone. If it was a test, I wanted it to end because I wasn't up for it. I was out of practice after so many years of calm. "Hang in there! Ricky will be all right," I said, using my son's nickname. "Erik will get your call and contact you," I added, referring to my husband. "Just hang in there for both of them. That's your job now." Yes, it was my job. I had to be strong and I had to feel confident that it would all work out for the best. I had no other recourse.

Dot finally called to say that she had arrived at the Medical Center and that Erik had been taken into a room in the emergency department, where she hadn't been able to see him yet. As far as she knew, he was doing okay. She, on the other hand, was a nervous wreck. "How do you do this?" she asked, knowing that I had been through what she was experiencing many times before.

"I don't know how. I just do it because I have no other choice," I said. I then told her that it was best not to think about what had happened or speculate on what might happen, and that she must concentrate on keeping calm. I told her that I knew she could do it and that Erik would be all right, even though I wasn't feeling so sure of that myself. I then told her that I wished I could be there; that being so far away made it very hard on me.

This confession took Dot's mind off herself, as she immediately understood what I must being going through. She sympathized with me, and we both allowed our tears to flow uncontrolled. It did us both good. I then told her I was going to check with the airlines to see when I could get a flight there.

Dot was silent for a moment, and then said, "No, Nita, don't do that just yet. I'll ask the doctor but I think they need you there to help coordinate for a while longer." Though I knew she was right, I didn't reply straight away. After a moment, however, I told her I understood and was glad she was there with Ricky. We talked for a little while longer before hanging up. I was alone again.

Unable to be by my son's side, I'd never felt so helpless. It was the worst! And what if he should … No, I refused to say it or even think it. I couldn't deal with those kind of thoughts. I paced about the house, stopping only long enough to make a cup of coffee before starting to pace again. I couldn't stand the waiting. I looked out the window; it was getting light and the sounds of morning would soon begin. I sat my cup on the counter and, leaving the bathroom door wide open, washed my face, trying to make myself presentable for the day ahead. I managed to find something to wear and then returned to the kitchen to refill my coffee cup.

The morning began. Through my living room window, I watched the cars being backed out of their driveways as my neighbors headed off to work. It was strange to see the world continue on with its usual routine, as though nothing had happened, while I was in such torment. I sat behind the desk in my office and tried to work, but it was impossible, so I wandered around the house, stopping in each room and looking about as if trying to find something. I ended up in Erik's bedroom. Surrounded by all his personal effects, I could feel his presence. I picked up the Hess semi-trailer he'd had since he was ten and turned it over, looking for the switch to turn on its tiny lights. Changing my mind, I returned it to its place of honor by the window. I opened his closet and looked at the clothes hanging haphazardly on their hangers. I reached out to straighten them but then pulled back, wanting to leave them just as he had placed them.

As I sat on the edge of his bed, I wished I hadn't washed his bed linen and dusted and cleaned his room. I wanted to be able to inhale his smell. But how was I to have known? How was I to have known that I would need the scent of him to help me through this ordeal. It hadn't been part of the plan when he left. I was sure I would miss him, but in a different way: the way you miss a teenage son who is on a short vacation; not the way you miss your baby, with that need to help them, protect them, and keep them safe at all times. But that was how I was missing him.

I left his room and wandered aimlessly around the house for a while before returning to the kitchen. I finished what was left of the coffee and again sat behind my desk, turning on the computer to defy my desire to not have to think. Soon I was lost in the work that had piled up in my tray, finding it soothing to take command.

When the phone rang I picked it up immediately. It was Dr. Cotanch, calling to explain what he had learned from the doctor in California. There wasn't much for him to tell me except that Erik was resting comfortably. Dr. Cotanch knew how much I wanted to be there but insisted I stay where I could be easily reached, as Erik wasn't out of danger yet.

Somehow the day progressed. Dot called to say she was on her way home to pick up some things and change her clothes. She told me she would call again once she'd returned to the hospital. Dr. Boettrich then called to advise me that she had spoken with the hospital and provided them with the required information. I returned to my work, which was becoming my salvation.

The neighborhood again came to life as evening descended. Cars returned home and people went about their normal routines: preparing dinner and asking each other about their day. I wished I could do the same, but it wasn't to be.

The phone rang again. Thinking it is was the hospital, I raced to pick it up.

"Nita, why don't you come over and join us for dinner?" I recognized the familiar voice of my neighbor Mary Jo. At that point, all she knew was that both my husband and son were out of town and I was home alone. She was about to find out a lot more.

When I told her what had happened, she said she'd come right over. Not only is she a close friend, she is also a nurse. As a friend and mother, she had an idea of what I was feeling; as a nurse, she wanted to help in any way she could.

Mary Jo and I have been friends since the day I moved into the neighborhood, and we have always been there for each other. I remember the time she was diagnosed with cancer, and within a breath learned she was pregnant. She and her husband had tried for years to get pregnant, to have a child between them to add to the children from their previous marriages. Two wonderful people, facing two extreme situations at once; but they came through it. They came through the cancer and they had a beautiful little boy.

As I waited for her to arrive, the phone rang again. It was Dr. Peterson. At the first sound of his voice, I felt a lump form in my throat and could barely say hello. I felt like a lawyer who thinks the jury has decided too quickly for it to be a favorable verdict. But I am not prepared for bad news.

Dr. Peterson took his time telling me that he had spoken with both of Erik's doctors in New York and that they had shared the information necessary to treat Erik. He then paused for a moment; I suppose to let the information sink in. I wanted desperately to blurt out: "So what does that mean exactly?" but I remained silent and waited for him to continue. When he did speak again, his words confirmed what I already knew but had been secretly hoping against— Erik was in a critical condition.

They had just finished a physical and a neurological examination, had taken blood for testing, and had him x-rayed. They were now waiting for the results. Since there was no known cause for the seizures, they were assessing their occurrence, nature and duration. Erik's seizures had been temporarily stopped through medication but had soon started again. Dr. Peterson informed me that he had placed another call to Erik's New York doctors in the hope that together they might be able to find a cause. Earlier, when Erik had been able to communicate, he had complained of a sore stomach shortly before vomiting. He had then fallen back to sleep before he could be questioned further. He was running a temperature, which could have be a reaction to the medication administered but the doctor wasn't sure. He asked if Erik had any drug allergies. When I told him I couldn't think of any, he requested I try and find out for certain.

I started to cry, which made me feel embarrassed, but I couldn't stop myself. Dr. Peterson tried to soothe me and told me not to worry. He explained that they were doing everything they could for Erik and that it was absolutely necessary for me to remain calm so that I could help as much as possible.

"I'm coming," I said. I could hardly speak for sobbing. "I'm calling the airport right now and getting a flight there."

The line was silent for a while, then Dr. Peterson told me I had to stay where I was.

"I want to come, doctor, and be with my son."

"I know," he said, "but there is nothing you can do here right now." He tried to console me by saying that Dot was there to watch over Erik, and that it was important for me to remain by the phone. Though they weren't sure what was happening to Erik, the test results would hopefully shed some light on things. In the mean time, Erik was being transferred from emergency to the ICU (Intensive Care Unit), and the next twenty-four hours would be critical; therefore, it would be wise for me to stay put for at least that long. The doctor then put Dot on the line.

Dot was beside herself as she explained how she had just seen Erik. "I am so scared," she said. "He didn't even know me, or react to my voice when I called his name. He was fine one moment and then the next he was like ... like he is now."

I could hear the helplessness in her voice and, taking my mind off myself, I tried to console her as best I could. Now it was Dot who was wishing I could be there, and I am the one who has to explain that there was nothing I would be able to do that she couldn't. I told her that I was depending on her to look after Erik and let him know we loved him, even if he didn't respond. I told her it would be comforting for Erik to hear her. This seemed to help calm her, and it wasn't until I hung up the phone that I allowed myself to fall apart.

Finally all cried out, I went to the refrigerator and poured myself a glass of water, drinking it quickly, as though replenishing the liquids I had lost through tears. The phone rang again, at the same time as the doorbell sounded. Hesitating for a moment, I answered the phone first. It was Dr. Cotanch. He asked if I was alone, and I told him that there was someone at the door. He said he'd wait while I answered it. As I went to answer the door, I wondered why Dr. Cotanch had asked if I was alone, and why he hadn't just told me what was going on. I opened the door: it was Mary Jo. She stepped inside and said, "I'm here to help in whatever way I can, so don't try and stop me." I closed the door and, taking her hand, dragged her with me to the phone.

During the conversation that followed, Dr. Cotanch told me that Dr. Peterson was doing everything possible for Erik, and that both he and Dr. Boettrich had informed him of their willingness to fly over there if they were needed. He explained that it was important for me to remain calm for Erik's sake. I said I would but it wasn't easy being so far away. I then asked if he had heard anything more.

Dr. Cotanch said he understood that I wanted to know how serious the situation really was, but still I had to assure him I could handle the truth. My hand began to shake, the phone seeming heavier as I struggled to keep it against my ear. I looked over at Mary Jo. Sensing immediately that I needed her, she brought a chair over next to me and gently guided me to sit down. She took my free hand and held it in hers, as though trying to transfuse her strength into me. Finally, after what seemed like hours but was only seconds, I managed to extract the words from within me. "Tell me. I can handle it."

"Mrs. Saxton, Erik is in a very serious condition, and right now it doesn't look good. They are trying to stabilize him. Until they do, they can't give any guarantees." Anticipating what I was thinking, he added, "I couldn't do any better than Dr. Peterson is already doing. Until we have the results of the final tests and can determine what lies at the bottom of the symptoms he is displaying, there is nothing anyone can do except wait and pray."

Mary Jo took the phone out of my hand and spoke with the doctor, explaining that she was a nurse and would be able to take care of me. Later I would learn the doctor had told her that the situation with Erik was so critical that even if I had flown down right at that moment I might not have made it in time. I couldn't even cry as I sat there beside Mary Jo, letting her take over while I wallowed in self-pity. I hated myself for being so weak, but I couldn't rally to the occasion. I couldn't be strong anymore. I knew why, too. I had someone next to me who was willing and quite able to take control, and I was leaning on her. I wasn't proud of myself, but Erik was out of my reach and it didn't seem wrong for me to let someone else take control.

Mary Jo stayed with me; answering the phone when it rang and relaying the message that Dot had called to let us know that Erik had been transferred to the ICU, which meant that they must have stabilized him, or he wouldn't have been moved at all. A few minutes later, Dot called again to say that Erik was unconscious. When she had asked the doctors if she should be worried, they had replied: "No more than before." That scared her even more, but Mary Jo told her that she needed to think about Erik being stabilized as positive, and not try to read anything into the words of the doctors assisting Dr. Peterson.

I spoke with Dot and she told me how hard it had been to watch Erik's body flopping around, out of control; his blank eyes and the strange sounds that came out of his mouth. I told her I understood what it felt like to stand by helplessly. I knew how useless it felt to have to rely on somebody else to take over responsibility. It was a feeling I knew well, and I was sorry she had to experience it too. From the tone of her voice, I could sense she was embarrassed to have sounded off like she did, but I continued to assure her that I really did understand. They wanted her to take a break, so she was going to go back to her apartment to make a few calls, and would return to the hospital later on. I agreed that was for the best. She needed to pull away from it all for a while and get her bearings. She promised to call on her return, whether anything had changed or not. Just before she hung up, Dot asked if I had been able to contact her brother (my husband) yet. I told her I hadn't but would try again shortly. He had left a few alternate numbers and I would try those also.

During my conversation with Dot, Mary Jo had made me a sandwich. I sat down and tried to eat, but I wasn't hungry. I tried to remain positive by remembering how many times Erik had gone through crises of this sort and had made it through. Why should this time be any different than before? He was strong and determined, and I knew he'd pull through this. He would be fine—he just had to be.

***

Throughout the rest of the evening I tried contacting my husband on the numbers he had left me. When not on the phone, I talked with Mary Jo. Erik was ten years old when we had moved into the neighborhood, so his past medical problems were unknown to Mary Jo. She had been divorced and remarried, bringing together her two children with her husband's three, and making it work so smoothly I would never have been able to guess. Adjustments had been made in her life, and managing to cope was a continual process. Though her struggles might not have been on the same level as mine, they were still significant for her. Being a nurse, Mary Jo had developed good bedside manners, and she displayed these as she tried to help and console me. Our children had played together, gone to school together, and had a very close friendship.

When I tried to get her to explain what the doctors might be doing, she was careful not to make any conclusions about the symptoms or say anything that might cause me to worry. Based on her experience in ICU, she tried to explain that patients who were sent there received more attention than those in any other wing of the hospital—which I should consider a plus rather than a minus. She managed to at least make me feel better about Erik being placed in the intensive care unit.

I was finally able to contact my husband and let him know what was happening. As I spoke with him I felt distant, unable to express my true feelings or understand his. Erik explained that he couldn't make it back to Rochester until the weekend, and for some reason I felt like yelling at him for saying that, even if it was true. He requested I call his hotel and leave messages as more information came through regarding Erik. Before we said goodbye, he told me he would call the following evening, if he hadn't heard from me already. Shortly after that I had to say goodbye to Mary Jo too. She had to get back to her family, but told me to call her if I needed her or had any news.

I was alone again, feeling even more depressed after having spoken with my husband. Things had been strained between us for some time, and his being away had proved a blessing, giving us both time to think about what we wanted to do. So much had happened during our marriage that it had been pushed to breaking point, and I could see no way of bringing us back together. Though he had certainly contributed his share, I didn't blame my husband for ruining our marriage. I didn't blame myself, either, because I had tried, but there comes a time when you need to face the truth. For us, this truth was the possibility of living separate lives. But right then, there was a more urgent issue facing us.

Deep down, I felt Ricky would be all right. But I had to admit that, on the surface, I was scared, which became more apparent as I found myself using his nickname again. I can remember the day he told us that he liked his name—Erik—and that was what he wanted us to call him. It had struck us as funny when he added that it was *his* name—meaning that his dad's real name was Harold, not Erik, though that was what I called him. He therefore saw no problem with claiming the name as his own. From that point on, he became Erik.

***

From three thousand miles away I could visualize Erik's surroundings. Having been inside so many hospitals, out of necessity, I know what the interior of a hospital looks like by heart. I had even stayed in ICU with Erik before. This experience has instilled in me the belief that nothing a hospital can provide in the way of technological and scientific marvels is as supportive as the atmosphere of compassion, both human and aesthetic, in these institutions where we all must spend time—to give birth, to be healed, or for some, to die.

The traditional hospital setting is typified by white, sterile walls and ceilings, surrounded by examining rooms, waiting rooms, corridors, areas for health professionals, operating rooms, recovery rooms, a central supply area and a pharmacy. The floor plan is perhaps the most important design element: generally a hexagon configuration or a circular design, with the nursing station in the center so that all rooms are equidistant and within view of the staff. All the corridors lined with patient rooms are visible from the nursing station, and there are no dead ends where patients are out of view while ambulatory. Oh yes; I knew the layout, the purpose, and the routines. With nothing else to distract me, I let my thoughts take over. The last thing I wanted was to be visualizing the building and walking the hallways I didn't need to walk. It was, I told myself, curiosity: a morbid curiosity, perhaps, but a curiosity nonetheless. The big rooms opened up like underground caverns, threatening to swallow anyone condemned to spend time there. Every few feet I saw cabinets with labels …

I didn't know this for a fact, of course. I had to assume how things were, but I did know there was truth to the way I felt. Even when devoid of people, a hospital doesn't fell empty, and there are always unanswered questions, like "Why did it have to be me?" That is the problem with hospitals: too many unknowns; too many stories; too many ghosts. The street might be a thoroughly frightening place but you could at least run from your fears, even if only for a while. In a building or a hallway, there is only so far you can run, and the only places you can hide are full of the things you are trying to get away from. I knew how crazy and unreal it was for me to think this way, but I couldn't get shake these images from my head.

There would be wide, tiled, institutional corridors with doors on lining both sides. There would be the main floor with its camouflaged lobby, reminiscent of a hotel until the staff passes through in their neat white uniforms, looking more like angels of mercy than actual human beings. And once you get a gander at the labels on the doors, you know this is not a place you care to linger. There are doctors' and nurses' offices and lounges; there are records and admitting rooms; x-ray and therapy rooms; clinics and dispensatories. And there is the ICU. This is a specialized area equipped to handle patients with a life-threatening illness or condition. Each patient is confined to a separate room and visitors are limited, to allow the patient to get the rest he or she needs.

In here you will see the patient looking completely transformed. There are often several intravenous, or IV, lines attached to different bags of medicine and fluid. These IV lines are inserted into veins in the hand, forearm, elbow, neck or groin. A cuff is wrapped around the person's arm to take blood pressure readings. Stickers are placed on the chest with wires attached to them to monitor the heart tracing, or electrocardiogram, also called an EKG. A device known as pulse oximeter, used to measure oxygen in the blood, may be placed on the patient's finger. Oxygen may be supplied to the patient through tubes connected to the nose or through a special face mask. Sometimes the patient is hooked up to an artificial breathing machine called a ventilator.

There always seems to be one or more machines beeping in the ICU. Occasionally these beeps represent a life-threatening situation. Patients and visitors in the ICU need not concern themselves with these—staff are trained to know what kind of beeps signal an emergency. However, these beeping machines are often a cause of concern.

Several hospital staff members attend to the patient at all times. Specially trained nurses generally work 8 or 12-hour shifts, with doctors often working during business hours and not on call at night. However, there is always at least one doctor assigned to be on call in case of an emergency. During shift changes, you can hear the staff pass on information about each patient and look over the patient's medical record.

Doctors, nurses, respiratory therapists, technical assistants, people who draw blood, and housekeepers may all come into the room at different times, ensuring the ICU isn't the most peaceful of places to try and sleep.

I could see it, visualize it, and even smell it. It was that vivid to me. I could never forget. I had tried, but here it was again, surfacing with all the familiarity and associated fear.

I find that whenever I lose control, it all tends to start with these sort of disjointed thoughts. Self-pity will then usually set in, and before I know it I have totally lost control of my physical and mental well-being. I had developed a self-defense mechanism to try and prevent this from happening, and though I hadn't used it for a long time, it had not been forgotten. I needed it then. I needed to play the Truth Game.

***

It's simple but it takes concentration. The idea is to come up with three truths which can occupy my mind until I am back in the driver's seat. So I began by saying it was true that everyone would expect me to be strong. I then paused and contradicted myself, thinking that though they may feel sorry for me for what I was going through, *I* wasn't allowed to be. I then tried to get back on track, saying, "So what!", and responding, "Well, for one, if you feel sorry for yourself you will be left alone with your feelings. No one wants to be around someone wallowing in self-pity." That seemed plausible. "Okay, right! It's true that this is not the first time you've been through this. Yes, it's different, but everyone sees it as the same. They really don't want to hear an analysis of the situation, or for that matter really want an explanation, which means you have only one alternative, right? Right! View this as an experienced person would, by not looking at it negatively. Erik made it through before and he'll make it through again."

Not quite satisfied with how the game was going, my mind became sidetracked. Was it important to tell the truth? The intellectuals of our time teach that there is no common truth; instead it is a matter of individual viewpoints. Can any social organization, including society itself, properly operate without some agreement on what is true? I wonder exactly what truth is. All I am sure of is that what is true for one may not be true for another, and there is no such thing as universal truth—something that is true for all people, all the time. Maybe instead of truth I should think about tolerance. If I were to ask what is deemed more valuable, truth or tolerance, what would be the answer? Is truth just a matter of personal opinion? Isn't one person's view of ethics just as valid as another person's? Are not all views, in essence, the same? And does the whole issue of truth and ethics really matter? Does it make any difference?

I have strayed so far from the point of the game that I am losing ground. I had to focus—it was the only mechanism I had to coach myself into acceptance of the situation. So I pushed myself by saying, "One more, and come on, think!" I became frustrated with this mind control and heard myself say, "I hate this game. I can't think this way yet. I'm too tired. It's still new, and I don't want to think anymore. I don't want to play the stupid game."

I lay down on the couch in the family room. I just wanted to close my eyes and go to sleep. But I couldn't. If I were to do that without having gained some kind of control, I wouldn't have been able to face the reality of my situation, and it would have haunted my dreams. I had to at least end the game honestly. I had to state three truths. There is a truth to be found, I told myself. "Let's see. I've got it! Okay, the truth is I want to escape the present, just for a little while; just so I can sleep." It was a copout, of course, but in all honesty it was the best I could do. I wanted a better answer but I couldn't find one, so I had to accept the only three truths I could consider for the time being. But I knew I had to occupy my mind in some way, so I turned my attention to thinking about all the information I had gathered about our families over the years.

Way back in the early days, when we first learned that Erik had physical problems, the doctors had asked about our family history. There were a lot of questions we couldn't answer at that point, but when informed that it could help diagnose Erik's medical problems, we began gathering details from family members until we had developed quite an extensive ancestral record. What had begun as a medical request became important on another level, as I became filled with a need to learn as much as I could about my own family and that of my husband's. Along with being a way to offer help to my son, it became a way to develop a legacy for him.

***

My given name is Juanita Baskerville, but I am called by the nickname, Nita. I married Harold Saxton on June 29, 1968, and soon formed a habit of calling him Erik, which presented a problem when we were blessed with our son. We both chose to name him Erik. So to avoid complications involved with having two Eriks in the house, almost from the day of his birth we started calling our son by the nickname Ricky.

What's in a name? Better yet, what's in a nickname? When I see quotation marks around a name that isn't a given name, I begin to wonder about that person and how the nickname came to be significant. Did it come from a joyful incident in childhood, or a bad experience he or she could never shake as an adult? Nicknames are like slices of life. When parents select names for their newborns, they usually try hard not to pick a name that will cause problems down the road. We can only hope. But even though my husband's name was Harold, he was known as Erik, and in many ways it was more 'him' than his given name. I found his nickname 'nice and cozy', while his given name seemed cold and distant, so I easily adjusted to using his nickname. Our son was too young to protest or have an opinion, so 'Ricky' it was.

Then came the time when little Erik was not so little any more, and he asked to be called by his given name. Now he had an opinion and was entitled to it, so we began to call him Erik.

But all of this is getting off of the subject. I settled back, drawing my mind into focus again.

***

There are many reasons to seek out our ancestors: the people of our history. They tilled the ground, spread the word, fought for freedom, braved oceans and mountains; they walked the plains, they settled the wilderness, and established homes and governments for the sake of their children and families. They are links in a great family chain of generations that connect you to the events of the past. You are a link in that chain and all future generations continue that linkage. It is where secrets as well as personal history dwell, and it can be a journey into wondrous discoveries of lost truths or forgotten legacies.

CHAPTER 2
OUR BEGINNING

Throughout my early adulthood I truly believed that destiny was linked to the undeniable factual circumstances surrounding birth, such as the exact position of the planets, the time and place of birth, and so on. I also believed in the more solid, yet still mutable, elements of religion, class and drive. Once these conditions were set, I thought, it was extremely difficult for them to be changed. This was how I came to explain the attraction between two individuals from different backgrounds and different parts of the country. With our hearts racing and common sense taking a temporary leave of absence, it was as though we were pushed together by an invisible force.

We met in April of 1968. I was working as a secretary at Xerox, and Harold for a security company. Broad-shouldered and muscular, he stood six-foot-four-inches tall; his weight hovering around 190 pounds. His hair was black and closely-cropped, befitting the style of the times, and his large, expressive brown eyes, with thick black eyebrows and long eyelashes, warranted a stare or two. He was handsome, and I couldn't help thinking that only a man of his build and good looks could carry off wearing a maroon-colored security guard uniform.

I, on the other hand, was hardly statuesque, standing only five-foot-three-inches. In my early teens I had been all legs and without curves; I was considered cute, but never sexy. I was one of those late bloomers, who didn't become popular with the boys until well into my teens. I mention this only because it heightened my appreciation when I eventually did blossom and begin to capture the attention of the opposite sex; though there was nobody's attention I appreciated as much as Harold's.

Whenever I saw him it was as though we were the only ones in existence; and when we talked, time stood still as his slow, purposeful conversation drew me into a world I couldn't have imagined. Harold's parents had separated when he was four years old. Outside of pictures, he had never seen his father again. My parents had separated when I was fourteen, and though I lived with my mother, I had regular visits with my father.

Maybe it all boils down to nothing more than the old adage that "opposites attract", or maybe it was these opposite forces that were later to draw us apart, taking us back to more familiar paths. Whatever the cause of our coming together, we would later be led to explore our pasts in an effort to save our son. This search indeed provided us with a deeper understanding of who we were, but also proved to be problematical. There were secrets that didn't want to be revealed, and time had erased many details that may have proven beneficial to our cause. But most significant was the fact that our grandparents had been the children of slaves, which meant there were no medical or other records relating to them or those who had come before them.

Faced with such monumental difficulties, we did our best in gathering information, not only for the doctors but for ourselves.

***

My grandmother, Mary Moorehouse, was born in the year 1900—the exact month and day of her birth are unknown to me.

Life wasn't easy for women during that time, nor was it necessarily happy. Being of the "Negro" race (as it was referred to then) meant it would be made even more difficult and out of her control. From an early age, her parents had taught her to remember her "station" in society, and so she always did.

Mary was short in height, not quite reaching five foot. Her weight, which was quite substantial, would be considered heavy today, but was seen as voluptuous back then. She was of light complexion, with a perky nose, full cheeks and twinkling dark brown eyes, though her pleasant manner made her features appear soft and pliable rather than impish and determined. Born in a small rural area, she quickly learned that she had no other option than to do what she was told. There were no thoughts of holding down a job, or any guarantee of twelve years' schooling. She was expected to develop the skills necessary to tend to the man she would one day marry and the children she would have to devote her life to raising and caring for. She could therefore cook, clean, sew and mend whatever needed repairing. Beyond that, there was not much else.

Seems hard to believe, but it is true. You, who have opened the lids on jars without assistance, mastered the remote control, survived in a working world, given birth, and can press the gas and brake while wearing three-inch heels, might have difficulty envisioning life for women in the 1900s.

It was indeed a real "man's" world, and a wise woman had no alternative but to accept it. From early childhood a woman was raised to manage her husband's property, while praising him as though it was he who did it. She was taught to suffer the pains of childbirth in silence, yet understand her husband's need to roar like a lion when he cut his finger or stubbed his toe. Her lot was considered easy. A woman must be kind, gracious, and have an exceptional ability to forgive and forget. And, of course, she must pass these traits on to each girl she bore. Mary Moorehouse accepted her role; she believed in it, and why not? Every woman she knew faced the same fate.

My grandfather, Frank Clark, was born on August 16, 1898. He stood five-foot-ten-inches, with a thick torso and sturdy legs. His light brown hair, which would later turn silver-white, contrasted with his gray twinkling eyes. He had a full face, a compact nose and dazzling white teeth. Frank considered himself an "experienced" man, as he had served his country in World War I. He was gentle, kind, and capable of making a good living for himself and the woman he chose to marry—Mary Moorehouse.

Frank and Mary Clark made their home in Penn Yan: a quaint New York village located on the edge of the northern tip of the east branch of Keuka Lake. When first settled, it was called Union, but the residents soon became dissatisfied with that name. The settlers from Pennsylvania wanted a name that reminded them of their native state, while those from New England wanted a Yankee-sounding name. A comprise was made—Penn for the Pennsylvanians and Yan for the Yankees.

My grandparents had a good marriage, surviving the loss of two of their four children. Frank Jr., born prior to 1929, died of pneumonia at the age of five; and Bertha Ann, a fragile child born in 1929, died at the age of three from an unknown childhood disease. The two surviving children were girls—the oldest named Blanche and the second-born Juanita.

It was while giving birth to her last child, Bertha Ann, that Mary Moorehouse passed away. At the tender age of 29, the woman who brought order, dignity and grace into Frank's household was gone; but not before completing her final duty in life—arranging for the care of her surviving children.

In those days, it was unheard of for a father to raise female children on his own. Mary had informed Frank that if anything should happen to her, he should allow the girls to be adopted by her uncle, Fred Maxfield, and his wife, Myrtle Grey Maxfield. It was in the winter of 1928 that Fred and Myrtle, with Blanche and Juanita in tow, entered the small courthouse in Penn Yan to sign the final papers for adoption. And so it came to be that Frank's daughters— when the oldest, Blanche, was almost nine years of age—became "Maxfields". When Fred died some years later, Myrtle remarried and continued to provide a home for her two adopted daughters. Myrtle would remarry four or five times throughout her life, but it wasn't until her final marriage, to William Dennis, that she was blessed with a child of her own.

My mother, Blanche, born on October 8, 1919, matured into a woman with a lasting beauty. Like her mother, her height never surpassed five feet. She was stoutly built, with smooth, taffy-colored skin; long black hair; a full face accentuated by high cheekbones; and expressive, light brown eyes. She had a calm and gentle nature that would later be passed on to at least three of her six offspring.

In 1943 Blanche was to participate in a pre-arranged marriage to a man named Pete Bliss, but this never came to be. Pete joined the army and, after basic training, was to be stationed in Germany. Though Myrtle and Edna, Pete's mother, brought the wedding date forward and sent Blanche to marry Pete in Philadelphia, his ship left port before the marriage could take place.

Luckily for Blanche she was born in an age in which women were offered alternatives to simply becoming a wife and mother. Blanche Clark-Maxfield took up residence in Philadelphia, where she worked at the U.S. Marine Corps base. It was when visiting her friend Mary Walker in Penn Yan that she came face-to-face with the man she would later marry: Sol Baskerville.

My father, Sol Baskerville, was born October 8, 1900. Standing six-foot-two-inches, he towered over Blanche, and was twenty years her senior. He was handsome, with a dark complexion; closely cropped dark brown hair; and extremely long, muscular legs supporting a trim, lean figure that had been developed from his physically demanding work as a carpenter. He seemed to overflow with energy and vitality. The two began dating, and on December 26, 1943—a cold, rainy day—they took a train to Elton, Maryland, where they were married. They returned to Pennsylvania and settled in a small town called Manyunk. Blanche returned to her job in the payroll Department of the U. S. Marine Corps until March of 1945, when she quit to begin a family. They would have a total of four girls and one boy before Sol died in June, 1965.

Their first child, Mary Moorhouse, whom they named after Blanche's natural mother, and who also carried the same name as the woman who first introduced Blanche to Sol, would later wed Isaac

Walker. On March 17, 1947, Blanche gave birth to her second child, who she named after her only surviving sister—Juanita—signaling the end of the namesake family tradition, as the generations to follow would only be blessed with one female child. Following Juanita was the birth of twin boys, born weighing only 1 1/2 pounds each. Both boys died within the fist eight hours of their birth. It was not until after the births of Dianne, on May 5, 1950; and Barbara, on December 31, 1952, that another son was born. On May 11, 1957, Odell became the only boy born to Sol and Blanche.

After the birth of their first two children, Sol and Blanche moved into a large house on Tuckahoe Road in Williamstown, New Jersey—an ideal place for raising children. Williamstown is situated on the outskirts of Camden, in the Delaware River Region, nestled in Gloucester County. The town is a part of the Philadelphia, Pennsylvania-New Jersey metro area. It has changed significantly since the time Blanche and Sol took up residency there. Back then it was farm country, with miles separating neighbors, and a road that supported very little traffic other than visitors to the local residents. The house itself was a two-story gray shingled farmhouse, sitting on ten acres of farm land. Its size would come in handy for the five children they would raise there.

Like all the women of her time, Blanche had expected her marriage to last forever. But in the summer of 1957, when I was 14 years old, they separated. I remember the event as though it happened just yesterday, though there are so many other memories from my younger days that I can't recall in such vivid detail.

I had been sleeping, and awoke to hear their angry whisperings from the kitchen. I couldn't make out what they were saying, but I knew they were arguing. I had never heard them argue before, and it scared me! I remember lying there, afraid to make a sound and wondering if my sister Mary was awake too. As I lay there, trying not to breathe too loud, so I could catch their words, I saw my heart beating outside my body—a plump red thing floating in the air as I fought hard to not cry or make a sound. I must have drifted off to sleep eventually, because the next thing I knew it was morning.

Dad was nowhere to be found when we kids got up and went to the kitchen. A man was sitting at the kitchen table with mom, drinking a cup of coffee. Without making introductions, mom hurried us around the table and fed us, then sent us to our bedrooms to pack some clothes. We were told we could only take a couple of toys each, but no one knew where we were going. Soon we all climbed into a van owned by the man and were driven non-stop until we arrived, exhausted and hungry, at my grandmother's house in Penn Yan that evening. Immediately after we had been fed, we were sent to bed. We stayed at our grandmother's for a couple of weeks, before moving to a house two doors down the street.

The name of the man who drove us to our grandmother's that day was Webb Jones. He stayed on for a little while to help mom, until one day he was gone too, and in October of 1958 we had a new baby brother: Robert Jones.

There were good times for us in Penn Yan. Evenings we would visit our grandmother and hear her tell of the times when our mother was the same age as us. She would often share with us how music played an important part in their life. Our Aunt Juanita played the violin; our grandfather Fred Maxfield played both the Spanish guitar and the Hawaiian guitar; grandmother played the piano; and mom played the piano and sang. There was one other member, a man named Clifford Peters, who played the saxophone.

***

It was a normal evening in 1959 when it happened. Mary and mom had gone to our grandmother's to do the laundry, and I was left at home to watch my younger siblings. We were sitting in the living room watching *The Ed Sullivan Show* when I heard a big boom. I got up and ran to the back of the house, thinking maybe something had fallen down, but instead I saw flames coming up through the floor of the kitchen. Careful not to excite my siblings, I tried to remain calm, telling them to come with me. I quickly slipped on their coats and boots, carrying my brothers and pushing my sisters through the front door. I managed to get us all outside before the whole house went up in flames. The fire took with it years of memories—all our photographs, childhood drawings and memorabilia were destroyed that day, never to be recovered.

This event changed our lives, again.

***

I missed those evenings at our grandmother's when we moved to Benton Center, about four miles from Penn Yan. The house we moved into was very large; filled with mahogany wood trim and doors throughout. We moved into the downstairs of the house, which was plenty big enough for all of us, but something had been lost that year … It was a time of family dysfunction. We were too far for our friends from school to visit us and, since we didn't have a car, we couldn't stay in town to visit with them. Teenagers can be cruel, and we openly blamed our mother for the problems we faced. We didn't want to be purposefully spiteful, but we were unable to control our anger at being unsettled yet again.

Mom was raising six children on her own when she thought she had fallen in love with Clifford Peters, only to find that she had mistaken love for friendship. From this union came our little sister Carol, who would be raised by our Mama Jenny and Daddy Milton: friends of our family who had never been blessed with a child of their own and wanted desperately to provide a home for Carol. We still managed to spend our summers with our father, who had settled in Scranton, Pennsylvania, until he made his final move to return to Philadelphia. In 1964 mom moved us to Fulton, New York; and in 1965 our father died.

***

My father was my tower of strength, and yet the gentlest man I knew. He liked to sit for hours watching us children play, with a coffee cup balanced in his hand. When he was not working on building sites, he spent his time taking care of the farm; sometimes allowing us to ride on the back of the tractor while he plowed the field. I remember mom taking us all to church on Sunday, to return home to dad standing in the living room watching television and ironing all our clothes, which would be hanging off anything he could find. I remember sitting in his lap and reading the funny papers with him, or watching cartoons as we waited for dinner. I remember waiting by the window to see him return after being on a job site for several weeks; and I remember holidays filled with gifts, smiles and happiness.

When he died, I felt as though a piece of my life had been snatched away forever. It was hard to believe that he would not see me graduate or know what I would become when I finished school. He would not be there to walk me down the aisle when I married, or see his grandchildren when they were born. I had taken it for granted that my father would always be there, and now I only had the memories.

After my father's passing, my mother took over the role of breadwinner. From a stay-at-home mom, she would now have to set off for work after hurrying us off to school At first she worked on the lines at the local canning factory, then later joined the literacy group to serve as an educator for the employed migrant workers. From that position she was later hired by the Fulton Middle School as an assistant to the special education teacher—a position she would remain in until she retired.

After graduating from high school in Fulton, I moved to Rochester to attend business school, and stayed on when I was hired by Xerox Corporation.

***

Harold's grandmother, Leora Parks, was born on November 17, 1889, in Maynard, a small town in Travis County, Texas. Leora was a tiny, dark-skinned woman with a beautiful laugh and smile. She was the oldest of her siblings—Beulah Lee, Hattie Jane, Amos Isaac Ilandis and Jessie James. The family made their living as farmers and worked three rented plots of land. The days began early, with a noon break for supper before returning to the fields again until eight o'clock in the evening. In 1903 the family moved to Oklahoma.

Although one of the youngest states in the nation, Oklahoma is a land that reaches far back in time. It is the site to which the Five Civilized Tribes of the south-east of the United States were forced to relocate, in designated Indian Territory, across numerous routes— the most famous being the Cherokee "Trail of Tears".

Forced off their ancestral lands by state and federal governments, the tribes suffered great hardships during the rigorous trips west. There was talk of using Indian territory for settlement by African-Americans emancipated from slavery. However, the government relented to pressure, much of it coming from a group known as "Boomers", who wanted the rich lands opened to white settlement. People came from all parts of the world to seek their fortune in Oklahoma's teeming oil fields. Cities like Tulsa, Ponca City, Bartlesville and Oklahoma City flourished.

The history of African-Americans in Oklahoma is a story unlike any to be found in the history of the United States. Initially arriving as slaves, the later African-American population would consist of cowboys, settlers, gunfighters and farmers. By 1907, the year Oklahoma was granted statehood, they outnumbered both Indians and first and second generation Europeans. They created more all-black towns in Oklahoma than in the rest of the country put together, produced some of the country's greatest jazz musicians, and led some of the nation's greatest civil rights battles. It was in this state, rich in historical significance, that Leora Parks found herself. Leora did clerical work at the church the family attended, and this is where she met the man she would marry.

***

Harold's grandfather, Daryl Hall, served as a superintendent at the same church where Leora worked. Daryl was well liked and was looked upon as a man who enjoyed life most when he was helping others. On July 22, 1911, he married Leora, and they had three children—Beulah Lee, Earl and Lena. Like their parents, Daryl and Leora returned to a life of farming rented land—raising corn, cotton and sugar cane. Their life was wrapped up in church, their children and farming the land.

Harold's mother, Beulah, born on April 27, 1913, had always been considered a stunning woman, and men took notice of her from an early age, discovering she was more than just pretty—she was also gracious. She stood five-foot-seven-inches tall, with jet black hair and skin the color of coffee beans. Though she was constantly being pursued by the local men, Beulah had little time for romance. As her father had passed away, by the age of 18 she was determined to take over the responsibility of providing for her mother and her grandmother. In 1931 Beulah moved the family to Bartlesville, Oklahoma, where through her income as a cook and house cleaner she managed to purchase a three-bedroom home for them to live in.

In 1936 she met Mr. Right. Beulah was 25 years old when she married Arthur Curtis Colbert, who would die of pneumonia after only one year of marriage. It wasn't until much later that she met and married Harry Saxton. Upon meeting Beulah for the first time, Harry was determined to spend his life with her. They would have three children—Harold Erik Saxton, born May 8, 1946; and the twins, Dorothy and Dwight. When the oldest, Harold, was five, Harry joined the army and Beulah became the main breadwinner again.

At the end of his army service, Harry returned home and began looking for a job. Leora, who had never liked Harry, now found him underfoot and didn't like it a bit. Hard as she tried, Beulah couldn't get to the bottom of the problem and ended up getting caught in the middle. She loved her mother and had vowed to take care of her; she also loved Harry, but he could take care of himself. That was the only reason given when Beulah asked Harry to leave.

Beulah continued to support her mother until her death, working at cleaning jobs and taking in ironing. Bartlesville was densely populated, making it easy for her to get work. When Harold joined the army he sent money home to help out his mother. Dwight did the same when he joined the navy as soon as he was of age.

***

Times were extremely hard for our parents and grandparents. The 19th century (1801–1900) is often referred to by historians as the "age of isms". No other century could boast the massive social changes that took place throughout this period. While the 20th century would evolve into the century of politics and science, the 19th was the "century of society". The rights of workers and the common man were questioned for the first time, and at no previous point in history had there been such a massive social movement, starting in Europe and spilling over into the Americas, and even parts of Asia. The 19th century set the stage for the beginning of the modern world. Though slavery had been abolished, there was by no means equal treatment of American blacks in most parts of the country.

Once Harold's term of service in the army was over, and with a need for further travel, he decided to try and locate the father he hadn't seen since he was five years of age. Based on information supplied by his mother, Harold decided to make his way to Rochester, New York, where he was eventually employed by a security outfit and assigned to Xerox Tower.

***

And so we found ourselves in Rochester at the same time and at the same place of employment. Rochester is a great place to live and raise a family. It's a beautiful old city located on the Lake Ontario border, with the Genesee River flowing through its midst, which enabled industry to flourish. It is not a large city, but a very prosperous one, with companies such as Kodak and Xerox having branches there and employing a large percentage of the population. The city was large enough to offer opportunity, but not so large that one felt lost, and the treatment of blacks was tolerable.

If destiny placed us in proximity, then fate took over from there. Maybe my role in our relationship was meant to be nothing more than the facilitator of Harold's reunion with his father. Early on in our conversations, Harold mentioned that he had come to Rochester to locate his father but was having a hard time finding him. So I offered to help, not quite knowing how to go about it but determined to support his effort. Harold showed me a photo he had of his father, Harry, and I tried to memorize the face that stared back at me. Harry was slightly built, with his Indian heritage evident in his facial features. He had long, wavy gray hair, high cheekbones, thin lips and wide-set eyes. Harold knew very little about him, which was one of the reasons he hoped to make contact.

Each day as I walked home from work, I kept my eyes open, scanning the faces of the people walking down the sidewalk. I had no idea where this man lived, so there was no reason to believe I would run into him. But that's exactly what happened. It turned out that Harold's father worked at the car wash located behind my apartment building. Harold and Harry's first meeting took place in my own living room.

Harry was a small man; quite the opposite of Harold. Where his dad was short, Harold was exceptionally tall. Where his father was thin, Harold was trim but muscular. Yet their facial features were one and the same. I played the spectator, watching from the side lines as they became reacquainted. Over the next few days, Harry quite often joined us for dinner and, as he talked, I learned about a totally different lifestyle than I myself had experienced. Though sweet and so very kind, Harry was what I would call a heavy drinker. He drank all day long without showing signs of being drunk. He drank all evening, continuing after the alcohol finally took charge of his body. But he was still able to participate in a conversation, captivating us with his charming remarks, accentuated by his winks and laugher. I couldn't help liking him even though I was anxious about his drinking habits. When I mentioned to Harold that I was worried that his father had a drinking problem, he just hugged me tight and said, "He's from Oklahoma, honey, and by Oklahoma standards, he's a teetotaler".

With so many forces pushing us together, it seemed only natural that after just two dates and having known each other for a little under two months, Harold and I married on June 29, 1968. I can't say that the two dates were so fantastic that they inspired me to want to spend the rest of my life with him. The first date was lunch at a local restaurant, where we sat talking about ourselves before returning to our jobs. The second date was longer. After work we went to dinner, and the conversation leaned toward our families, our likes and dislikes, and what we wanted out of life. After dinner we saw a movie. I remember it was a western, *The Wild Bunch*, starring John Wayne. I used to watch westerns with my dad—not because I liked them, but because he did. Now, I was again watching a western for basically the same reason—because Harold liked them, and I enjoyed his company.

When he asked me to marry him a few days later, at first I was speechless, unable to understand why he was asking me. But then I wondered, "Why not?" He had a job—not a great one, but a job—and I enjoyed being with him. These were minor reasons compared to the fact that he had told me he loved me and was the first man who had ever asked me to marry him. So I said yes, and we were married in a small Presbyterian Church in Fulton, with my family and his mother and father in attendance. Later, after everything settled down, I asked myself if Harold and I had actually fallen in love at first sight. Can a complicated process like love occur so quickly and yet be real? Can a marriage between two practical strangers, who have known each other for only fifty-five days and have had two certified dates, survive the trials of marriage? Only time would reveal the answer to that question.

Meeting his mother for the first time made me remember what Harold had said about Oklahomans and their drinking. Beulah also drank what I considered to be an excessive amount, but I kept my remarks to myself. After all, she was very nice and I liked her. Here was a woman who had struggled all her life to keep a roof over her family's heads. A woman who had loved and lost, yet kept on going as though she truly believed that it would all sort itself out eventually. She was a pretty woman who, despite her struggles, had refused to develop a hard edge or wear a mask of hopelessness. Because of all she had gone through just to survive, I could sincerely overlook her drinking.

***

Though I did give it a moment of thought, I can't say that it seemed like a mistake as we began our lives together. Sure, there were things Harold did that I disagreed with, but I told myself it was because he had been raised differently, and that we would now grow into our own lifestyle. As for his drinking, I saw it as sociable. He drank when he was around either his father or his mother, but not when we were alone. He sometimes had nightmares in which the horrible images of his experiences in the Vietnam War were brought to life, and these left him full of rage when he finally woke up. It was during these times that I saw how powerful he could be. But these were isolated instances, and not truly representative of his personality, as Harold was genuinely kind and loving. He was attentive when he wanted to be, as well as understanding.

I wasn't perfect by a long shot. Professionally, I was ambitious and thus very committed to proving myself, and this spilled over into my personal life. Everything was a challenge, and all challenges must be met with strength and perseverance. I had my own method of overcoming challenges, and that was to determine if they could be turned to my own advantage or if I must compromise in order to level the ground.

What Harold and I seemed to have in common, beyond physical attraction, was the need to live for the moment and not question its validity. I think I was always this way. I think Harold was too. A characteristic of people who live their lives from moment-to-moment is their difficulty in recalling a specific moment once it has passed, because they tend to float right through it.

Time, it seems, is not only out of our control but actually controls us. Time seemed to control me from when I first met Harold. I found that I did not have enough time to get to know him, and then there wasn't enough time to prepare for a family. It just was not in the cards. Why? It was a question impossible to answer in relation to our meeting, our life together, or the birth of our child. Almost from the beginning I would ask myself why, yet find no answers. But at first the whys are fun to ask. Later the whys would cause pain and suffering, but that is still part of the unknown.

What I did know was that, though my life seemed to move quickly through the stages of adulthood, I enjoyed being married and playing the role of a wife. It was new to me, but I had learned from my mother the routine of wifehood and I enjoyed having someone to cook for and someone to talk with each evening. I found it refreshing to hear the opinions of someone who had a stake in my future, instead of those of a friend who merely sympathized, saying what they thought I wanted to hear. I concentrated on making each day count, since I expected our relationship to continue on the rapid treadmill on which it had commenced. Here we were: two individuals who, before having even gotten to really know each other, had become husband and wife, trying to learn how to live together.

I was the first to admit to the oddity of the relationship, particularly the swiftness of our marriage, but I believed then, as well as later, that it seemed right—and it was exciting. The excitement came from all angles. Here was a man who had grown up in Oklahoma and had served four years in the army, stationed in places I had dreamed of visiting, and others that I could not even envision. As a soldier in Vietnam he had learned of hunger, killing, dying, and knowing what it was like to be afraid to fall asleep. I, on the other hand, had lived what could only be called a "sheltered" life. My life lacked exposure, while exposure was what his life had been all about.

In the beginning, things were so hectic that there never seemed to be enough time to sit down and share all the facets of each of our lives. But when the tailspin did finally slow, we were able to retell, as they floated to the surface, our various past experiences, and in this way we slowly developed a familiarity with each other, and were able to form a picture of each other at the different stages of life.

To Harold, living in New Jersey on acres and acres of land, with clean air and only the sound of crickets and birds, seemed like "Hicksville", even compared to living in a small town like Bartlesville, where there was always somewhere within walking distance to go. The thought of my mother always being there when we came home from school, a father who was still part of the picture, and everyone sitting down for dinner together was something that Harold could appreciate. In his home, his grandmother was the one who had always been there to keep them in check, while his mother would rush in, change, and go out again.

Maybe that was part of the attraction. In Astrology, destiny is believed to stem from the strong feelings of our past, thus bringing us back full circle to the question of our fate. Destiny is our final calling to resolve old issues and to complete cycles started long ago. Maybe that explained what life had in store for us.

I was just getting used to coming home to be with my husband, when that changed too. Shortly after our marriage, he was hired by Xerox to work in the copier lab. It paid substantially more than the security guard position, but it had a downside. He was placed on the second shift, so I was faced with spending evenings alone. Then, before we had time to adjust to that change in our lifestyle, we found out we were to become parents—mother and father. What should I do? It was a pointless question, as the roles would soon be forced upon us and there was no choice but to adapt quickly.

41

It was a happy time, probably the happiest time we shared, as we prepared for our baby. We both had well-paying jobs with good medical benefits—which we would soon learn to value. I spent a lot of time in my doctor's office and was following a regimen of vitamins and exercises to improve our chances of having a healthy baby. My obstetrician explained the whole process to me and showed me pictures of what I could expect to happen to my body.

I had the best obstetrician ever. I'm sure a lot of women feel just the same way, but I couldn't be persuaded to believe there was a better baby doctor than my own. He was open, honest, never rushed through my appointments and had a wonderful bedside manner. I trusted him and was open to his suggestions and advice, which he gave often. This was exactly what I needed at that point in my life, because there was only a short time to adjust.

There really wasn't any time to analyze my thoughts or feelings on whether I wanted to be pregnant or not. Harold didn't have the time to sit down and contemplate either. Instead we were forced to just begin preparing for the new addition in our lives. For me it would mean taking care of myself and a lot more visits to the doctor. For Harold it would mean trying to fit into the role of father and breadwinner. That's where our priorities were as we prepared to take the next step forward in our life together.

You would think one would learn from the past, but I don't think I did. When my father died I lamented not having savored each minute that I shared with him, but I continued to let moments pass without taking the time to appreciate the time spent with Harold. In my defense, I was trying to cope with the kaleidoscope of changes that were so rapidly taking place in my life.

After the checkup and confirmation of the pregnancy by my OB-GYN, I was on cloud nine. I was 22 years old, married and pregnant—could it get any better? There was a new purpose to my life and it filled the evenings, leaving no time for feeling lonely while Harold continued his evening shifts at Xerox. There were books to read, plans to make and habits to break. No more smoking, no more caffeine—this was the first order of business. The next was the food cautions—which I didn't question, only followed, even though some seemed strange.

Never eat raw meat or eggs. Always wash your hands after preparing food, between foods, and after visiting the restroom. To avoid contamination, don't mix foods together. Always use clean utensils and cooking equipment. Avoid dented cans. Eat or drink only pasteurized products, including apple juice. Completely defrost foods, especially meats, prior to cooking. Do not refreeze anything that has been defrosted. Reheat food only once, and then toss it. The list went on and on, but I was determined to follow each one of the recommendations. I was set on doing everything I could to keep my baby healthy. I was responsible in a way I had never been responsible before. This baby was in my body and was depending on me to keep him or her safe.

Along with the changes on the outside, there were also changes on the inside, with some unpleasant results. During the first trimester, vomiting became a part of my morning ritual. I started taking the bus to work instead of walking, as I felt nauseous and dizzy throughout the start of each day—though the doctor assured me this would pass. It was suggested that deep breathing sometimes helped, so I did a lot of deep breathing between trips to the ladies room.

I kept mints everywhere—in my purse, my pockets, and in my desk—to freshen my breath. I was also thirsty all the time, so I made sure I always had a thermos of iced water with me. Somehow I managed to get through those first few weeks of my pregnancy, until the day when the morning sickness, fatigue, cramps, and the all other causes of discomfort were gone and I could start enjoying just being pregnant.

Thankfully, for the rest of the first trimester I was feeling like my old self again. I began walking to work and busied myself reading about baby-safe furniture while beginning to visually design the nursery. By the start of my second trimester I was on to less serious matters, like how to prevent stretch marks and ensure I was getting proper nutrition and exercise. It was around this time that I was introduced to *Baby and Child Care* by Dr. Benjamin Spock.

"Trust yourself. You know more than you think you do." Those were the opening words of Dr. Spock's book, and they instilled within me the confidence that I knew how to be a mother; which was fine, but I still needed a boost from those I knew personally. I read the book from cover to cover and then read it again, marking passages that I found particularly interesting.

I talked with my friends and asked them for suggestions on baby-related reading material. I was constantly pressuring my mom and my sister for details on their experiences, bombarding them with questions I would later discuss with the doctor. There were so many issues to cover: How often should my baby eat? How do I know if my baby is getting enough milk? What is the importance of breast milk or formula in the first year? When should I introduce solid foods? When would my baby start getting teeth?

I asked my sister, "What is labor like?" To that she replied, "I am going to tell you what mom told me. There is a pre-ordained plan for pregnancy, and that is to fill your head with all sorts of matters requiring your attention so that there will be no thoughts of labor pains. Then, when it is over and you have your child next to you, all is forgotten. You know," she then added, "I guess if the pains of labor were on the minds of pregnant woman from conception to delivery, there wouldn't be many babies born." I was sure she was right, but I made a mental note to add this to the list of questions to ask my doctor on my next visit.

Was I the worst pregnant woman ever? I was a barrel of questions, but at least I had categorized them from the beginning, keeping basically to one topic area at a time. In this way, I was able to glean more information, as I wasn't jumping from one topic to another—such as diet, to care of the baby, to a host of other matters that puzzled me. I planned to use my upcoming visit with the doctor to ask questions concerning the changes going on inside my body and to discuss the topic of labor pains.

The physical changes in my body during the first six months took some getting used to. I found it impossible to lean over to tie my sneakers, and that standing on one leg was just not going to happen. I wanted to diet but I knew I must eat the foods my doctor had listed and stick to the portions he had outlined. The foods were nutritious but not what I considered "dieting". I managed to convince myself that the weight gain was the result of a human being growing within me, and that once the child had entered the world my body weight would drop appreciatively.

Waves of depression came over me; I found myself crying a lot and not knowing why. This was a happy time, so what was the matter with me, I wondered.

My obstetrician, Dr. Hamilton, was becoming my best friend, and why not? He met all the criteria. How would you define the word friend? Ralph Waldo Emerson, the famous American essayist, said, "A friend may well be reckoned the masterpiece of nature"; and according to an old Arab saying, "A friend is one to whom we may pour out all the contents of our hearts, chaff and grain together, knowing that the gentlest of hands will take and sift it, keep what is worth keeping, and blow the rest away."

Dr. Hamilton was experienced in working with pregnant women, had the medical knowledge to instill confidence, and possessed a genuine desire to make the experience as wonderful as possible. For me this qualified as a friend.

***

The scales were tipped in my favor. With morning sickness behind me and the feelings of depression on the back burner, it was smooth sailing. Harold and I budgeted our money carefully, since we would be without my paycheck once I reached my seventh month. The year was 1969 and there was no paid maternity leave. The rule was that if there were no complications with my pregnancy, I could continue to work right up to the start of the seventh month, but then I would have to leave work. This was the policy of most companies. Then, I would not be able to return to work until eight weeks after I had given birth. This meant I would be without a paycheck for at least four months.

Luckily, Blue Cross would cover the hospital expenses as well as part of the costs incurred for the obstetrician, which allowed us to come through the pregnancy clear of any debt. Since I saw my obstetrician on a regular basis, I made payments at each visit so I could settle this account before I took my leave of absence.

I was taking my prenatal vitamins, drinking milk and watching what I ate. I continued to get in as much exercise as possible, being sure to wear my pregnancy girdle and support bra at all times. It was a case of being uncomfortable in order to lessen the "scars" of birth and provide a safe environment for my baby. At least I was feeling great.

I enjoyed my checkups. Dr Hamilton examined me and said that I was coming along nicely, and he never made me feel as though I was a bother with all my questions. This was good for me, since most of my friends were childless and, though they tried to show interest, were unable to hide their boredom with the subject. Married or unmarried, women of my age were not starting families just yet, and I had exhausted my mom and sister to the point that they had started finding excuses to not have to talk with me.

My delivery date was set for April 15, but as for the baby's sex, well, not knowing was the norm in those days, as ultrasound's were not yet in common use as a means of determining the baby's gender. From 1966 there was a significant increase in the research and application of ultrasound technology in obstetrics and gynecology, and there followed an upsurge in the number of centers and people studying the application of ultrasound diagnosis across Europe, the United States and Japan. For me, gender wasn't an issue. All it meant was that I had to buy yellow or light green, instead of blue and pink, before my baby's arrival. I thought the colors would look good on my baby anyway.

As my pregnancy progressed, the roles were reversed between Dr. Hamilton and I—he became the one who controlled our conversations. I seemed to have exhausted all the questions I could think of, so I was a willing listener as he explained that, most likely within 2 hours after delivery, I would be moved to a hospital room that I would share with another new mother, and that our babies would be cared for in the nursery and brought to us for feeding and for the commencement of the bonding process. On this advice, I went on a tour of the maternity ward, delivery room and nursery at the Genesee Hospital, chatting with the nurses and doctors. I learned there were no set visiting hours for family members and that I would stay at the hospital for two or three days before returning home. When I asked how long it would be before I was back up and around, the doctor replied that my body would let me know when. I would find myself extremely tired after delivery and want to sleep, but I would be encouraged to take a short walk several hours afterwards.

Of course, I told Dr. Hamilton what I had learned, and he said that I would most likely remain in the hospital for between 2 and 4 days after delivery. He cautioned me to tell anyone who had a cold or was not feeling well to hold off visiting until they felt better. It was during one of these later visits to my doctor, when most of the major details had been covered, that I ventured to ask a question that I had so far been holding back. It seemed relatively unimportant, but I still wanted to know. So I finally asked, "Doctor, when can I expect to get my figure back?"

Dr. Hamilton replied, "Although your uterus will no longer be carrying the baby, your abdomen will still be extended, taking approximately 6 weeks or thereabouts to shrink back to its normal size." He added that I could help the process along by starting light exercises once I was home and felt up to it. Regular exercises to tighten the abdominal muscles should wait until after my postpartum checkup. Then I could pick up on my regular routine. As for dieting, that should wait; instead I should just keep up the good food habits that I'd maintained during pregnancy.

One question always seemed to lead to another. I think this was because I didn't want to find myself worrying about anything, so I just presented all my concerns to the doctor for clarification. One cause for concern was how much I was sweating. I was pleased to learn that this was normal; though it didn't please me to learn that it would probably continue after the baby was born. Before I left Dr. Hamilton's office that day, I remembered something he had said early on, which was that no matter how many questions I asked or how much I talked with other parents, it all boiled down to me. How it might be for me could be totally different from the experiences of another woman, and I should keep that thought in my head.

For example, I heard that constipation might be a problem during the first weeks after my baby was born; to try and reduce the chances of this, Dr. Hamilton said that I should eat plenty of high fiber foods, such as whole grain cereals and breads; raw fruit and vegetables; and drink plenty of water. Yet my sister said that I could eat all the fiber in the world and still have the problem. I was also told that I might have difficulty urinating, and when I put this to Dr. Hamilton, he replied that it might be a problem as a result of the anesthetic, the pressure on my bladder during labor, discomfort from stitches, or for a number of other reasons. But, again, this may not be part of my experience.

I liked the way the doctor explained what could cause a symptom to present itself. For instance, when I asked about bleeding after delivery, he explained that it was due to the placenta, or "afterbirth", being attached to the inside of my uterus. For the first few days, it would be bright red, changing to a pinkish-colored discharge by the end of the first week. This could continue for up to 3 weeks after delivery, decreasing gradually until finally stopping.

By now I had heard the worst and the best experiences of pregnancy and birth, but it was all put into perspective when in my readings I came across something about people's recollections of the past often being prejudiced, and that this prejudice has two causes. The first lies in people's perceptions of events; that is, people more often tend to perceive events as pleasant rather than unpleasant. The second cause is the fading affect prejudice; that the affect associated with unpleasant events fades faster than the affect associated with pleasant events.

Why do pleasant events outnumber unpleasant events? It is believed that people seek out positive experiences and avoid negative ones. This explained a lot about mothers who claim they can't recall the pain of labor. It also reinforced the truth that one's opinion is just that: one's opinion.

***

As the weeks past I tried to stay focused on getting the apartment ready for the baby. My head swam with all the things that needed to be done. Knowing my limited "recall" on details, I plastered notes everywhere for easy referral.

"Are you planning on breast-feeding?" my friend Barbara asked one afternoon. We were seated at lunch, talking about nothing in particular, when she laid this bombshell on me. All I could do was look up at her, with my mouth agape and half-chewed food there for her to view. I must have been in that trance for at least ten seconds before I was able to make a connection between my brain and my mouth. I hadn't thought about it, until then.

I gave her the intellectual response, "I don't know."

Barb then spilled out the purpose of her question. Being all about fashion, she told me I should be prepared—whether or not I decided to breast-feed So, forcing me to quickly finish the rest of my meal, she then dragged me to the maternity store and, shoving her way through the throngs of pregnant women, placed me in front of a rack of nursing bras. Barb chatted away about the need for a well-designed and quality bra, adamantly proclaiming that I not scrimp on the purchase or I would regret it later. The nursing bra must have great support, or I would be complaining about back aches. Its design should allow for nursing without having to go through a lot of maneuvers. I took her advice and purchased what Barb felt was the best of the bunch, stunned by how much I was spending on a bra that would later find its way to the bottom of my dresser drawer.

Driven by a need to justify such an extravagant purchase, I began reading about beast-feeding. It was all there, down to each grim detail, starting with the fact that my breasts would be larger and heavier when they were filled with milk, and then continuing on to explain the intimate details. For the first few days, a liquid called colostrum would flow from my nipples. Colostrum was nourishing and contained substances to protect the baby from infection. True breast milk would come approximately three days after the baby was born.

I read on and learned that I should expect some discomforting pain on the second or third day, when colostrum changed to milk and there was more fluid in my breasts. Frequent nursing of my baby or expressing the milk by hand would offer relief from that pain. On my next visit to the doctor, I sought his advice on the matter. Dr. Hamilton confirmed the information and then gave me pamphlets on nursing. He agreed that a good nursing bra would help in alleviating the pain, but if it persisted I could put ice packs on my breasts. I silently prayed that the ice would not be necessary.

On the upside, the doctor told me that I could expect the discomfort to ease within 36 hours. Then, as an aside, he added that not every mother was able to nurse their baby, and that we would have to wait until later to determine if I fell into that category. If it turned out that I did, I would then be given a prescription for medication that would dry up my milk. I was embarrassed by how interesting I found that notion to be.

***

As my delivery date grew closer, I began making arrangements for getting to and from the hospital. I packed and unpacked my suitcase, trying to make sure I had everything I would need for myself and for bringing my baby home. I arranged for my mother-in-law to come stay with us for the first week, and for my sister and mother to take over afterwards. Then, I went back again to checking the suitcase.

I kept getting bigger and clumsier every day. I not only had trouble putting on my shoes, I couldn't even see them any more. No matter how I sat or lay it was uncomfortable, and I would have given anything for a good night's sleep. I kept alternating between sitting and standing, but I couldn't stand long before my legs became weak from the combined pressure of my weight and the baby's. All the novelty of pregnancy had worn off as I suffered through the sleepless nights and uncomfortable days. I constantly wanted to eat but knew gaining too much weight would make the delivery harder. That was the only thing that kept me out of the refrigerator.

To keep my mind occupied and off my discomfort, I began making a list of names for our baby. Each evening I would press Harold for names and add them to the list. We put the list aside for a few days, pulled it out and presented each other with our choices. It worked well on all counts. It kept me thinking about the wonderful gift I would have at the end of this ordeal instead of how I was feeling getting to that day. We finally settled on a boy's name: Erik Scott. The problem was finding a girl's name. We toyed around with a few names but couldn't reach any agreement, so we decided to ask friends and family for their input.

Time marched along and, as my final day quickly approached, I was kept busy with last minute details at work. My co-workers surprised me with a baby shower at my last official lunch hour. Everyone from the 1st floor to the 28th floor was there, and by the time it was over, the list of items I still needed for the baby and nursery had been greatly reduced. Then, after having been home a week, I was given another baby shower; this time by my old room mate, Fran. She invited my family and our friends, and I was able to cross off the last of the necessary purchases. I could now relax and take it slow, making several small purchases at my leisure.

Each evening and all during the weekend, Harold worked non-stop on the nursery. He painted, papered, carpeted and dragged in the furnishings. Each day before he left for work, he cautioned me to stay out of the room so I wouldn't breathe in the paint smells or carpet fibers that he insisted were floating in the air. I obeyed him because he was only thinking of my welfare, and I felt he was probably right. I had to be careful, but it wasn't easy. Finally, when he was sure the fumes were no longer an issue, Harold allowed me to supervise the positioning of the furniture, the hanging of the curtains and the placing of all the baby items in convenient locations. After that, he insisted that I concentrate on just taking it easy.

"Read something you like," he would say, "and stop scaring yourself trying to become a pro on having a baby."

Good advice—and I felt comfortable accepting it.

***

My final month of pregnancy finally arrived. I was still exercising, if you could call it that, and still trying to waddle around the apartment. I was definitely ready to go back to being one person again, instead of two and looking like three. Thank God, I thought, there were only five days left until the delivery. I couldn't get much bigger—I hoped.

On April 10, 1969, I forced myself to wake up and see Harold off. He had offered to work a day shift for a friend, along with doing his afternoon shift, which meant he needed all the sleep he could get. I had experienced one of those restless night's that are common for pregnant women; trying every position possible to get comfortable but not succeeding. Probably because of all the tossing and turning, I found myself waking up with a backache. I managed to sit up long enough to have a glass of water while I watched my husband drink his coffee. Early in the pregnancy I couldn't have been in the same room where coffee was brewing. Having been a coffee drinker for such a long time, I was surprised that the smell could make me sick. But it was true, and I had little trouble giving it up.

As soon as Harold was out the door, I lay back down—something I never did. Only I couldn't get comfortable, so instead I went about cleaning up the kitchen and the rest of the apartment. I kept looking for things to keep me busy, until finally I was tired enough, I thought, to fall asleep. Just in case I turned out to be wrong, I took my book with me.

No matter what I did, I couldn't get comfortable, and I couldn't focus on reading my book. This could be it, I thought, but that was exactly what I thought four weeks ago when I had Harold rush me to the hospital in the middle of the night. I was prepped for delivery, only to spend an uneventful night in a hospital bed. False labor pains they called it.

***

"I feel ... funny?"

"What do you mean by funny?"

"I don't know. Sort of different."

"Okay, I'll be right over."

I was so glad to have my sister near. Mary answered the phone on the first ring and in no time she was at the apartment, taking charge. Sisters are wonderful, as they have a way of understanding you even when you seem to have lost touch with yourself. All those years of living under the same roof makes them an expert in interpreting unspoken feelings.

As soon as Mary arrived I felt safe. I knew she had no experience with anything remotely like delivering a baby; it was just having her with me that made all the difference in the world. Every now and then I experienced a sharp pain, sort of like waves of indigestion, but they passed quickly and I felt fine again—not great, but at least bearable. I soon fell into what was quite an unpleasant pattern—a few moments of relief followed by waves of indigestion. I thought that maybe I should eat something, and turned to offer up the suggestion to Mary. It was then I noticed that she was watching me closely. She only took her eyes off me to check her watch.

"How do you feel?" she asked

"Okay, I guess."

"Did you just have another one?"

"Another what?"

"Labor pain."

It was only then that I realized what was going on. I was in labor and didn't know it. After all the questions I had asked and all the books I had consumed, I never once figured I was in labor; probably because I had five more days to go. How could I have

53

forgotten something as important as timing the contractions? Easily, I told myself, since I was the 'contractionee' and had never had contractions before.

Mary talked into the phone while I lay there wondering what should happen next. She'd had two children so I figured she knew what she was doing, and she did it so well that I found it difficult to interfere. I looked at the clock; it had been almost an hour since she had come over. I seemed to have lost all sense of time as I continued to steel myself for each new wave of pain, which were becoming more regular, and waited for her instructions.

"I'll call Harold once we're at the hospital. Right now you need to get dressed. I'll get your suitcase."

It was like I was in a tunnel, unable to think clearly and far from comprehending English. My only aims were to try and recall the Lamaze breathing techniques and to try and stay focused. Somehow Mary managed to get me ready, get the hospital bag out of the closet and get us both out the door to the waiting taxi where, upon seeing us, the driver immediately jumped out of the cab. He took the bag from Mary and helped me settle in the back seat. In one quick motion he got back in the driver's seat, and we were on our way. I heard Mary tell him to take us to Genesee Hospital. I wanted to say something but I didn't know what, so I concentrated on not letting out any embarrassing screams or moans.

It was becoming difficult, and I was finally starting to know what it felt like to be in labor. I needed to lie down and fold my body up into a ball. I needed to yell and scream out with each wave of pain, but I still had some pride left. I tried desperately to keep in control, dreading every pot hole we hit on our way and grateful that the hospital was not that far.

When we pulled up in front of Genesee Hospital, Mary jumped out of the cab and rushed up to the entrance, returning with an attendant pushing a wheelchair. Carefully, they worked together to help me into the chair. I heard Mary say she would handle the check-in while they took me directly to the labor room.

I had just enough sanity left to enjoy a moment to shine. I reached into my purse and presented Mary with a manila envelope, marked "hospital sign-in". Inside were all the relevant signed papers, a list of personal details, my license and insurance card. Although I wanted to stick around and be complimented for my incredible foresight, I was in too much pain to do anything more than appreciate the smile of gratitude on my sister's face.

By the time I had been wheeled into a curtained-off cubicle, all I wanted to do was climb into the bed and rest. But though I was helped up on the bed, instead of being able to rest I was told to undress and put on a hospital gown. I did this as quickly as I could, which wasn't very quick at all. By the time I had accomplished that feat, the doctor was in the room. He monitored my progress, timed the contractions, and checked my heart rate and blood pressure. He then checked my cervix. Even though all of this had been explained during my prenatal visits, he let me know what he was doing. The baby's heartbeat was checked with a fetoscope (a type of stethoscope). When he was done, he said that everyone was doing just fine, and then turned to talk to the nurse before easing out of my cubicle.

The nurse was doing an efficient job of shaving and prepping me when another nurse came in to hook me up to an IV. All of this had been explained to me as well, and came as no surprise. I also knew that they would be giving me an enema, and I steeled myself for this, but neither nurse seemed to remember this part of the procedure. Not that I was a glutton for punishment, but I had to ask when the enema would be given. The nurses glanced at each other, but before I could panic, Nurse Peterson said, "You're too far along for that." This was the best news I'd heard all morning.

"Who will be with you during labor and delivery," Nurse Peterson asked, and I told her my sister would fill in until my husband was able to get to the hospital. Then they questioned me on what type of pain medication I would be requiring. I wanted to say something to knock me out until it was over, but replied an epidural block. This was what my doctor and I had discussed when I was naïve about labor pains. The epidural would numb only the lower part of my body, giving some relief from pain while allowing me to do my job in delivery.

Mary soon joined me, letting me know that my husband was on the way and that she would be able to help me through the labor pains if he didn't make it in time. I knew she had been told how close I was to delivery. So I lay there wondering what I should do next, but it wasn't to be my decision; I had joined the chorus of screaming and moaning women around me.

The doctor returned to check my progress and then called a nurse to assist. "She's ready; let's get her to the delivery room." For the first time, I became scared. Until that moment, the delivery room had just been a word, with little practical meaning. Now the reality sunk in that this was the room where the real pain would begin. I tried the Lamaze breathing to remain calm. I told myself that this was what it was all about and there was no turning back. But I was scared, and in so much pain that I didn't dare speak or move. As I was wheeled out of the labor room, I caught a glimpse of Harold in the hallway. He saluted me before going with the nurse to put on his delivery room clothing.

I was hoisted into the bed; my legs were put into the stirrups and a sheet thrown over me. In a daze, I watched the flurry of activity around me, asking if my husband was there yet but not hearing the reply, as a wave of pain knocked the breath out of me. My doctor performed an episiotomy to widen the opening of the vagina and to prevent bowel movement. This was the big moment. The second stage of my labor, which can last less than 30 minutes or over 3 hours, was upon me. I prayed for it to be fewer than 30 minutes.

I was told that though I would feel the urge to push with each contraction, because the cervix had opened, I must wait until cued to do so. When is heard a voice say "push", I did so gladly. Each subsequent time I heard "push", I followed the command. An hour and forty-five minutes would then tick by before the delivery of my baby. I became aware that Harold was in the room. "Encourage her to breath. Say 'breathe with me … BREATHE WITH ME' … That's the way … just like that … Good … STAY WITH IT … just like that … LOOK AT ME … Stay with me … Good for you … It's going away … Good … Good … Now just rest; that was so good

With my husband there, I managed to obey; until I heard someone say that the baby's head was emerging. Then Harold told me that the doctor was easing our baby's body out of the birth canal and into the world. I heard a loud cry, and then my baby was passed across a pool of white uniforms until he came to rest on my chest.

Finally it was over; we had a baby boy. I couldn't stop crying as they laid him on my chest so I could feel his soft skin and touch his naked body. I was in the final stage of labor: the period immediately after giving birth. It could last a few minutes or up to half an hour. The contractions continued, and although they weren't as hard as before, they were still very painful. We had talked about this, so I knew it was necessary to suffer through as it would help push the placenta and amniotic sac (also called the afterbirth) out of the vagina. I felt a little lost when they cut the umbilical cord and took my baby away.

As I stretched out to watch, I could hear my baby crying while they checked his heart rate, breathing, muscle tone, reflexes and skin color. He wailed loudly when he was given a sponge bath to clean off the thick, creamy substance known as vernix, which protected his skin while in the womb. He announced his disapproval when weighed and measured for length and for head and chest circumference. He began a nasal whimpering as his nose was suctioned to clear the airways to enable him to breathe more easily. Antibiotic eye ointment was applied to his eyes to prevent infection; then he was given a vitamin K shot in the thigh to enhance the clotting of blood. His tiny heel was pricked to extract a blood sample to test for phenylketonuria (PKU), a metabolic disorder, and other conditions. Finally, before leaving the delivery room, Erik's footprints were recorded and he was cleaned up, and both he and I were given wristbands in order to identify us.

I was given a final examination before I could leave the delivery room. My blood pressure, pulse and temperature were all checked. Then I saw Harold holding his son. I was tired—drained of every bit of strength my body once possessed—but I was happy; so very happy. Harold came over to the side of the bed and lowered the baby into my arms. He was perfect—two arms, two legs, with all his fingers and toes. I hadn't held him long before he was again whisked away; this time into the arms of a waiting nurse.

"Rest now; you've been a busy girl."

I closed my eyes. All I could feel was the motion of the gurney as I was transferred to another area. I tried to sleep, but every time I did, someone came along and started pushing on my stomach. And then I could feel motion again. I was lifted up and transferred to yet another bed; but I didn't open my eyes, as it took too much energy. Finally I was left alone, and fell into a deep, restful sleep.

***

One of the first things I did while preparing for the birth of the baby was talk with both my obstetrician and medical doctor, to get a recommendation for a pediatrician to care for our baby. I wanted the best, and though several kinds of physicians provide medical care to kids, pediatricians are medical doctors who are specially trained in children's health. Pediatricians are often regarded as the first choice for a child's doctor, because they have at least three years of specialized education in children's health after they complete four years of medical school. Pediatricians are trained to diagnose and treat illnesses and injuries commonly seen in children, and typically emphasize disease prevention through initiating a healthy lifestyle, safety precautions, and regular check ups on a child's growth and development. They also provide advice on child-rearing and behavioral issues, which can be helpful to first time parents. I knew that there would be around six well-child visits in the first year of our baby's life. This would be followed by three visits the next year and then one yearly visit for our baby when he was aged between three and six; with a routine well-child examination at least every two years, and then annual checkups at predetermined milestones. During the examinations, the pediatrician performs a complete physical examination and evaluation of a child's height, weight, physical development, blood pressure, vision, hearing, diet and sleeping habits. There are also a series of immunizations done, which are updated at a later stage. So, while I slept, the pediatrician I had chosen, Dr. Boettrich, performed the first checkup.

She checked Erik's reflexes, breathing, heart sounds, and weight (which usually drops after birth). The doctor also checked the umbilical stump (a clamp will be left on for about 24 hours) and looked for conditions such as possible dislocation of the hips (hip dysplasia). When the examination was completed, she had a full history of this new human being.

It was around noon when I finally woke up and realized I was in a hospital room and on a bed with rails along the sides. I rang the buzzer that had been placed next to my hand and a nurse came. She helped me out of the bed and into the bathroom. I splashed water on my face and padded it dry before I allowed myself to look into the mirror. This was not my face! The face reflected in the mirror was old and worn out. I didn't look like that, but it was my face.

Exhausted, I climbed into the shower and washed my hair and my body, then climbed out and dried off. Wanting to lay down again, I forced myself to slip into a nightgown and robe, fix my hair, and camouflage my face before leaving the bathroom. When satisfied I could do no more, I returned to the room to find that my bed had been remade and the nurse was waiting for me.

"How do you feel?"

"Better, thanks."

She helped me into the bed and I immediately fell back to sleep. When I awoke again it was to the sound of voices in the room. The nurse was talking with Harold.

"She's doing just fine. She's a little tired, but that is to be expected."

Seeing that I was awake, Harold came over to sit on the edge of the bed. He gave me a big hug and kiss, smiling all the time. Finally he released me and brought over flowers and a card. The nurse left us alone and then returned with little baby Erik, and all the attention was focused on him. No words can describe the feeling of looking down at a small child that you have created and brought into the world. It is even more impossible to describe the feeling of touching such an object of love!

Too soon little Erik was taken away again, and I was forced to perform the menial task of eating, which I did quickly so that Harold could take me to the nursery to look at our son crinkling up his face and fidgeting in the tightly wrapped blanket. We watched him until it became too uncomfortable for me to stand. Then all too quickly it was time for Harold to leave, with the promise that he would return in the morning. He took the rest of the week off.

Nancy and George Anderson, Erik's godparents, spent as much time at the hospital as Harold did. I had met George when we were in business school, and our friendship developed into more of a brother-sister relationship. We were inseparable and looked out for each other. When George met Nancy, he immediately introduced us; and George was one of the first people I introduced Harold to.

When George and Nancy married, we were part of the wedding party. When there was a great movie or a show, we all went together. We liked the same food and the same games, so we double-dated and spent the majority of our time in each other's company. They became a necessary part of our lives and, of course, we hoped that they would become as important to little Erik. There was no question that they would be our choice for his godparents.

I remained in the hospital for the allotted three-day period before I was released. We pack up my belongings, the flowers and cards that friends and family had dropped off, and our baby boy. Motherhood and fatherhood was about to begin.

***

Friends and family were constantly dropping in to see little Erik; commenting on what a beautiful baby he was. "And so good!" they'd say. That he was. Most of the time I had to wake him up for his feedings, as he slept constantly. Harold and I spent more time standing over the crib looking down at his peaceful form than we did holding him. He seemed to want only to sleep, and we consoled ourselves by saying that we should be glad he was such a good baby. Other couples walked around like zombies when their newborns came home. We, on the other hand, seemed to get all the sleep we needed. But we didn't really want it like that. Erik woke up sometimes when we changed him, but even this disruption didn't always disturb his sleep. I put in a call to his pediatrician, Dr. Boettrich, but she didn't see it as a problem and told us all babies were different.

We spent our time planning for the months ahead; both of us knowing that I had to return to work. We discussed this with my sister, Mary, and she offered to watch little Erik for us. Harold and I didn't have to discuss sharing the responsibility of having a baby in the house. It wasn't necessary. We set up a schedule so that we were both given equal time with Erik, as we found that we were both responding to Erik's infrequent cries. At first it seemed appropriate and didn't upset anything, so we would both end up at the side of his crib; but later we decided each of us should have some time alone with Erik.

I looked down at our baby; his body comfortably curled—formed into the same position in which he had spent the previous months within my uterus. All that crib, and there he was, "scrunched up", with his arms and legs not fully extended. He appeared to be bowlegged but, according to the books I had read, he would stretch out, little by little, and by the time he had reached his half-birthday, he'd be fully expanded.

By the end of his first month, Erik still wasn't lifting his head even briefly, nor turning from side to side; and his movements were still jerky. Sleep was the most important thing in his life, with food running a close second. Sleeping schedules are intermittent and quite variable from one infant to another. He slept for a total of 16 to 17 hours in a 24-hour period, but it was usually broken up into eight or so naps, with us waking him every few hours around the clock for feeding.

Erik continued to be "a good baby". He slept through the night and through most of the day. I would wake him to feed him and show him off. I wanted to wake him just to play with him during the day, but the pediatrician advised against it. She told me to let him sleep, and only wake him for his feedings or when he needed to be changed. Dr. Boettrich said that it wasn't at all uncommon for a baby to sleep most of the time; she even said she could quote mothers who would envy my situation.

As Erik wasn't a light sleeper, I could do my housework and anything else I needed to do, without disturbing his sleep. I continued to spend a lot of time in the nursery watching him and wishing he'd wake up, and sometimes he did. Sometimes he smiled or drew his little mouth into a pout while he slept. The pediatrician said it was gas; it could be, but I liked to think he was smiling at me. Sometimes I wondered if he had memories and dreamt. Why not? I answered myself; he's had a few experiences in his life to dream about, and even think about.

I watched him and smelt him. I loved being with Erik and felt warm and content in the nursery. I would sometimes sit in the nursery with a book, or just watching him. He was so soft and cuddly, smelling of the baby powder and baby lotion that scented his room. I loved the pleasant smell and I loved being with my baby. I tried to look into the future and plan what we would do together. There was so much to share with him beyond the walls of the apartment.

As spring started to settle in, it was becoming quite pleasant outside. There was a glassed-in sun porch at the front of our apartment, and I spent many days sitting there with Erik so he could enjoy nature at a distance. The grass was green, the birds were singing happily in the trees, and the sun had managed to shine for most of the days since Erik's birth. Sometimes I would step outside so we could just smell spring and feel it around us. When he was five weeks old, I dressed him warmly and took him out for a short spin, before returning to the sun porch, with the windows open. Spring is a nice time of the year to be out watching nature wake up, and knowing that summer is just around the corner. Winter is okay, but can be a real drag, as it hangs on for what seems like an eternity.

Playing the role of doting parent, I started taking pictures of Erik both inside our home and outside, as soon as the pediatrician said it was okay. By the time he was six weeks old I had managed to fill several photo albums, which I kept out so visitors could look through them. Being proud and showing off a baby is acceptable; probably because parents can't help it. But taking care of a baby requires attention to more than just how cute they are.

By his 1-month birthday, Erik's neck muscles were getting stronger, allowing him to occasionally hold up his head for a few moments while lying on his stomach. He could also turn his head from side to side. When we entered his room, we often found him in the midst of exploring his body; mainly discovery of his hands and feet. I began playing baby games with him: holding his arms above his head and asking, "How big is baby?"; or reciting "This Little Piggy" and counting his toes. He made such cute sounds when he gurgled, cooed, grunted, and hummed to express his feelings. Sometimes he even squealed or laughed when we talked to him face-to-face.

Even though they said Erik had been able to recognize us since he was just a few days old, by the end of the first month he was showing it with a big smile each time he saw us. We sang to him and played classical tapes for his enjoyment, which became obvious as he cooed, smacked his lips, and his legs and arms moved spasmodically. When I held him in my arms while sitting on the sun porch, the sound of the wind chimes or the ticking clock amused him. Sometimes I would take his rattle and move it in front of him, and his eyes would follow it around while his body squirmed in motion.

***

On May 15 I took Erik for his first visit with his pediatrician since his in-hospital checkup. I dressed him in his finest baby wear and checked outside to see what he would need to keep warm. He was looking so sweet I couldn't stand it. I quickly slipped into my clothes so as not to be late. I was excited about the visit, and I wouldn't be disappointed. Watching your baby being examined is quite special, and I know it is something I will never forget. I had made sure I was prepared for his first visit. I told the obstetrician how he was sleeping and eating, and related my observations about his demeanor. I had no concerns to share about his development. The doctor then proceeded to examine Erik. She did a general physical examination, took growth measurements (head circumference, length, and weight) and checked for heart and lung function. She checked the healing of the umbilical cord area and the circumcision.

I watched as she checked Erik's startled responses to noise; his ability to follow movement with his eyes; his skin tone; development of the genitals and the abdominal organs. I even took pictures during his first visit to the pediatrician, and she accommodated nicely, working around me as she asked about Erik's feedings—including how often he ate, whether I was breastfeeding or bottle-feeding, the number of wet diapers, and the frequency and characteristics of Erik's bowel movements. She also wanted to know about his routines, including active times and fussy periods.

"Babies have no privacy" ran through my head as I supplied the doctor with personal details while she checked over Erik's naked body; lifting and probing while he squirmed under her gentle hands. When my son was again released to my care, he was whimpering, and though I didn't like my baby crying, I had to admit I liked Dr. Boettrich very much. I found her to be gentle and efficient, but also able to administer the proper dosage of care and concern.

She asked if I had any questions and, when I said I didn't, told me that Erik seemed to be doing fine and complimented me on my care-giving. She informed me that the next visit would also include a test of Erik's blood for hemoglobin (the oxygen-carrying part of red blood cells) and lead level, and that she wanted me to take note of his sleeping times and positions. I had read that at that visit he would be checked for his muscle function and tone, as well as his hearing, which was checked by the way he turned toward and responded to voices speaking at normal volumes.

I already knew that I should keep track of certain developmental milestones, including when Erik lifted his head, rolled over from front to back and back to front without assistance, sat up unassisted, grasped a small object with thumb and fingers, bore some weight on his legs, and cooed and babbled in nonsense syllables. But most of that would happen later on in his development. For the time being, the most important thing, medically, was to ensure he made his regular visits to the doctor's office.

When Harold arrived home, I shared the full details of Erik's first visit to the pediatrician with him, which made him anxious to join us for the next one; scheduled for July 14, 1969.

CHAPTER 3
1969

Erik rewarded all our loving care with a beaming, toothless, just-for-you smile that totally disarmed us and brought tears to my eyes. I was the first he smiled at, and when his dad arrived home that day, I handed him Erik, who looked straight at his father and smiled this gorgeous all-gums grin. He was still sleeping for long chunks of time, having to be awoken for feedings, and still not staying awake for long intervals. I noticed his movements were becoming less jerky and more coordinated; his arms and legs moving in smoother, more circular motions. When I held an object in front of him he would try to grab it.

By the time he had reached his three-month birthday on July 10, Erik was able to independently support his head, and I had caught him lifting his head and chest, as if he were doing mini-pushups, in his crib. I continued to encourage his eye-hand coordination by holding out a toy to see if he'd grasp it, clapping my hands in approval when he did. By the look in his eyes, it was clear that Erik could recognize us; and he would smile when friends visited, but it was easy to tell he was beginning to sort out who was who in his life, and he definitely preferred some people over others.

Each time Erik heard my voice he would look directly at me and start gurgling or trying to talk back. I spent a lot of time reading to him, varying the pitch of my voice and watching his reactions. I talked to him constantly as I went about caring for him or fixing meals, and he seemed to enjoy the conversations immensely. Sometimes he would get distracted by an object in the room, or his attention would be caught by a sound. At such moments I would tell him that he was just like his father, and we would laugh together.

Harold or I read to him each night; his baby book library growing at leaps and bounds, though at his young age reading the same book to him would have been okay.. We exposed him to new sounds and new words as often as possible, and stimulated his sense of touch by handing him furry, soft, rough or bumpy objects. He communicated his preference through his expression, and his different reactions would often make me laugh. I loved to hold him up to a mirror and watch him smile at himself; his eyes adverting to my mouth as I talked or laughed at him. The fun of parenthood just kept unfolding, and I was excited about what would happen in the months ahead.

On July 14, I dressed Erik and, along with his father, we left for the pediatrician's office, located in the downtown area. As it was such a beautiful day, I managed to get us all ready early enough so we could walk instead of taking the bus. In terms of natural beauty, there is very little in the Rochester area to compare with the Genesee River Gorge and its 96-foot high falls. One of the features that sets Rochester apart from other cities is the way it is integrated with the water. From the Genesee River flowing through the center of town, to Lake Ontario forging its borders, there are few areas of the city that don't call your attention to the beauty of the water, and walking downtown always seems to soothe my soul.

Outside, the sun was shining; the air hot and humid as we headed down Main Street with Erik in his carriage, crossing over the interloop bridge and then down past the many restaurants and boutiques that line the sides of the street, until we turned into Alexander Street. We passed the fashionable old building store fronts until we had reached the entrance to the doctor's office. The doctors in this office are associated with the Genesee Hospital next door, where Erik was born. On more than one occasion I had seen the convenience of such an arrangement. One time when I was at my obstetrician's office, which was also in this same building, one of the women in the waiting room entered the final stages of labor. In a matter of seconds the receptionist was making calls and one of the nurses had told the doctor what was happening. A wheelchair soon appeared in the lobby and, accompanied by the doctor and an attendant, the woman was wheeled out of the room and taken to the hospital. I felt secure knowing that the hospital was so close, and how perfectly the situation had been handled.

I entered the pediatrician's office with my husband and baby, acting like an old pro. After letting the receptionist know we had arrived for our appointment, I cautioned my husband to mind his step as I guided him around the toys in the waiting room until we had sat down in one of the comfortable chairs. Harold held Erik in his arms and glanced around at the surroundings, just as I did. It looked like a big nursery. There were nursery rhymes and cartoon characters on the walls; on the floor were toys which the older children played with; and waiting mothers and fathers were seated around the perimeter, either reading or watching their children at play. I reached out and took Erik from Harold's arms, glad it was warm outside and we didn't have to fuss with coats and boots. Harold sat beside me, stiff at first but then finally relaxing.

They called Erik's name. "Come on, dear, it's our turn," I said, anxious to get started; probably because I thought Harold would enjoy seeing how they examined our baby; but most likely because I wanted to see it all again. I had watched very closely during Erik's first examination, fascinated as the doctor moved her hands over Erik's frame, probing gently and then moving on until she had examined every inch of his body. I could have recited each movement she would make and in what order, assuming the process was done exactly the same each time. I smiled, thinking that it probably wasn't quite so robotic yet followed a pattern of some sort.

The nurse showed us into a different examination room than we had been in the first time. I looked around as I entered, enjoying the pleasant way the room had been decorated with the children in mind. The room in which Erik had had his first examination was decorated in a Minnie Mouse theme; this room had Sesame Street characters.

When we were all settled in the room, the nurse said, "You can get Erik undressed; Dr. Boettrich will be with you shortly." The door was gently pulled closed and we were left alone. I started undressing Erik while his father looked through a pile of magazines; not finding any to his liking, he stood next to the padded table and played with Erik.

Dr. Boettrich entered and I re-introduced her to Harold, who she had met briefly at the hospital after I had given birth. Dr. Boettrich had a heavy accent that I believed to be Swedish, and I had informed Harold of this earlier. "Sometimes she is hard to understand, but I think it will be much easier once we become accustomed to her. Just listen carefully when she speaks and when you don't understand, ask her to repeat what she said. She won't mind."

We stood close by as she examined Erik, watching as she measured his head and looked for any abnormalities. She checked his fontanels, also known as the soft spots, and felt the roof of his mouth to ensure that it was complete. She then listened to his heartbeat and checked his lungs. "I was checking to see if Erik had a heart murmur," she told us, "as it's common among newly-born infants and nothing to be alarmed about; but Erik doesn't."

Dr. Boettrich began touching Erik's tummy, making sure all the abdominal organs were of the right size. She then felt the pulse in our baby's groin and checked his genitals, explaining that she was checking whether the testicles had descended. She then moved on to examine his navel—the umbilical stump had dried up and dropped off 16 days prior to the visit. Next she checked his limbs, moving them to and fro. She checked that the lower legs and feet were in alignment and that the legs were the right length.

With the examination almost complete, Dr Boettrich gently turned Erik over on to his stomach and felt along his spine to ensure that all the vertebrae were in place. She then asked about his bowel movements, and for this I was prepared. In order to keep track of his urinating and his bowel movements, I had tacked a tablet to the wall near the changing table, with a pencil attached. Having brought it with me, I handed this information over to the doctor. Dr. Boettrich nodded approvingly.

She then checked his soft spots and measured his head and legs again. Suddenly I began to feel concerned, but I couldn't put my finger on the reason for this feeling. I continued to watch Dr. Boettrich carefully, searching her face for an explanation as she proceeded with the examination. I couldn't read her expression. Harold seemed to be calm and enjoying the scene, but then he hadn't watched her examine Erik the first time. Something seemed different.

What was this feeling—what caused it? I wondered. I felt sort of tingly, like I'd had an electrical shock. Maybe I was just nervous. No, I thought; she seemed to be repeating certain steps in Erik's examination, as though she was not quite sure of the results she was getting. When the doctor started to speak, I felt myself stiffen in preparation for bad news, but all she said was, "You can get Erik dressed now. When you finish, come down to my office. You remember where it is, don't you?"

"Yes, yes, I remember," I announced hastily, managing to smile confidently before the doctor left us alone.

It amazed me how quickly I was able to make it all seem right again in my mind, just by telling myself it was silly of me to be so worried. I could tell just by looking at my sweet baby that he was fine, so why should I worry? Besides, shouldn't I be glad that the doctor was so thorough, instead of being alarmed?. Dr. Boettrich was just doing her job. I started to relax, and chatted happily with Harold as I dressed Erik. I told Harold that the doctor would review everything she had done, as well as tell us Erik's weight and length, and that after sharing her findings she would ask us if we had any questions. "You can ask her anything, so don't hesitate," I told him as we started down the aisle to her office. "And remember that she can be hard to understand if you don't listen carefully."

I could see the grin on Harold's face as we advanced down the hall. He had once asked me if I realized how many words I wasted in making sure that he understood me. I did know, but I just couldn't seem to stop myself. That was one of my flaws that he sweetly overlooked.

71

The three of us entered the pediatrician's office and sat in the chairs in front of her desk. Dr Boettrich looked up from the papers spread out before her and paused slightly before she began to speak. Just as I had promised my husband, the pediatrician reviewed her examination of Erik and told us his weight and length. But she didn't finish up with the words I'd been expecting—"Be sure to stop at the receptionist desk on your way out and make the next appointment." Instead she continued in a calm voice, saying she was concerned by the increase in Erik's head measurement and his soft spot. Then I remembered how she had measured Erik's head twice, which she hadn't done during his first examination. Panic was apparent on my face.

"Are you all right, Mrs. Saxton? Can I get you a glass of water?"

"No, I'm all right. What does this mean?" I glanced at Harold out of the corner of my eye—concern was etched on his face too. I watched the doctor closely as she tried to explain.

"An infant's skull is composed of six separate bones." She moved her hands around Erik's head, pointing as she spoke. "The frontal bone, the occipital bone, two parietal bones, and two temporal bones. All of these are referred to as cranial bones. These bones are held together by cranial sutures, which are strong, fibrous, elastic tissues called fontanels, or 'soft spots'. There is an anterior fontanel and a posterior fontanel. The cranial bones remain separate for approximately 12 to 18 months before fusing, and will remain fused throughout adulthood." She paused to see if we were taking everything in. "The fibers (sutures) and spaces between the cranial bones are necessary for the child's growth and development. During childbirth, the flexibility of the sutures allows the bones to overlap their edges so the baby's head can pass through the birth canal without compressing and damaging the brain. Then during infancy and childhood, the flexibility of the fibers allows the rapid growth of the brain without constriction. It also protects the brain from minor impact to the head (such as when the infant is learning to hold his head up, roll over and sit up). Without the flexibility of the sutures and fontanels, the child's brain would be constricted within the cranial bones and could not grow adequately, which may cause brain damage."

All of this explained the importance of the opening, and I determined that she wasn't really worried about Erik's soft spot. I wanted to ask her to get to the point, but realized that was exactly what she was trying to do. I was pretty sure her concern was related to the size of Erik's head; even my untrained eye could tell it was large. So wouldn't this mean that his brain was growing and that his head was therefore expanding? I didn't know so continued to listen.

"Feeling the cranial sutures and fontanels is one way that physicians and nurses determine the child's growth and development. We are able to assess the pressure within the brain by feeling the tension of the fontanels." I still had no idea where this was heading, but her final words clarified the matter. "The fontanels should feel flat and firm. Bulging fontanels indicate increased pressure within the brain. Sunken, depressed fontanels indicate dehydration of the brain. Erik's fontanels seem to be bulging slightly, and I would like to have this checked, as a precaution. This would be best done in the hospital."

I could sense Harold sitting up straighter in his chair, but was afraid to look over at him right then because I knew my face showed my concern. I slid my hand over the arm of the chair and found his hand waiting.

"There is no causes for alarm; I only want to be sure everything is okay, and that can be best done at the hospital."

Dr. Boettrich had spoken very clearly to make sure we heard her every word. Being slightly medically challenged, but no more than the general public, I understood the basics but not much more. I was glad she took the time to provide the information to help us identify the importance of her findings, but we really didn't comprehend the significance of what she had told us.

"Do you have any questions?" she asked.

I had no idea what to ask, and I could tell Harold didn't either. We both shook our heads.

"Fine," she said. "If it is all right with you, I would like you to wait out front while I make the arrangements for little Erik to be admitted to the hospital."

"Okay," Harold and I replied in unison. Dr. Boettrich stood up from behind her desk and moved closer to our little family circle. "Please don't worry," she said. "I just want to be sure Erik is okay, and I can do this best if he is in the hospital."

We gave her a weak smile and thanked her. Can you believe it? We thanked her for what she had just told us. We then stood up to leave, all confused and filled with apprehension; and wanting to ask a thousand questions but not having enough medical knowledge to formulate what to ask or say. Yet even though we didn't understand her concern exactly, we did understand that she had told us all she could for the time being.

This wasn't the way it was supposed to go, and I had difficulty accepting it. It was supposed to have been a wonderful experience; something we could share with Erik when he was older. As we sat there amongst all the other mothers with their babies, I couldn't say a word. All I could do was wonder what lay in store for each of those parents when they walked through the door. Would they return shocked or elated? Would they be able to remain as calm on the outside as Harold and I pretended to be?

We seemed incapable of speech as we waited for further instructions. We didn't have to wait long; we were soon summoned back to Dr. Boettrich's office and supplied with the details for admitting Erik.

***

It was like a dream; a terrible dream that holds you in its grasp until you are so frightened you must wake up; then it becomes like a play that opens up and presents you with enough of the story to mesmerize you so that you can't wait to find out the ending. But this was no dream that would end when I awoke. Nor was it a play to which the actors and writers already knew the ending. This was real—a real life experience that was unfolding in a hospital: an institution built, staffed and equipped to identify, diagnose and treat the sick or injured! A place that looms frightening, even if it is a place of healing.

What was it like? It was like nothing that you will ever wish to experience. You feel helpless, confused and worried about the outcome. No amount of words can comfort you, nor can you succeed in comforting each other. You try to tell yourself to not worry and not think the worst, but you can't help it. You look around at the other actors participating in this experimental play and can actually read their inner feelings, which are similar to your own. And somehow you know, without being propped, that you cannot share your feelings with them. They are enveloped in their own roles, restricted to offering only words of encouragement. We were really completely alone. No one, including family or friends, could enter the drama and provide solace. Our role would force us to interact with doctors and nurses only, and we would have to take our cues from them. How long would it take? Well, that was a question best left unasked.

X-rays, tests, examinations, consultations! These became the norm. Somewhere in between the activity, we managed to eat and feed Erik. Home? Home didn't fit in to the equation. The hospital became our home. Work? Harold went to work while I roamed around the hospital each day until he returned. I made sure I listened to the instructions, the information shared during consultations, so that later I could tell him what had transpired. When any new doctor was assigned to the case, I noted his or her name and role in the ever-increasing cast of characters.

There was a weird sense of being alone, yet feeling as though there was someone always watching you. It was only a feeling, with no genuine basis for concern, but yet I felt uneasy and, quite frankly, scared. Scared because there had no doubt been deaths here and, at moments when I felt the most useless, this thought preyed on my mind.

Idle minds and hands are a bad combination, especially in this place where the feel of those who have come and gone permeate the air. I looked at my watch; the sun would be setting soon. Despite the fluorescent lights It had been a dark day already and I knew that without sunlight the hospital, would become a more threatening place without something to do. The echo of my footsteps down the hallway sounded even louder and hollower than before as I pretended to have somewhere to go. The feeling of being observed remain constant as I sought for something to keep me occupied..

The part I played was small, my responsibilities limited to feeding, changing and providing most of Erik's personal care—this all seemed so insignificant compared to the responsibilities of the doctors and nurses. In all fairness, I must admit that I was able to spend more time with him than anyone else, and I was happy for that. Actually, I was the one who was suffering—not my child, who spent most of the time sleeping peacefully, unconcerned that he was not in his own crib in his beautiful nursery at home.

***

At first I observed those around me, watching what they did and what they said. I watched the doctors, the nurses; but most of all I watched the other mothers and fathers so that I could mimic their hospital etiquette. There is an unwritten form of etiquette for all those who become part of the hospital environment; and to preserve yourself, others and your child you learn it early. I soon learned the golden rule was don't try to relate. Keep conversation uplifting. Rather than relating stories about who went through the same procedure and what complications they had, direct the talk to cheerful topics.

When I had become more adjusted, I talked with the other parents who had children in the pediatric wing, being careful not to unload my problems on them. I also knew to not ask why they were there or what was wrong with their child. It was okay to tell them I had seen them with their child and comment on something special about them, like saying their child had lovely eyes or pretty hair. Whatever I said had to be innocuous, or else I risked making them suffer more than they already had.

It seemed everyone knew what was appropriate to discuss and what was off bounds. Some of us watched as parents took their children home, leaving us to greet the newcomers and make them feel less alone. Daytimes were the worst. There were usually only a few of us, and all you could do was roam the corridors until settling in the lounge, trying to appear as though nothing was wrong. Yes, the days were long. I found myself trying to initiate conversation by offering words of encouragement. When these attempts fizzled, I would watch television. Erik slept most of the time, and I was asked not to wake him. When he did wake, it was usually to be changed or fed. Once these needs had been attended to, he would fall back to sleep, leaving me alone.

I had read every magazine by the end of the second day and had started rereading them, until Harold finally remembered to bring me a book. I saved it for the times when there was nothing else to do, not wanting to read it too quickly. I had no idea how long we would be there. The nurses told me to go for a walk outside if I didn't want to go home. It would do me good, they said. I took them up on their offer, glad to feel the warmth of the sun on my face and cocoon myself in the routine of everyday life that span around as though all was right with the world. When I returned to the floor, I must admit I felt refreshed and better equipped to cope.

Dr. Boettrich was in Erik's room when I returned from one of my short walks. She had just finished examining him when I entered.

"Mrs. Saxton, I wonder if I can have a word with you," she said in a calm voice.

We walked out of the room together and down the hall to a small, empty room. She turned to me and asked how much I knew about our family history, meaning both Harold's and mine. I told her I knew some but not a lot. She then asked if it was possible for me to gather up some information for her.

"What exactly are you looking for?" I inquired.

"Just everything you can find out about any family members—when they were born, their medical history, any known complications with their birth, or early deaths." She wanted whatever information I could find, to help the doctors determine if Erik's situation was something to be concerned about.

"What is Erik's situation?" I asked.

"That is what we are trying to determine. If you can do this for me it may help in diagnosing Erik quicker."

She explained that she understood I would rather be there with Erik, but that I would be of more help to him by gathering together the family history, which would be easier for me to do at home.

She was right. I didn't want to leave, but I had finally been given a chance to help my son so I had to take it. I told her I would do it. That evening, when Harold arrived at the hospital, I filled him in on the doctor's request and we left together. I began making calls that night.

***

Between visits to the hospital, I began in earnest to gather all I could about our families. I noticed that some branches of our families had lived longer than others. Many of the men on my mother's side had lived well into their 80s, whereas it was not unusual for men on my dad's side to have passed away in their 60s. Why the difference? What caused their deaths? Were there common health characteristics? What did this mean to me and my immediate family? I did not know. I only knew that it must have some bearing on our health or the illnesses we suffer, because we inherit from our ancestors.

I began with what I already knew—birth and death dates, if deceased, along with cause—and worked back from there. I asked various family members about ethnic background; major illnesses such as cancer, heart disease and diabetes; and general patterns of illness, like chronic sore throats. I asked about birth defects and allergies, both environmental and drug related. I probed their emotional or behavioral problems, such as depression, heavy drinking and anxiety. I asked about chronic health problems like asthma or high blood pressure, and their vision and hearing problems. Though I stressed the urgency of gathering the information, I had a feeling that some held back in telling details. Other family members were not really sure of their history, medical or otherwise. There were also many who had passed away without anybody knowing the cause of death. It was frustrating and I dreaded each call. I didn't have time for formalities; I only had time for information.

Inside my head I began to wonder if all this was necessary or just a ploy to keep me occupied.

I was notified each time a new doctor was brought in to look at Erik, and I was aware of the tests that were being performed—but that was all. I had no idea of the results or the findings yet. Dr. Boettrich was the central point of contact for everyone involved, but no one was saying anything until all the results were in. I was desperate to know the unknown, because the waiting was frightening. Then a diagnosis was made.

***

Harold and I both formed a protective bubble around ourselves. There was to be no talk of our baby's situation, only about the happy times we shared with him. There was to be no mention to anyone of what we were going through, because we couldn't hold up under pity. That was how Harold saw it and I respected his wishes, though inside I cried out to be able to talk about it so that maybe I would understand. We had become so closed off that when we were finally summoned for a consultation with one of the specialists, it wasn't easy to pull back the veil of protection and come out in the open. We were told that the private consultation had been set up to advise us on one of their conclusive findings. One finding, I thought: how many problems did they anticipate?

I thought back to that second examination performed by Dr. Boettrich, recalling each movement she had made, so when we were told that the consultation was with a bone specialist, I immediately thought, his head! Something was wrong with his head. I focused in on the soft spots. I had felt them and thought they seemed to be smaller, but I wasn't positive of that. I tried to envision what would happen if the soft spots did not close up totally, only it was too much drama. I decided it was best not to try and figure it out on my own, or else I'd be a real basket case by the time we met with the bone specialist. But like a little child that you tell, "Stop that or I'll spank you!" I couldn't seem to obey.

***

So I invented the "Truth Game". I never sat down and designed the way the game would be played, or the rules to follow. All of that sort of shaped itself to meet my needs. In any case, to keep my thoughts focused only on what I know to be certain, I force myself to state a fact, without being influenced in any way by speculation. After stating the fact I next state a real problem resulting from the knowledge of the fact. The problem also has to be in line with the truth as I know it. Then I have to formulate as many reasons as I can as to why this is a problem; again based on only what I know. I find it works best to try and come up with three stated truths to analyze. In the case of Erik's condition, as I am not an authority in the medical field, the only truths that could be dealt with related to how the situation made me feel, and my reaction to those parts of the medical terminology used that I had an understanding of. It wasn't much to go on, but I found the Truth Game to be an excellent tool for dealing with facts rather than speculation.

***

All the family medical history we gathered was immediately passed on to Dr. Boettrich, with the more interesting details filed away for future use. Harold and I finally had our meeting with the bone specialist. The doctor informed us that he had been studying Erik's x-rays and that his purpose in meeting with us was to see if we could add anything further to the details of the family history we had already provided. After examining Erik, consulting with other doctors, and reviewing the x-rays, the doctor had determined that Erik was an achondroplasic dwarf.

I wasn't prepared for this and neither was Harold. What in the world were they talking about? A dwarf? What did this mean and was it a problem? While I tried to make sense of it, I could vaguely hear the doctor's words filling the room, but it was as though he was speaking in a foreign language.

He began by saying that achondroplasia was the most commonest cause of dwarfish, which to me then meant that it was the most easiest to cure. As he continued the doctor explained that the disorder was characterized by a lack of cartilage cells so that bones that depended on cartilage models for development could not grow.

So, I surmised at this point that the clue to correction must have something to do with cartilage, which didn't seem too drastic.

I listened closely as the doctor talked, noting that he called it a disease that was hereditary and that those affected would have short limbs, an almost normal truck in size and an enlarged head as a result of some overgrowth of the vault bones following premature closure of sutures at the base of the skull.

The picture that began to form in my mind wasn't that bad as I meshed it with the face and body of my beautiful baby boy. The doctor continued to diagram out the face stating that the forehead might bulge out with a saddle nose, and full-sized jaw, which didn't frighten me a bit.

It was then on to his body development. The doctor continued explaining that they would expect to see a deeply incurved lower back with prominent buttocks and a narrow chest. I had seen people who fell into this descriptive category of body shapes and found it to be quite common and in cases, quite an attractive figure.

By now I was somewhat less afraid and this feeling grew when the doctor stated that achondroplastic dwarfs were of normal intelligence and had otherwise normal health, which meant to me that once this visit to the hospital was over, there would be no reason to foresee another. But then came the shocker as the doctor added that about half of affected infants die before or soon after birth. This information took my breath away and I sat now without analyzing each word.

I heard the explanation that achondroplasia appeared to be transmitted by a single dominant gene that acts to impair the growth of specific cartilages in the body as the bones are being formed. Single genes frequently have more than one obvious effect and multiple effects of single genes are just about universal. He explained that genes operate by affecting developmental processes, and a single gene change may eventually affect a number of bodily or behavioral characteristics. All this meant was that in achondroplasia, not only is the process of bone development altered but the consequent dwarfism affects the size, distribution and function of the muscles and internal organs as well.

I could see the seriousness of what the doctor was now saying, and more so as he continued to explain that Mild to moderate hypotonia is also common. He immediately explained that hypotonia is a condition that often signals an abnormality in the case of a newborn or older infant, and may suggest the presence of central nervous system dysfunction, genetic disorders, or muscle disorders. For example, hypotonic infants rest with their elbows and knees loosely extended, while infants with normal tone tend to have flexed elbows and knees. Head control may be poor or absent in the floppy infant, causing the head to fall to the side, backward or forward. Motor development is usually delayed. Intelligence is normal unless hydrocephalus or other central nervous system complications arise.

And at that point the fervor rose. Complications might arise!

"Your son's type of dwarfism stems from abnormal development of cartilage."

"Give it to us straight, doctor, what can happen to my son?" I pleaded.

The doctor paused for a moment before mentioning he had spoken with Dr. Boettrich, who had stated our wishes to know exactly what to expect, so he would tell us the limited information he knew. In 1966, a Doctor J. A. Davis claimed to know of at least five cases of achondroplasic dwarfism. The five infants with the condition were located in various parts of the world and no details of their medical history had yet to be accumulated. Beyond explaining what it was, there was no available information to determine what would happen in the future.

So now I knew that though this was the most common form of dwarfism, it did not mean that there was a magical cure or bank of knowledge that would guarantee our son's survival.

"What should we do now? Take Erik home?"

"No, not yet."

The bone specialist informed us that the neurosurgeon assigned to Erik's case would also like to speak to us. I had been advised that a neurosurgeon had been contacted, but I had yet to meet him. As we waited, I turned to Harold; though he tried to comfort me, he was obviously worried. We both knew that we were going to have to contact relatives again, to ask if there had ever been a case of dwarfism in the family. That would not be easy, for many reasons. First of all, of course, we would have to tell them that Erik was in the hospital and listen to their reprimands for not having told them. Then we would have to answer the question of why were we asking about cases of dwarfism in the family. No, it wouldn't be easy.

I wanted to ask Harold what he was thinking, but thought better of it. The only thing I knew about neurosurgery was that it somehow dealt with the brain and nerves. I wasn't actually sure of that, but it was all I could come up with. I glanced over at Harold but could read nothing in his face as he stared off into the distance. That made me angry for some reason, but I held it in. I had a feeling there would be a lot more to prepare for, and that I should allocate this block of time to absorb the information that the bone specialist had shared with us.

So we sat there, trying not to look at each other at first but eventually having to. We were both afraid to express our feelings.

Finally Harold said, "Let's see what the neurosurgeon has to say, okay?" I nodded.

Unbeknownst to us then, we were about to meet the doctor who would play a major role in our lives for many years to come. The neurosurgeon and the pediatrician would become more like family members as the years passed by. They would spend more time with our son during his developmental period then we would. Their beds would become more familiar to him than the one we had created in our home. Erik was more theirs then ours, and this frightened me on one level; while on another it made me angry. This was not the way it was supposed to be.

Even in my confusion, my first thought when Dr. Cotanch entered the room was, what a gorgeous man! He was young, muscular, of medium height, well-built, and had a thick head of hair. His face was not only handsome but filled with expression, from his blue eyes to his perfectly shaped mouth. There was an aura about him that took command of a room instead of becoming a part of it. A sense of security came over me and instantly I felt hope. Harold, on the other hand, took a little more time for acceptance.

Dr. Cotanch introduced himself and took a seat near us. He then verified that we were little Erik's parents. Then, still not ready to talk "medically", he said, "That's quite a little guy you have there!"

We knew that. But even if I hadn't, I would have believed it. The doctor had charisma; even stripping him of his medical title and making him a bum on the street would not change this. It was not only his good looks, soft-spoken voice and friendly attitude, it was just his presence. As he prepared to talk with us "medically", he leaned forward, as though becoming part of our little family grouping.

He told us the consensus was that Erik might have an abnormal accumulation of cerebrospinal fluid in his cranial vault. The condition itself is called hydrocephalus and frequently occurs in newborn infants. Since the bone of an infant's skull is not fused together, the pressure of the accumulating fluid forces the head to actually enlarge, sometimes tremendously, making the forehead become prominent. Though rare, in a hydrocephalic adult there will be no cranial enlargement, since the cranium is fixed in size and cannot give.

Harold and I sort of nodded together, anxious to hear more. I wasn't sure that Harold and I were on the same page, that he was recalling the bone specialists words, "Intelligence is normal unless hydrocephalus or other central nervous system complications arise." Yet I listened carefully. After having already heard so much bad news, I was surprised that we were so eager to hear more.

Dr. Cotanch continued. "In any case, whether in an infant or an adult, the mounting pressure caused by the excess fluid squeezes the brain tissue against the skull, causing tissue atrophy and tissue death. If allowed to continue, there may be convulsions and mental weakness." He paused, waiting for our reaction.

By now we had learned how to mask our faces so that the information was given to us straight. We could always ask for verification later, we knew that, and we also knew that if we showed signs of breaking down, the flow of details would immediately be halted.. Dr. Cotanch continued. "When present at birth, hydrocephalus is considered congenital—primary or chronic hydrocephalus. When diagnosed in the early stages, and with the advancements in the medical field, the results are very promising."

His last statement prompted a reaction. It was hope and I immediately reached out to grasp it. "Are you saying that this disease can be cured?" I asked.

"It can be cured. Various surgical procedures have been developed to treat hydrocephalus by implanting artificial drains in the brain and creating new paths of circulation for the cerebrospinal fluid."

Harold then came to life, asking if he would share more information to clarify the importance of the cerebrospinal fluid.

The doctor replied that hydrocephalus is often referred to as "fluid on the brain".

I had heard this term before and it seemed that Harold was familiar with the term too. I wasn't at all surprised when he asked, "Where does the cerebrospinal fluid come from and what's its purpose?"

Dr. Cotanch told us that cerebrospinal fluid, sometimes referred to as CSF, fills the ventricles and the canal within the brain stem. CSF surrounds and bathes the spinal cord and the brain, acting as a lubricant and a mechanical barrier against shock. The fluid flows slowly from the ventricles and continues down through the canal of the brain stem to ultimately pass out into the tissue spaces surrounding the central nervous system. CSF performs many chief functions mechanically, such as bathing the brain and spinal cord areas, helping to bear the weight of the brain, lubricating the surfaces between the brain and spinal cord, lubricating the bones that encase the brain and spinal cord as well as others.

Dr. Cotanch, who had been leaning toward us throughout his report, lifted his shoulders slightly as he stretched, still maintaining eye contact with us. He let us know that he was aware that it was a lot of information to absorb and that we may not entirely understand all of it. Yet he wanted to give us as much information as possible. He further said that he realized the bone specialist had been to see us, and encouraged us to try and obtain a more complete family history.

I had one question—were they sure this was what was happening with Erik?

After a moment's hesitation, Dr. Cotanch explained, in carefully chosen words, that it wasn't a firm diagnosis, yet; and that was because an enlarged head was characteristic of dwarfism. However, he believed that Erik was hydrocephalic, though the results weren't verifying this and without more tests it was not conclusive. Dr. Cotanch told us that he would be keeping a close eye on Erik. This meant that Erik needed to remain in the hospital a while longer. We understood.

***

After several days, all of the tests had been reviewed but there seemed to be no further conclusions. Dr. Cotanch's second talk with us was sympathetic. He explained that he understood how we felt not knowing for sure if Erik's diagnosis was accurate or if there was something else wrong with him. He then assured us that he would be reviewing all the information again and talking with colleagues to get their opinions. In the meantime, we could take Erik home. If any further information came to light, we would be contacted. But for the moment we should try not to worry.

"I will do all the worrying for you," he said. "I want you to just try and enjoy your son."

Erik was released and we took him home.

***

On August 1, 1969, we moved from the city to a suburban apartment, based partly on an unspoken decision to control our own destiny, resolve problems as they arose, and not let anything stand in the way of our desires; which right then was to keep Erik safe.

We had slowly watched the deterioration of our first home, which was owned by Mr. Volpe, a prominent businessman in Rochester. It was a lovely, two-story house of old mahogany wood and stained glass windows. The sturdy central staircase was solid, with no creaking steps, leading to a wide marble-floored foyer. I had fallen in love with the structure the first time I laid eyes on it. The house had been renovated from its single family layout into a four-apartment building. The atmosphere of the neighborhood had changed along with the architectural changes; once a peaceful, middle-class area, the conversion of homes into apartment dwellings attracted a different kind of resident—and the neighborhood was still adjusting to these changes.

Since Mr. and Mrs. Volpe were living upstairs when I first rented the apartment, I felt safe living in the building. Later, when my girlfriend Fran, who I had met when going to business school, became my roommate, it was even better. Once Harold and I married, it seemed ideal for us to stay in the apartment. It was close to our jobs and located right on a bus line, making it easy to get around without a car. Plus there was plenty of room for a young couple just starting out. But there were changes on the horizon that would force us to reconsider this location.

First the Volpe's moved out, and we found ourselves as the only tenants in the building until several months after Erik was born. People were constantly moving in and moving out, with no regard for the beauty of the building or, for that matter, their fellow tenants. The turnover was so rapid we didn't have time to make the acquaintance of our fellow residents before they were replaced by others. That was just the beginning of the need for change; as roaches started to appear, and then rats in the backyard having a picnic in the uncovered trashcans. Neither Harold nor I were use to sharing our home with bugs or rodents, and we had no desire to put up with this, even though the house was convenient for work and larger than any other apartment we would be able to find. We had to make a decision. So we did. The house on Union Street would always have a special place in our hearts. It was the place we shared our first time alone; where I carried our child; and the home we brought our baby to. But it was time to move on.

This was not going to be easy. When you are forced to give up something you really like, it becomes extremely hard to accept a replacement. But after making many calls and visiting one apartment after the other, we finally moved into the third floor of a well-kept Holyoke apartment development in the suburb of Greece, on Milford Street. The rent was reasonable and in line with what we had been paying, and though there were no stained glass windows, no pantry or maple sliding doors, we rallied for the move which would put us in a save environment. Though the buildings were nice, they held little charm beyond being clean and well cared for, but the area and the tenants made up for this. There was an expanse of grass and trees for the children to play safely away from the streets. Trees shaded the buildings and the grassy knolls, making it a pleasant setting. And there was the added bonus of having a laundry room on the premises.

It didn't take long to realize that the laundry room had more than a practical use. This was a meeting place where the neighbors came to socialize. The first meeting was an introduction and questions about the family. The next added a personal note about work, interests and friends, and by the third wash day you became a part of the clique.

We developed lasting friendships on Milford Street. It was a self-contained community where everyone knew each other and was there to help you. We took turns watching each other's children, had parties and game nights at each other's apartments, and we discussed our dreams of the future, which for the majority was to purchase a home in a nice neighborhood and near a good school system. Not much to ask for, but when you're young parents just starting out, it is just a dream.

***

A new home, friends, shopping and work kept our minds full. We were beginning to feel just like any other young couple with a young baby. But reality always has a way of poking its ugly head out.

Shortly before September 19, a little over a month after our move, we received a call from Erik's pediatrician. He informed us that they wanted to hospitalize Erik for a week of further testing. All the arrangements had been made for us to check Erik into the hospital. With that quick return to reality, we transferred our thoughts to getting Erik ready for his readmission.

As promised, this stay was one week to the day. Again we met with doctors while nurses attended to little Erik. But when we finally had our meeting with Dr. Cotanch, he had nothing further to report. Again we were asked about our family history. Having not concentrated too much on learning anything more than we already knew, we could only repeat the information we had already shared. I felt as though I had done something wrong. I had been so caught up with the move that I had not taken the time to continue digging up family details. I wanted to apologize for my seemingly uncaring attitude and to ask for forgiveness, but I was too embarrassed to do anything more than promise to find out whatever more there was to learn.

Harold was quiet. I wondered if he felt responsible in any way, but I was too afraid to ask him because, by then, I knew that it was not in his personality to show his feelings, or even talk about them. I tried to respect this, though I needed words from him to help me understand, by reminding myself that he was a wonderful father and he cared for us both.

Harold and I took Erik home again, and I promised myself that I would be prepared next time. I knew for certain now that this was not the end but only a beginning, and I had to somehow find out as much as I could to help the doctors.

I tried not to miss Erik's advancements as I balanced work and home. Since reaching nine months he had been crawling and moving around upright while holding on to the furniture. Several times I caught him taking a couple of steps while clinging to his support, and I could tell he was getting closer and closer to full-fledged walking. I would stand or kneel in front of him and help him walk toward me by holding both his hands, before letting go and holding out my hands in encouragement. I began to learn the value of childproofing the apartment, placing latches on the doors of off-limit cabinets, as Erik made a beeline for such things. I asked the pediatrician if I should put shoes on him, but she told me it wasn't necessary until Erik was walking around outdoors, explaining that going barefoot could help strengthen his arches and leg muscles, while feeling the texture of the different surfaces he walked on could help his balance.

Erik's play was becoming more advanced; he could put objects in a container and even remove them. To encourage him, we gave him a plastic bucket and some blocks so he could practice this new skill. We found that he also liked toys with wheels, levers, or doors that opened and closed, so we bought him plastic cars that he could roll around on the floor.

Neighbors brought their children over to play with Erik and he didn't seem to mind when a toy was taken away from him. He would sit there for a while as if thinking about it, then he'd go off to find something else to occupy his time; which might be exploring the hair, arms or legs of another baby.

I began to notice that the other babies would stop now and then to find their parent before moving on. Not Erik; he seemed content without the security of knowing where I was. This bothered me at first, but then he had to depend on a lot more people than most babies, so I just tried to accept it.

The words that Erik had been hearing since birth were now beginning to work their magic, as he demonstrated his understanding of "no", ma" and "da." But his understanding of the words far outpaced his ability to use them. I realized it was more the tone of my voice that he could comprehend rather than the actual words I used, but the more I talked to him while preparing dinner, driving, or getting dressed, the more he learned about communication. I admit that though he seemed to understand the word "no," he didn't necessarily obey me each time he heard it, while he would always respond to his name by looking around or stopping what he was doing to see who called.

During the days that followed our most recent visit to the doctor, I developed a process for the work ahead of me by first outlining all the sources for information, such as medical records and the recollections of Harold, myself and our living relatives. I would then go on to gather information about our deceased ancestors by checking death certificates to see if they listed the cause of death. I also read through obituaries, in case they yielded any further information, and checked pension documents, Social Security applications, family bibles, diaries, old correspondence and the like, plus military records.

I made a note to be sure to record any medical conditions I came across, and when they had occurred. For example, did Grandma have diabetes as a child, or did it develop later in her adult life? Every bit of information would be helpful, I kept reminding myself.

It might help Erik, or who knew—maybe the information I found today would save a life tomorrow.

Between working and caring for Erik, Harold and I made calls to members of the family, filling them in on what had transpired and recording any more information that they could supply. Now understanding the need for our probing questions, once the shock wore off the family willingly participated. There is so much buried in the past that can remain unspoken, but each of our families realized the importance of providing any piece of information they could. Taken in small doses and placed in its proper historical timeframe, it is powerful information; but when dropped all at once in the context of the present, it was like a bombshell.

Once I had returned to work, I found it necessary to focus on the positive sides of our life, not just the conflicts, or else I would go crazy. For a while I managed to appear as though everything was under control. I did my work, kept up with friends and remained part of the team until the workday ended. Then it was all about Erik's discovery of his toes as I dressed him, or his laugh when I tickled him. Each evening when I returned home I was not preoccupied with all the things I needed to get done. Instead I enjoyed cuddling Erik, singing to him, bathing him and wishing I could stay home with him but knowing we were going to need all the money we could earn to make sure we could meet all and any expenses.

It was hard. I asked my mother, "How did you do it? How did you study for your career and keep us fed? How did you complete your courses and proofread our homework? How come your generation did it and mine is losing its collective mind?"

In the world according to mom, the answer was threefold. First, she said, my life really was more complicated. She was a mother first; her career came second. Also, she hadn't prepared for her career until I was a freshman in high school; and when her youngest child left for college, mom did things serially, while my generation did them simultaneously.

***

By the time he was ten months old, Erik was crawling well on his hands and knees. He could also sit confidently, and continued to walk while holding onto furniture, sometimes letting go momentarily and standing without support. He would take steps when held in a walking position but immediately get down on all fours if he saw a toy he wanted.

Erik's fingers were becoming more agile. Using his pincer grasp, he could pick up a piece of cereal or some other small object without having to rest his wrist on his high chair tray. Tiny things seemed to intrigue him, and he was still likely to give them a taste-test, so I tried to make sure that non-edible objects were always out of his reach.

His personality was really starting to emerge. He was very sociable, granting broad smiles to everyone he met. He repeated sounds and gestures for our attention, and waved goodbye when he saw us head for the door. He was also developing a mind of his own, which revealed itself each time we tried to put him in his stroller or even his high chair.

I kept an eye on him to identify objects or sounds that seemed to frighten him, but they were few and far between; and as soon as they were gone or had stopped, he seemed to forget and continue on his merry way, constantly chattering in clear words and phrases—a result of our constant conversations as well as the hospital personnel he had been in contact with. His need to be understood seemed to be developing at a rapid pace.

It was also around this time that I had finally exhausted all avenues for gathering information about the family history. There just wasn't anything there that added to what we had already learned. This wasn't to say there definitely hadn't been a case paralleling Erik's at some point in our family's medical history, but it may have occurred so long ago that there was no record of it. So, thinking the information I had already recovered was all that I could hope to obtain, I set the project aside. I had learned a valuable skill in gathering information, and now I used it to help me learn more about dwarfism; something I knew nothing about. I hadn't even known anyone who was a dwarf. If I wanted to help my son fit into the contemporary world, I knew I would have to begin first by understanding this disease. Once I had understood what I was dealing with, I could then prepare us for what lay ahead. So I began in earnest to learn more. I first wanted to know everything about the disease, and then see if I could learn more from someone who was actually raising a dwarf. This would be the hardest part of my research, since I would first have to find the parents and then hope I could get them to share with me, a stranger.

I began by setting up an appointment with the orthopedist who had diagnosed Erik. He was willing to repeat much of what he had already told me, then went on to suggest the names of other doctors who might be able to provide me with more information. I immediately began setting up appointments during my lunch hour; my shorthand pad filling up with details that I later typed up and added to my file. Each doctor I saw had another suggestion for me. I was directed to other hospital personnel and eventually found myself seated amongst more medical reports and books than imaginable when I was sent to the medical section of the library.

My head swam with all the terms and all the case studies, but I began to realize that most of the sources contained the same information, only expressed differently. It helped to know this; especially when struggling through medical cases that seemed incomprehensible.

I wrote down names and hunted for the referenced reports, hoping to be able to track down the individuals and talk with them personally. By the time I had exhausted all avenues for gaining information, I had a better understanding of what dwarfism really entailed. Essentially, dwarfism is a general classification for literally hundreds of conditions characterized by short stature. Beyond this similarity, however, there are a diversity of clinical features. Achondroplasia can be diagnosed by characteristic clinical and radiographic findings in most affected individuals. In individuals who may be too young for an accurate diagnosis, or in individuals with atypical findings, molecular genetic testing can be performed. As for the number of achondroplasic dwarfs, this was unknown.

I learned that achondroplasia was definitely a genetic disorder, but nearly 80 percent of cases occur from spontaneous gene mutation rather than from direct inheritance, so most achondroplastic children come as a surprise to their average-stature parents. This genetic disorder is not operable in the sense of being cured, but with the advances in medicine and early detection, the medical world now knew what to watch for and how they could help these children survive into adulthood.

***

I was becoming a glutton for punishment as I switched gears. I had contacts now; medical personnel who knew me and were willing to help. This would be the best time to complete the process and learn all I could about the currently undiagnosed disease called hydrocephalus. It was during this second process of information gathering that I understood the dilemma cloaking the discovery of the illness. The diagnosis had not been obvious because Erik was a dwarf, and the symptoms of hydrocephalus were also the symptoms of achondroplasic dwarfism.

A variety of medical problems can cause hydrocephalus. In many children the problem is present at birth—this kind of hydrocephalus is referred to as congenital, and most cases of congenital hydrocephalus are thought to be caused by a complex interaction of genetic and environmental factors. Hydrocephalus is believed to occur in about 2 out every 1,000 births, and is generally diagnosed at birth or shortly after, though sometimes it is not diagnosed until the child is a little older. In an infant, the most obvious sign of hydrocephalus is an abnormally enlarged head. The soft spot (fontanel) may be tense and bulging. The scalp may appear thin and glistening, and the scalp veins may appear to have unnatural fullness (prominence). The symptoms to watch for are vomiting, sleepiness, irritability and downward deviation of the baby's eyes, known as the sun setting sign.

***

When we finally brought Erik home after that first hospital stay, we were all craving a good night's sleep but felt uneasy that first night at home. With the lapse of time between this and the next hospitalization, we were all better equipped to experience the "normal" routine of home life.

Though I had heard the doctors, I still couldn't see any evidence of Erik being different from other children, so it was easy to ignore their findings. Only I was definitely concerned, as I found myself constantly checking on Erik, up to a dozen times at night, to make sure he was breathing and that he hadn't turned over onto his stomach. My concern grew from a fear of losing him, and that fear was present during every waking moment. His crib was cozy and safe—I had taken care to make it so. There were no pillows, quilts or stuffed animals around him—those I placed at the foot of the bed. The hanging mobile was secure and out of his reach, yet I still felt a need to check on him.

So I sat by his crib, thinking there must be something more I could do. This time became my quiet time. I read passages of the Bible in hopes of finding an explanation or at least a reason for all of this; but each time I gazed at Erik's face or heard his laughter, I began to doubt that the doctors knew what they were talking about. Erik was just like every other baby. Somewhere in the back of my mind I held on to the possibility that there really was nothing wrong with Erik; that the doctors who had examined him had made a mistake and any day now they would confirm it. Only it was not to be so.

A routine began to develop—Erik was in and out of the hospital, though for shorter periods of time than in the preceding months. These hospital visits became a formality which we quietly accepted without discussion. Erik was beginning the first stages of his transition to a more independent soul. When I looked at his cute baby face, all I could see was beauty. Sure, his head seemed larger than that of other babies, but not in a grotesque way, and not enough to suspect there was anything wrong. He seemed to hold it up with pride. It was impossible for me to imagine, either emotionally or intellectually, that there was something different between my baby and those of my friends or family. I just couldn't reconcile Erik with the symptoms of his dwarfism. He had the cutest face ever, and a smile that could light up the world. Still quite small in stature, it appeared as though his development was advanced as he began to crawl and walk around the room with the support of furniture.

I wanted to pick him up and hold him close all the time. He would let me have a moment of closeness before struggling to be set free and explore his world once more. I loved him so much it hurt. I loved to hold him and care for him, finding joy in everything he did. When he began eating solid foods, just feeding him could be so much fun. He'd crinkle his nose with the first mouthful, as if he was pretty sure he wouldn't like it. Then a smile would breakout as he swallowed happily and opened his mouth for more.

Making the transition from milk to cereal and finally solid foods was a big event, so we had a little celebration for Erik's first exciting introduction to the world of new flavors and the enjoyment of chewing and eating. Each meal was an adventure in different tastes and textures so that he could experience as much as possible. It was just one of the many ways we learned to enjoy all the experiences of our life with Erik.

Terrible though it may sound, we were becoming "used to" this type of existence. We were no longer frightened by Erik being hospitalized, just determined instead to remain calm and try to make each day memorable, because it was Erik that was important and not the diagnoses. I had no previous experience with hospitals. I could count on one hand the times that a member of my family had to be hospitalized, and there had been no occasions when anybody had had to stay for long periods of time. I remember one time in New Jersey when my sister Dianne fell under the plowing discs while riding on the back of dad's tractor. She screamed and cried for some time before we heard her over the loud engine of the tractor, and when she was rescued there were cuts all over her body. The doctor was called and came to the house to examine her. He told my mother to keep her awake for the next few hours, but was certain she would be fine.

I remember the birth of my younger siblings; they were all delivered by a midwife at our home. I remember the time that my father was on his way to a jobsite and was struck by a truck door opening, causing him to fall face down on the pavement. My mother mentioned that he was in the hospital, but we were never taken to visit him there. By the time he returned home, most of his scars had healed, and he looked as though nothing had happened at all. There was one change though, which we would later learn, and that was dad had become blind in one eye. And, sure, there were all kinds of scrapes and bumps, but it took only a little disinfecting, a kiss and a bandage for them to be all better again.

Harold, on the other hand, was better equipped. He had seen horrendous things in Vietnam in 1965, when the United States began air raids on North Vietnam and on Communist-controlled areas in the South. Harold had witnessed blood baths and death. Then, after serving his country in the Navy during the Vietnam War, Harold's brother, Dwight was returned to his family with a brain tumor, and spent his last days in the hospital, waiting for death to claim his body while his family helplessly looked on. So whereas hospitals up to this point in my life had represented a safe haven, for Harold they meant something entirely different. .

When we had to take Erik to the hospital after his second well baby checkup, my world had blurred into a mass of pain, confusion, denial and shock; my life was forever changed. At first it didn't register as I sat stunned, wondering what was happening. Then when he was diagnosed as an achondroplastic dwarf, I had no idea what it meant, so I imagined it to be a death sentence. But I had come a long way since then. I knew that achondroplasia dwarfism did not have to be a death sentence, and that Erik would otherwise have normal health. But we also knew that though this disease had been known since antiquity, because about half of affected infants die before or soon after birth, there were not a lot of medical studies around.

As I think back I ask myself how I could not have seen that something was wrong when it was happening to my own child; but then, how would I have known? I wasn't a doctor, or even an authority on babies; I had just read a lot, that's all. Even so, as much as I wanted to deny or forget, I knew that I must keep an open mind from here on out. I knew that no matter how much it hurt to think that Erik might be in for a bumpy future, I had to be strong for him.

CHAPTER 4
1970

When Dr. Cotanch summoned us to his office after Erik's latest stay, I felt exhausted after all we had been through. We had one diagnosis under our belt and were probably about to hear another. Whatever he had to say, we didn't think it could be all that bad. Only it was.

Dr. Cotanch responded as we had asked him to, providing us with as much detail as possible. He began by saying that birth defects do not all have the same basis, and that it is possible for apparently identical defects in different individuals to be due to totally different causes. Single genes frequently have more than one obvious effect. Since genes operate by affecting developmental processes, a single gene change may eventually affect a number of bodily or behavioral characteristics. To clarify this further, he explained that in achondroplasia, not only is the process of bone development altered but the consequent dwarfism affects the size, distribution and function of the muscles, as well as the internal organs.

He further stated that given the genetic complexity, it is frequently difficult to distinguish between the primary and secondary effects of the action of a gene. Genetic conditions are usually named for their most easily recognizable phenotypic sign. This serves as a convenient label but by no means describes the full genotypic effect. To put things into perspective, human characteristics are often attributable to a single dominant gene.

Dr. Cotanch then started to focus on Erik's specific problem, saying, "Mr. and Mrs. Saxton, I still believe your son is hydrocephalic."

"I thought it had been determined that the size of Erik's head was due to this dwarfism," I said. The doctor explained that was a possibility, only he still believed that there was a need to check for fluid buildup. Though Erik had demonstrated only the minor symptoms, it still seemed to be a possibility. "So, where do we go from here?" I asked, though I didn't really want an answer.

Dr. Cotanch replied that more invasive tests would have to be performed, and if fluid was discovered, this would mean surgery.

Our early optimism was crushed by the devastation of the unexpected. They were talking about surgery on our baby, who had only just begun finding his way in the world outside the womb. He was too young to have surgery. I found myself floating in and out of blankness, trying to disguise the fact but unable to conceal it. It was the sensation that somehow we had lost something, and that our experience had isolated us. I felt as though we were alone, belonging to no one and no place.

I had to ask the question, though I wasn't sure I was ready to hear the answer. "Why surgery, and what would the surgery entail?" By now familiar with our need for him to not hold back on the information we were given, Dr. Cotanch explained that the most common surgery for the treatment of hydrocephalus (fluid on the brain) is the insertion of a shunt, which is a device that diverts fluid from the brain into the abdominal cavity, where it is safely absorbed into the blood stream. A shunt may be inserted into infants, children and adults; and the procedure is essentially the same regardless of the size of the patient. Without treatment, the brain will be damaged as pressure inside the skull enlarges the ventricles, causing compression and, ultimately, death of sensitive brain tissues.

I tried to hide how scared I was, how impossible it all seemed, as I asked him if that would be it; if the surgery would take care of the problem and Erik could go on from there.

He hesitated a moment. "Believe me, I know this is very hard on you, and I can understand your feelings, but I must be honest with you: no, that would not be the end of it. Most patients with hydrocephalus can look forward to a normal future. Shunts are expected to perform reliably over a long period of time. However, because hydrocephalus is an ongoing condition, patients do require long term follow-up care. Having regular medical checkups at intervals recommended by the neurosurgeon is sensible. Occasionally, patients with shunt systems require revision: a surgical procedure to modify, repair or replace a shunt system due to complications or changing patient conditions. Once inserted, the shunt usually remains in place for life—with periodic adjustment—and continuously regulates intracranial pressure. What this means is, as Erik grows, shunt revision surgery might be necessary."

I can't believe it; it can't be corrected with one operation! This might lead to further surgery down the road! It took everything I had to keep from shouting it out; but I had to be calm in order to be prepared. I finally asked Dr. Cotanch to explain everything that he anticipated to take place. Dr. Cotanch paused for a moment then said, "We will do the exploratory surgery and if fluid is found the shunt surgery will begin immediately."

Dr. Cotanch could see through our pretense of strength but understood our need to fully understand what needed to be done. He was accustomed to being totally honest with us and at this point he was quite sure that there would be a need for a shunt. As he turned towards Harold, he sympathized with our feelings, telling us that, generally, patients with an implanted shunt system were not restricted in their daily activities—except those involving great physical exertion—so for the time being he could see no reason for any restrictions. He went on to say that hydrocephalus is a complex and unforgiving condition. The more we knew about hydrocephalus—its side effects and how to live with the condition—the more we would be able to prepare for the road ahead.

***

Erik was allowed to come home with us that day, but it was hard to see the joy in this. We were taking him home only to await word from Dr. Cotanch on when to bring him back. In order to keep my mind clear I remembered that throughout the months that Erik was with us he was not sick and encumbered, and that was something to be thankful for. On the other hand, Harold and I were encumbered, but our experience wasn't bad across the board—there was joy for each frustration. There was good as well as hurt in knowing our child's health and care was out of our hands.

***

That evening, when everyone was asleep, I sat by the window thinking about the road ahead. I had been in this conundrum for almost a year and would remain there for who knew how long. As I treaded through worry and disappointment, the world continued its progress toward the future and I had to make my choices in life. I was a part of the world outside, and as it evolved, I had to also. But I was discouraged. Not with God; not with my circumstances; not with my choices—but with my lack of options and control.

It was a bleak time in my life and trusting God was about the only thing I had left. Nothing else made any sense. I wanted it all to be behind us so that we could fully enjoy Erik and not have so many interruptions in our parental role. I wanted to feel the joy of being a parent without having to turn over my responsibilities to a nurse or a doctor. I wondered when it would always flow along normally.

***

Now more than ever there was nothing like a family and friends gathering for Thanksgiving with all its trimmings. Starting with greetings and seating arrangements, followed by roast turkey with giblet gravy, cornbread stuffing, cranberry and orange Sauce, homemade rolls and candied yams, and finishing off with a selection of desserts, smooth pumpkin pie, scrumptious sweet potato pie, mincemeat pie, carrot cake and white cake, all served with lots of laugther and conversation.

At ten o'clock that Thanksgiving morning, I had begun preparing the food to take to my sister's house, where we were all gathering. Our family nucleus had expanded to three and we were thankful for that. By noon we were excited by the prospect of dinner, the smells of my cooking making it harder to wait, until finally it was time to leave.

Harold and I bundled ourselves up in winter clothing and then got Erik ready for the trip to my sister Mary's house.

It was cold and a light snow fell as we made our way up the front porch steps and rang the doorbell. Within seconds the door flew open and the warmth and smells inside were only outdone by the warm family welcome. There were hugs and kisses all around. Someone took Erik while Harold and I took off our coats and then all that was unhappy in our life was quickly put aside as we entered into the fold.

Conversation was nonstop as I moved toward the kitchen with my sisters, assured by all the oohs and aahs coming from the living room that Erik was in good hands. We talked as we put the final touches on the dinner, setting the table and counting and then recounting chairs as we ignored the voices coming from the living room asking if it was ready yet. And finally we were ready to gather around the table, say grace and then pass the food around. Erik laid quietly in his car seat enjoying his bottle, and for everyone the meal held no disappointments. Such a dinner! The Baskerville sisters and their mother had surpassed themselves on this occasion, producing a dinner never to be forgotten by those who enjoyed it. Altogether, the day was a very pleasant one.

After dinner the men took the children into the living room with them to watch the football game, while I answered questions on what was happening with Erik.

That was Thanksgiving that year.

***

Every family seems to have a different way of celebrating Christmas. Each one has special traditional Christmas foods, special Christmas customs, and our family was no different as we looked happily toward this very special holiday.

From the day after Thanksgiving, it is impossible to forget that Christmas is coming. Colored lights decorate many homes and stores, along with shiny decorations, and artificial snow painted on windows.

It had become the tradition in our family to make a trip to Midtown shopping plaza at the start of the holiday season. It all began with Santa Claus and his helpers seated amidst the fake snow welcoming the children to sit on his lap and share their secret Christmas gift desires. Though Erik was too young to want for anything beyond sleep, food and clean clothes he nevertheless was taken with his cousins to the Midtown Plaza.

The older children were able to ride the monorail that was assembled above the shopping floor and then waited in line to see Santa Claus. Later we stood watching the mechanical dolls in the store windows as they hammered, cooked, ate and played.

There was the lighting of the Christmas tree in the center of the mall and the pre Christmas sales to attend. Shopping centers became busier as December approached and often stayed open till late, their sound systems playing Christmas 'carols' to entertain the shoppers. Somehow I managed to mail out our Christmas cards and get my Christmas shopping done.

We attended Christmas parties at work and with friends in a steady stream and by the week before Christmas the celebrating slowed down giving us time to decorate our first Christmas tree with Erik. There were colored lights, glass and wooden ornaments, tinsel and a lighted star placed on the top of the tree. There were candle lights placed on each window sill and a Christmas wreath hung on the door.

On Christmas Eve we again gathered with the family at my sister Mary's house, to exchange gifts and celebrate. The older children made themselves heard as they played loudly together or ran through the house spilling drinks and dropping food as if marking their passage. Erik and his cousin lay in the padded playpen between Mary and me as we enjoyed conversation with the family and ate the sweet cookies and cake while sipping on non-alcoholic eggnog until it was time to return to our homes and get ready for Santa Claus.

With Erik being so young, we could just put the gifts under the tree as we purchased them; but it would not be as much fun as having to do it in a rush late at night, as our parents did before us.

Erik was already asleep when we arrived home, so I carried him to his room, where I undressed him, changed his diaper, washed him and gave him a good night kiss. Harold then came in to take over, putting on his pajamas and tucking him in while I made us some coffee. I put the gifts we had received that evening under the tree, adding them to the ones I had purchased for Harold and Erik. I arranged them in sorted piles and then sat down to enjoy the tree lights. Harold entered, taking wrapping paper and scissors into the kitchen. He hadn't wrapped anything yet, so I offered to help him with Erik's gifts. When everything was finally under the tree, we were able to sit and enjoy the effects in silence. I sipped my coffee, Harold adding a boost to his before sitting on the couch beside me. In this way, we let the evening pass.

The next morning, I cooked eggs, bacon, pancakes and coffee for breakfast. Erik had rice cereal, which he seemed to enjoy the best of all the baby cereals he had tried. He was in such a great mood: laughing out loud as Harold teased him, making his arms swing around and knock the spoon out of my hand. Finally I gave up and started clearing the table.

I knew that, at seven months, Erik did not know what Christmas was all about, but he did know that he really liked paper. We were constantly taking the paper out of his mouth as we tried to get him to open his packages. The whole unwrapping ritual took most of the day and several rolls of film. These were priceless moments, and helped me feel as though everything was back to normal, and that normal was a good place to be.

It was easy to think that everything was normal, since Erik did not look or act sick, beyond wanting to sleep all the time. When he was awake, he was a joy: a wiggling, giggling bundle of joy. He smiled readily and seemed to be comfortable being the center of attention that babies always seems to become. I kept telling myself that God had given him to us and that God was now allowing us to enjoy him and fall deeply in love with him; therefore God wouldn't take him away.

We didn't treat Erik any differently than you would treat any child of his age. We were careful not to drop him or put him in a place where he might fall. We had childproofed the apartment to make sure he would be safe, and we kept him in eyesight as much as was humanly possible. And we still made those constant trips to his nursery and felt the need to wake him up—which wasn't exactly normal behavior. When at work, we made unnecessary calls throughout the day to Mary, who was quite capable and experienced with taking care of children, since she had three of her own. When it was time to pick Erik up, Mary had usually already told us all about his day over the phone, so we could talk about other things besides the children. Routine was setting in. We got up each day, ate, dropped Erik off at my sister's, worked, picked up Erik, ate, played with Erik, went to bed and then started it all over again.

Over the weeks that followed, I began to wonder about certain things. I had my game, the Truth Game, that I played whenever I needed to control my thinking pattern; but what did Harold have to keep him from feeling as though the world was about to fall apart? Was it the constant glass of liquor that fortified his soul, allowing him to function like the future offered nothing but hope? I always wondered about that but never asked, which might of meant that

I really didn't want to know. Whatever he used to help him get through, it worked—and that was the important thing, right?

Strange as it might seem, we could not talk about Erik's health problems with each other. We had tried early on, but the need of one of us to console the other always meant that the one doing the consoling ended up bearing a bigger load. Some things are best left alone.

***

We had lots of pictures; so many of them that we were constantly filling up albums and having to buy more. It wasn't long before we started to fall behind in putting the pictures in the albums in their order of event. There was such a mass of them that it became impossible to identify the exact situation in which they had been taken. Did that make me a horrible mother, or was it a common occurrence among parents with too many pictures and not enough time? I figured I had more important things to worry about than whether or not I was doing a disservice to our baby by not categorizing photographs. Soon I began letting them stack up, promising myself I would take care of them later.

There was so much more to be appreciated. Our lives were growing in the right direction and it all was accredited to having Erik. It wasn't obvious at first, as it seemed to happen in bits and pieces each day. The change manifested itself in simple situations, such as when I found myself in the grocery store happily relinquishing a ripe cantaloupe I had spent some time searching for to a confused fellow shopper. Erik had changed every facet of our lives in a positive way. We could sit in traffic without feeling frustration. We didn't stress out over situations at work or worry about finances. We were stronger, more tolerant, and were even polishing our sense of humor. We had developed into the kind of people that wanted everyone around them to feel comfortable and happy. We were becoming more tactful, seeing it as a personal gift to our fellow man, and we were able to sympathize with those who were less fortunate. I liked the changes that the experience had manifested in our personalities and I knew that deep down the reason was that if we did good deeds we thought that they would be rewarded. Even if it wasn't admitted openly, deep down in our hearts we still felt that we had done something that had displeased God and now we needed to make up for whatever that something was.

In January of 1970 Harry Saxton passed away. This was a great loss for Harold; and for me, as I had learned to love him too. The strange truth was that Harry had not seen his grandchild since his birth. At one point, before the baby was born, Harry just stopped coming over and, even though we resided in the same city, we had not been able to locate him again. We would later learn that Harry had started a new family in Rochester and for some reason hadn't wanted his children or wife to know about us. If our attitude towards life hadn't changed, our first impulse would have been to become furious; only later would we have thought about it more rationally. Maybe Harry felt he had to keep his life separate so that he could deal with it on a plane where he felt confident. After all, he had left his family in Oklahoma, without ever sending child support or presents on special occasions, and when his two worlds later clashed, those children had become adults with minds of their own.

The separation of our lives had begun when Harry left his job at Volpe Motors prior to Erik's birth. I was pregnant when he came to tell us he would not be working there anymore and was not sure where he would be going. We assumed he would let us know at a later stage. But later never eventuated, and the next we heard of Harry was a call notifying us he had been hospitalized. It was a troubled man we saw lying on crisp, white sheets in the sanitary atmosphere of the hospital room. He reached out to us for forgiveness, which we willingly gave, and we pacified him as he asked for our understanding. He died the next day.

Having lost my own father, I thought I knew what Harold was going through—but I was wrong. I had been lucky to have spent almost fourteen years under the same roof as my dad, and had seen him on a regular basis right up until his death. Harold, on the other hand, only had fleeting glimpses and memories of his father—a few little plugs that couldn't possibly fill all the gaps in his life. The relationship they had developed in the months following their reunion had not been that of a father and son, and it wasn't as though Harold had lost a father, rather a friend he was just getting to know.

***

Friends and family continued to play a vital function in our lives, becoming the one constant we could depend on to help us sift through the realities of life—to separate what had been from what remained; what was real from what had been imagined; and what was of value from what could be relinquished. With their support and faith, we were able to keep our sanity during that period of our life.

On the heels of the death of Harry, we received another phone call from the doctor. Erik was to be re-admitted to the hospital on March 2nd.

***

We awoke with a feeling of dread, and the weather outside held no promise whatsoever of lifting our spirits—it was a bleak, dismal, snowy winter day that greeted us, with no hope of a ray of sunshine pushing through the clouds hovering above.

It occurred to me that in thirty-nine days Erik would be one year old. On the tenth of each month, we celebrated Erik's birth by having a little family party. We would gather together with family and his godparents, George and Nancy, and do something just a little special. We would have a special dinner for us and baby food treats for Erik. Or we would buy him small gifts and watch him open then.

Some celebrations were spent in a park or at the zoo; anything that we thought would make him feel special.

You would think that all this special attention would spoil our child, but it didn't. He remained sweet, innocent and a joy to be around. He only cried if he needed his diaper changed or if he was hungry; and he would lie in his crib for hours at a time, staring up at the mobile, if we let him. As months passed, he enjoyed playing with the other babies in the apartment complex. We often had two or three friends over with babies his age, and they would crawl around together, making the sweetest sounds as they laughed and chattered in their baby babbling way.

If any child deserved special attention, it was Erik, and I wished that we could have rescheduled this hospital stay to have him home for his monthly celebration, but I knew that would not be possible. What if he was hospitalized right up until his one year birthday? It could happen, and if it did, what would we do? Nothing! It was out of our hands. Anyway, it was ridiculous for me to get so anxious about what *might* happen when there was already enough that actually *was* happening for me to be anxious about.

To help me focus on what was, rather than what might be, I played the Truth Game. The truth was that this could be the solution to Erik's physical problems. It would also be possible to have a small celebration right on the pediatric floor, if it came to that; and the final truth was that Dr. Cotanch hadn't mentioned anything about it being an extended stay, so it was assumable that Erik would be home before his first birthday.

We decided to start the day off just like any other. I got up first and went in to say good morning to Erik. Harold got up right after me and went into the bathroom to take his shower. It was my turn to prepare breakfast, and Harold's to give Erik his bath. Later we were all in our robes sitting around the kitchen table. Harold and I lingered over our morning coffee while Erik played with the leftover cheerios on his tray. We were silent as we each became lost in our personal thoughts of the forthcoming hospital stay. Several times I had wanted to openly discuss my thoughts with Harold, but something held me back. Instead I tried to brighten my mood by thinking about happier things.

So much had changed since Erik's last hospital visit. He was almost walking now. He would crawl across to a chair, couch or table, pull himself up and hang on until he had mastered the balance thing, then look around for the next available support before letting one hand go. He would then reach out as though he had seen an invisible object and then slowly release his other hand, but before he could take a step he would be on his way down to the floor, crawling as fast as he could. To encourage him, I would take his little hands and hold them tightly, letting him step proudly across the room as his laughter filled my heart with joy. These were the moments that I would treasure forever.

Erik still slept quite a bit for his age, but he was up and about when he wasn't sleeping, acting like most baby explorers and getting into as many things as he could find. Some mornings we had to wake him, but there were other mornings when we found him already up: jumping up and down as he held on the side rails of his crib. On those mornings his arms were out, ready to be picked up and cuddled.

I began to realize that all of these developmental changes might make it harder for Erik to be in the hospital, but we'd find that out soon enough.

I continued to reminisce, barely hearing Harold when he asked, "Do you have everything ready? We had better get a move on."

I nodded, watching as Harold went about putting the kitchen in order, before rising to go and get dressed. When Harold had finished in the kitchen, he entered the bedroom and, like ships in the night, we passed each other as I headed for the nursery to get Erik ready. Having done it all so many times before, we performed our duties like well-oiled machines, without having to think what to do next. I put Erik in his crib and made sure the side was secure before going to his closet and getting out his clothes for the day, along with his snowsuit, boots and hat. I then lifted Erik out of the crib and carried his wiggling body over to the dressing table, where I took off his night clothes, changed his diaper, cleaned his bottom, put on a fresh tee shirt and his outfit, and finally his snowsuit, boots and hat; all while he kept trying to wriggle away. In soothing tones I told him where we were going and what he would see, but I knew he didn't understand.

When I emerged from the nursery with our baby, Harold was already in the front room with Erik's suitcase, which had been packed with a few toys, his baby toiletries, his favorite blanket and his pacifier, in case he needed it. I put on my coat and finally we walked out the door.

We arrived at the hospital on time, quickly going through the admission procedures before being escorted to the pediatric wing. That was when it hit me—this had all become a familiar routine too. Erik had spent almost half of his young life in the pediatric wing, so it was most likely as comforting for him as being at home in his own bed. He was too young to distinguish this visit any other way. As depressing as it might seem, Erik was at home in the confines of the hospital, amongst all the other children and the familiar faces of nurses and doctors.

While Harold and I unpacked his little bag and placed objects in his assigned crib, the nurses came and said hello to Erik. He was his usual self, smiling and laughing with such warmth that they couldn't resist picking him up; and when they do, he becomes even more animated with the attention. Just when we had begun to adjust to the need of our baby having to stay here again, we were informed that the neurosurgeon wished to speak with us. We left Erik in the nurses' capable and willing hands.

We remained placid during the walk to the lounge, trying not to think ahead and afraid to speak in case our voices gave away our concern. There had been a few tests that Dr. Cotanch needed to review after we had taken Erik home, but he had told us that he would discuss the findings on this day. So we were either going to hear that they had found fluid on Erik's brain or that they were going to run more tests. It was a Catch-22 situation, with no positive outcome either way as far as we could see. Even if Erik was found to have hydrocephalus, it was incurable, though it could be effectively controlled. It was this need for a definite solution that held us at bay.

Though we trusted Dr. Cotanch completely, and believed him, we couldn't help feeling frustrated as he explained that further tests would need to be done, repeating that disorders of the brain were more misleading and frustrating to diagnose than any other organ in the body. In other words, they were still trying to find the fluid.

***

We found Erik waiting impatiently for our return. With just one look at his happy disposition, all thoughts of what we had just heard moved to the back of our minds. How could we remain wallowing in sadness when before us our baby was laughing and demonstrating how anxious he was for our attention? So, putting our problems aside, we went to Erik and lifted him out of his hospital crib, talking to him and tickling him as he squirmed in our arms. We then set him down and joined him playing with the toys we had brought from home. When he tired of this entertainment, we took him for a walk up and down the hallways and then to the waiting room, where there were other children, as well as a children's show on television.

The day passed swiftly as we entertained our son. We fed him lunch, and then before we knew it was dinner time. We filled each minute showering our attention on him until we saw that he was tiring. We then took him back to his room, washed him and put on fresh clothing. He then yawned contentedly, ready to be put back in the crib to sleep.

Finally it was time for us to leave the hospital and get a good night's sleep before going to work the next day. Erik was already asleep when we entered his room, which was good. Being the night before his tests and possible surgery, he cannot eat or drink anything, and we had been informed to let him sleep. It had been a long day for him, so we let him remain asleep as we kissed him good night and then drove home, discussing our plans. Harold and I agreed that it would be best for me to take the day off from work so that I could be with Erik before and after his surgery. I would keep him informed of any news so that he didn't have to miss any more days from work.

When we returned to our apartment this time, neither of us wanted to sleep. It was a monumental situation, beyond anything we had thus far experienced. Our baby was going to have surgery, if we believed as Dr. Cotanch did, and it seemed we did. Though we had suspected it all along, it was different now that we knew it was really going to happen and all that it would entail. Dr. Cotanch had gone over the details of the surgery with us as thoroughly as he had explained it earlier. It was frightening, and yet a relief to know that they were prepared to proceed with surgery. If Erik had fluid on the brain there was nothing that we could do for him except love him, pray and be with him to offer any comfort he needed.

Neither Harold nor I got much sleep that evening—we kept going over the facts of the surgery again and again. We asked ourselves if having our son undergo surgery was the right thing to do. We were going to allow the doctors to cut open his skull, for God's sake, and if something should go wrong, could we accept that we had allowed the operation to take place? We tried to combine our strength and confidence that everything would be all right as we outlined all the pros and cons. It was after midnight before we finally fell asleep.

***

The days that followed were a whirlwind of tests and conferences with the doctors as they reviewed the results. Each day that passed I became more passive and accepting because I knew there was nothing I could do or say that would be more beneficial to Erik. They had the ball in their court and I just had to play along.

***

It was Erik's eleven-month birthday. I arrived at the hospital long before the sun had fully risen and went immediately to Erik's bedside, where I found him still sleeping. There was a sign over his bed announcing that he was not allowed any food or drink, and the whole room was bathed in darkness; with the only sound being that of the babies breathing as they slept in their cribs. Not wanting to disturb him or any of the other children, I decided to take the elevator down to the cafeteria and get a cup of coffee, which I hoped would relax me.

From experience, I knew that once I had returned to the children's wing it would only be a matter of minutes before the whole room was awake, because it was in the early morning, before the arrival of the breakfast carts, that the nursing staff began their rounds of temperature taking and blood pressure reading. Once one child had woken up, that child's laughter or cries of impatience usually made sure all the other children in the ward were woken soon after.

When I returned to the pediatric wing, the nurse was one bed away from Erik's. Then she was with Erik; I watched as she took Erik's temperature then placed a blood pressure cuff on his arm, pumping the little ball in her hand until it fit tightly around his little arm, waking him. "It's all right, Erik, I'm almost done," the nurse said soothingly. Erik gave her a sleepy smile. Then finally the nurse moved aside and it was my turn to be with Erik.

I smiled down at him before lifting him into my arms, snuggling into his neck and whispering how much I love him as he flashes me one of his wide, innocent smiles. I continued to play with him while removing his pajamas and changing his diaper and undershirt. A pair of hospital pajamas was laid out at the bottom of his crib; I put these on over his diaper and undershirt, trying to keep him busy so he wouldn't realize he hadn't eaten yet. I felt a need to hold him close to me, so I gathered him up and took him over to the rocking chair that they kept in the room. I rocked my baby in my arms, holding him close to me and whispering how much I loved him. Erik wiggled around as though he wanted to play, but I continued to hold him close.

There was very little time for Erik and me that morning, and too soon he was given a sedative. His little body was unable to fight off the effects and he quickly fell asleep, unaware of the motion of the gurney wheeling him to surgery. I walked alongside as it made its way down the hall to the bay of elevators. While we were waiting, I leaned over Erik and continued to let him know how much I loved him, though he was sound asleep. I stepped into the elevator, telling the attendants I would be fine but had to be with Erik for as long as I could. No one objected as I continued beside the gurney until it was outside the surgery room. Everybody paused to allow me to say my last goodbyes. Then Erik was whisked away behind the double doors of the surgery unit.

Alone this time, I waited for the elevator to take me back up to the waiting room in the pediatric wing. Once there, I placed a call to Harold to let him know that our son was in surgery. As I sipped my coffee, I sensed the eyes of the other mothers in the waiting room on me. Through the hospital grapevine they were made aware it was the day of my son's surgery. I acknowledged their looks of sympathy with a smile and then tried to concentrate on the television, but my mind was far away, trying to picture every detail of the surgery, each step that was to be performed, as though I was by my son's side in the operating room. It was my way of continuing the feeling of holding him close to me.

Nancy, Erik's godmother, arrived at the hospital to wait with me. She kept me talking, trying to keep my mind off what was happening with Erik. I pretended to listen to her chatter, knowing that she was talking as much for her sake as for mine; and since she didn't seek any response, I could easily fake attentiveness. The clock ticked and the room filled will children laughing and crawling about; I couldn't stand it, so I asked Nancy if she wanted to sit in Erik's room, away from all the children who were in the hallways and in the lounge with their parents.

I wanted to wait somewhere quiet, and Erik's room seemed to be the most peaceful place on the whole floor. Nancy agreed and we walked back down the hall. Once settled, Nancy suddenly remembered she had brought Erik a present, which she had left by Erik's bed in the baby ward, having arrived earlier and finding he wasn't there. With nothing better to do, we decided to open the present ourselves, knowing that Erik wouldn't be in any condition for opening gifts.

It was a stuffed gray mouse with big pink ears, whiskers and a long, skinny black tail—Erik would love it. We set it up in the crib then, as if thinking the same thoughts, both placed our hands on the bed, feeling where Erik's small body had lain and envisioning his presence.

We were careful not to look at any clocks or wrist watches. When you watch time, it seems to pass more slowly. The neurosurgeon had said that if all went well Erik would be down in surgery for approximately three hours. That's a long time to watch the hands of a clock crawl around the dial, and unsettling if the doctor didn't appear at precisely the designated time.

We busied ourselves in conversation, trying to block out everything else and just focus on each other. It seemed to work right up until we were joined by a staff intern who had been asked by Dr. Cotanch to give us a progress report. The intern told us that they had found fluid on Erik's brain and Dr. Cotanch was now performing the surgical insertion of the shunt. He asked if we had any questions and though I had many, I decided to give him a break and save them for Dr. Cotanch. Having delivered this news, the intern excused himself and returned to the operating room.

As the time progressed, it became easier to distract ourselves. We talked about the ingredients in a shrimp dish that Nancy and George had prepared for Harold and me. We talked about the time, before Erik was born, we had gone to an amusement park. Then the conversation turned to Erik's birth, and funny little anecdotes about him, like how he had started out crawling with one knee and hand on his left side, and one foot and hand on the other. Our hearts and minds were flooded with joy as we recalled those precious moments. Then a nurse approached us, informing us that Dr. Cotanch would be up shortly and that she would take me to a room where I could wait until he joined me.

I was confused—I had been told that Dr. Cotanch would talk with me once the surgery was over. Had something gone wrong? It couldn't possibly be over yet! My worry was apparent on my face and the nurse saw it. She said, "The surgery went well and it is over now. Erik is on his way to the recovery room." Relief flooded my body as I turned to Nancy. "Go ahead, I'll stay here in case Erik gets back before you do," she said. With that, I let the nurse guide me down the corridor.

I didn't have to wait long before I was joined by Dr. Cotanch. I could tell by the smile on his face that he was happy, and this was soon confirmed when he told me the news. The surgery had gone well and Erik was doing just fine. I wanted details so that I could feel a part of the episode, so I asked Dr. Cotanch to tell me everything as it happened in that room. He did.

After a general anesthetic had been administered, Erik was positioned on his back, with his head turned to one side. The hair over the scalp incision area was then clipped and shaved. Two incisions were made: a small incision in the abdomen and a curved incision in the scalp, creating a flap. This scalp flap was turned back to expose the skull, into which a small burr hole was drilled to uncover the dura, the brain's covering, over the enlarged ventricles. The shunt was then inserted first into the abdominal incision and brought beneath the skin over the abdomen, chest and neck, into the scalp opening. After the tubing and reservoir were in place, a small cut was made in the dura and a ventricular tube inserted into the brain's right ventricle. The reservoir was then attached to the ventricular tube and fitted into the opening in Erik's skull. Once the surgery was completed, the shunt system was completely inside Erik's body, where often it cannot be detected by others and might not even be felt by Erik himself.

That was what I wanted and I thanked him for being so thorough.

Dr. Cotanch then went on to give me an overview of what would happen next. Erik would be under constant neurological observation for the next 24 hours and kept flat in bed until nearly all the subdural air introduced during surgery had dissipated. The bandages placed on his head and abdomen, covering the incision sites, would be monitored for signs of infection, and there was a possibility Erik would have to stay in the hospital for between three to seven days longer before we could take him home. Afterwards, follow-up visits would be required to check his post-operative status and the resolution of symptoms. Dr. Cotanch cautioned that although shunt surgery was a relatively simple neurosurgical procedure, the insertion of a shunt should not be taken lightly.

I took notes as he spoke, so as not to forget anything when I relayed the information to Harold. The doctor allowed time for me to write everything down, before continuing on, stating that the potential complications of shunt surgery were twofold: those directly related to the surgery and those that might occur days to years later.

I asked him to explain and he told me that potential complications included infection of the surgical wound, possible bleeding into the brain or ventricles, and even a seizure.

I asked him how would I know and he reported that a shunt infection may be indicated by fever, or redness or swelling along the shunt track. He added that fortunately these complications were uncommon and if they occurred they could be managed successfully in most cases. Another problem might bean obstruction and they can occur multiple times.

Dr. Cotanch asked if he was scaring me; I stopped writing, thought for a moment, and said that yes, it did scare me but it would be worse if I was not informed about what to expect. I asked the doctor if Erik would require any special care, and was told that beyond what had already been mentioned, no special care would be required after Erik's release; apart from making sure he was taken to his regular follow-up visits and that any relevant observations on Erik's health were reported, no matter how subtle, as they could be indicative of a shunt problem.

I played with my pen then blurted out, "What caused this to manifest itself in Erik". Dr. Cotanch gently explained that it may have resulted from defective genes, or some kind of accident or trauma during his embryonic development. There could have been one or multiple causes, but that was not what really mattered. What mattered now was that Erik was doing fine, and what he had gone through was not to be considered anyone's fault. Harold and I had done nothing to cause this to happen. Dr. Cotanch then went on to prepare me for Erik's return.

All surgery results in bruising and swelling that may remain for one or two weeks after the operation. Some patients remain bruised for longer, and though rare, the swelling can still be apparent for up to a month. With that said, Dr. Cotanch warned me that Erik's face would be swollen and that he would have an IV in his ankle. I was not to worry, as this was normal after surgery. He added that though the hospital staff would wake Erik before he was returned to the pediatric wing, he would probably spend the rest of the day catching up on some much needed sleep. The intravenous tube would provide his nourishment, as well as medication, so there would be no need for him to be disturbed.

I finally left the office and started down the hallway to Erik's room. As I approached the elevators, the doors opened and a gurney was pushed into my path. I stopped my progress, somehow sensing it was my child on the gurney. As soon as it was close enough, I grabbed the side and looked down at what appeared to be my child. A large bandage was covering the right side of his head, with a half Dixie cup hooked to the center. Further observation revealed there were bandages on his neck as well. At the foot of the gurney, a nurse was holding an IV bottle up over her head. I followed the tube running from the IV bottle to Erik's ankle, locating the point where the needle was inserted. I continued to hang onto the side of the gurney—no longer for a better look, but more for support. Someone asked if I was all right and I nodded my head affirmatively; but I was not all right. I hadn't expected this transformation in my son. His face was so swollen that I, his mother, was having trouble recognizing him. I continued to hang on as the gurney proceeded down the corridor.

We arrived at the pediatric wing to find an anxious Nancy waiting for us. She took one look at me and told me to sit down. As she guided me to a chair she told me she had just received word that Erik was on his way up. Someone handed us each a glass of water, which we accepted gratefully. The gurney moved closer. Nancy was then the one in shock, as she peered down into the face of her godson. We watched as Erik was gently lifted from the gurney and placed in his pediatric crib. A hanger had been brought in and the nurse attached Erik's IV bottle to its top hook. Another nurse started restraining Erik's arms and legs to the crib rails. Then aware of the impression this was having on Nancy and I, she paused and told us the bindings were necessary to keep Erik from turning onto his side or possibly tugging at the IV or bandages.

I finally asked why the IV had been put in his ankle.

"Sometimes it makes it easier for children of your son's age to accept being bedridden if they can use both of their hands," the nurse explained as she continued to make Erik as comfortable as possible.

"But he can't. You have them tied!" I said in frustration.

"Oh, this is just for now, so that he stays on his back and doesn't roll over. When he is awake and someone is with him, these restraints can be released."

It made sense. Well, at least I had to believe it did.

I was shaking and my legs felt weak as I sat there watching the nurses put Erik in his bed. Finally I found my legs again and managed to get up. Nancy was right there beside me, barely holding her own as we both walked to the side of Erik's crib and looked down at him together. He looked so helpless lying there: his lips dry and his eyes puffy, as though he had been crying. I wanted to hold him close so he felt protected. The nurse, as if reading my thoughts, told us it would be best for him if we let him sleep. She suggested we go down and get something to eat, and told us they'd let us know if there was any change.

In the cafeteria, Nancy and I were unable to eat. Instead we drank coffee in silence until Nancy had to leave, making me promise to call her if there was any change, no matter how late it got. We rode up in the elevator together so that Nancy could look at Erik one more time before we said our goodbyes. Then I was left alone in pediatrics. I let the nurses' station know that I would be in the pediatrics' waiting room.

***

The waiting room was full of the sound of children playing; a sound I welcomed as I picked up a magazine and idly turned the pages. It was not until one of the parents asked how little Erik was doing that it finally dawned on me that he was really doing fine now that the surgery was over. I began to relax.

The television was on; watching the screen soothed me. I wasn't really absorbing what I saw, rather using it as something to focus on while my mind wandered. Periodically I got up to check on Erik, only to find him still sleeping soundly. That was how the evening progressed; though I must have drifted off at some stage, because I later found myself wiping the sleep from my eyes as my name was being gently called out. Harold stood in front of me with a worried look on his face. I sat up and stretched, removing the lingering traces of sleep. I asked him if he had seen Erik yet. Of course he had, that's the first place he would go. Harold waited patiently until I was awake enough to tell him that Erik was doing fine; he didn't look like he was fine, but Dr. Cotanch, the nurses, and everyone else were pleased with the results.

Harold relaxed and sank down on the couch next to me. I told him everything that I had been told throughout the day. As I could see that he was anxious to go to Erik's room, I warned that we had to be careful not to disturb him—he needed to sleep. Harold understood, and together we went to see our son. He was still sleeping, so we sat by his bed, holding hands and just looking at him. We stayed that way for some time before realizing how late it was getting. As we were leaving I let one of the nurses know that we were going home and that I would be back the next morning.

Erik slept for the next two days, waking for only short periods before falling asleep once again. But by the third day after his surgery, he was finally fully awake. He had managed to slip from the bindings during the night and had removed the IV needle. When

Harold and I arrived at the hospital after work, we saw three stitches marking the spot where the IV needle had once been. The bindings had been removed, so we were able to pick Erik up and hold him.

At the end of each day, the nurses would relate Erik's activities to us in minute detail. He seemed to be doing fine, though he'd been suffering headaches—they'd caught him rubbing his arms across his forehead. His temperature was constantly being taken by one of the nurses; he was registering a fever but it was going down. They had been giving him Tylenol.

Harold and I were advised that headaches and fever were normal occurrences after a surgical procedure and did not present a problem. We were also told, as if offered as a consolation prize, that as long as someone was with him, he did not have to be bound to the bed. They had only been binding his arms at night so that he wouldn't remove the bandages.

***

During the days that followed, Erik kept improving. There was a noticeable reduction in the extent of the swelling. He was starting to look more like himself. His activity increased but, as the nurses had told us, he hadn't yet regained his full strength and therefore still needed as much rest as possible. Erik was matching the amount he slept to the requirements of his body.

By the middle of the second week, Erik's chart showed no sign of fever or headaches. The doctor was pleased with his progress. Erik started spending his mornings in the play room and going for stroller rides up and down the corridor. Harold and I could see that he had fully recovered. He was as active as he had even been.

His bandages were removed, then finally the stitches—to Erik's dismay. And then came the good news—Erik was being released. He would be able to go home with us on March 17—my birthday! Taking my son home was the best present I could have ever received.

***

It's really a feeling that is hard to put into words. I guess that I had never felt parental responsibility fully, since Erik had been away so much. I hadn't been able to really get used to being a mother; accepting all the responsibilities that come with the title. But, as a result of Erik's hospitalization, I began to feel less like a mother and more like an inactive stranger. I had given birth to him, but then others, more qualified than me to attend to his needs, had entered the picture.

It wasn't fair! Didn't giving birth to a child make you the person most responsible for their existence? I wanted to give him his bottle; I wanted to change him, bathe him, and be the most familiar "face" in his life. It was my right to lay claim to Erik. But circumstances had taken away a lot of my controlling influence. I understood the necessary part the doctors and nurses were playing in this true life drama, but I couldn't help feeling a selfish loss.

Erik was growing up with doctors and nurses as his parental figures—the ones who looked after his well-being—while my husband and I had to push our way in for a moment of mothering and fathering. How would Erik learn what a normal relationship between parents and a child was like when there had been so much intervention? Time would tell.

With all my heart I prayed that Erik would continue to improve and that we would soon be able to take him home. When Erik was given a clean bill of health and we were told he would be released on schedule, I experienced the selfish joy of having won the prize intermingled with a feeling of respect and thankfulness for the parts played by the other actors. Nothing could have made me happier.

***

I remembered reading somewhere that adults may get a cold every winter, the flu once in a while, but that babies get sick a lot, so be prepared to be on a first-name basis with your pediatrician or nurse practitioner. These relatively frequent bouts of illness are necessary to buildup their immune systems against viruses and other germs that share our world. Most of the illnesses they contract are minor, but babies are much more—and much less—than just tiny humans. They're tiny, underdeveloped humans, particularly when it comes to their immune systems. That's why even the slightest fever may be cause for worry. They can become jaundiced, which generally goes away without any special treatment. And it often seems that, as soon as you've finished feeding your baby, everything you worked so hard to get down comes right back up—all over your shirt. Spitting up is as endemic to newborns as the soft spot on the top of their heads. These "wet burps" usually occur shortly after feedings. Babies spit up because, in about half of all infants, the valve at the upper end of the stomach (the esophageal sphincter) hasn't yet closed properly; but this should change by the end of the first year.

Babies may suffer from croup, fevers, colic, and ear infections. Rashes may also appear—no matter how careful, or whether you use disposable or cloth diapers, it's nearly inevitable that at some point your baby will get diaper rash. The article I had read finally cautioned that very young babies can become dehydrated or suffer diarrhea, and that there's nothing as heartbreaking as a baby with a cold.

I was the second oldest of six kids, and I did my share of caring for the little ones. Changing diapers, rocking them to sleep and keeping them entertained were chores shared by everyone. With that many kids, for many years there was almost always a baby in diapers; and though we didn't call it frugal baby care at the time, that's exactly what it was.

Most of the childhood illnesses I had been exposed to when young now seemed minor, and having to share the standards of child care would have made me feel less equipped for full time motherhood had it not been for my brothers and sisters.

***

After Erik's release and return to our care on March 17, we began the business of celebrating his one year old birthday. All preparation had been held off waiting to see if he would be indeed up to a party. We were finally getting down to the business of being a family on a full-time basis and loving every minute of it.

By the time Erik's next appointment with his neurosurgeon rolled around, we had already given him a clean bill of health. Dr. Cotanch only verified our findings.

Life took on more meaning. Though our feelings and experiences were no doubt similar to those of other young parents, our relationship as a family had far more meaning. There are those who might disagree with this, but it can't be denied: trauma forces one to become more involved with life, and we had no problem, no problem at all, dealing with this deep involvement in each other's existence.

Our baby was no longer a helpless infant unable to do anything without us. He still needed plenty of care and support, but his growing independence was becoming apparent. He could walk while gripping our hand, and would hold out his arm or leg to help us dress him. At mealtimes, he could grip a cup and drink from it independently, and hand-feed himself an entire meal. It was also around this time that he developed a new form of entertainment. He liked to drop objects for someone, usually us, to pick up. He enjoyed looking at his books, and many times we had found him leafing through the pages, though he wouldn't always turn them over one-by-one. Before our eyes, and in spite of his setbacks, he was developing nicely. He loved playing with other children, and we encouraged it. We knew it was the time to set limits, but limits had been set for Erik since birth, so we used our best judgment as a guideline.

He was talking, using meaningful words as opposed to babble, and it was obvious that he was developing the ability to reason and speak, imitating word sounds and inflections as well as actions. He also had the ability to follow simple one-step directions, such as "Please bring me the ball" or "Pick up the spoon". He was, out of necessity, becoming a social animal and that was a good thing that the hospital visits created and exactly what encouraged us to plan for a big party, but that had to change.

***

Erik's one-year-old birthday plans had to be changed. Since the event would be taking place so soon after his release, the doctor advised us to cut down the guest list—no children and as few adults as possible. Understanding how much we had looked forward to the event, Dr. Cotanch sympathized but felt it was in Erik's best interest health wise to confine the celebrations to just ourselves. Though he appeared to be fully recovered, Erik needed rest and should not be overly excited. As for eating cake, well, a crumb or two, but no more. At first the news was quite a let down, but then appreciating that Erik was home it soon didn't matter. Even with the restrictions we were determined to make the day as eventful as possible.

It was hard, to say the least, to contact the family and tell them that we would not be able to proceed as planned. At Dr. Cotanch's suggestion, we were about to pick two adults from our large families to share Erik's birthday with us. We started with our mothers.

We found that Harold's mom was unable to make it up from Oklahoma until later in the year. My mom, who had been shuffling back and forth from Fulton to Rochester over the past months, needed some time to recuperate. So two family members eliminated themselves. This left us with brothers and sisters to choose from. Because we had to be careful to not allow Erik to come in contact with any viruses, even the common cold, we were met with understanding. But how do you pick from so many loved ones?

We gave the matter a lot of thought and finally came up with the ideal solution—George and Nancy would be the other couple to attend Erik's birthday. They had been around Erik so much already that their presence would not overly excite him, as he was used to seeing them. This choice meant we didn't have to pick between our brothers and sisters, and surprisingly, everyone felt it was the best choice.

We went all out, purchasing a complete ensemble of party goods—table cloth, napkins, plates, cups and plastic cutlery. We blew up an endless number of balloons and hung them throughout the apartment. We ordered a cake, and prepared fruit punch and snacks. Of course Erik would have his picture taken amongst the party array, even blow out the one candle on the cake, but that would be as far as it would go. While we indulged in the pleasure of eating the party food, Erik would have to settle for milk, fruit juice, water, and a few crackers. At first it seemed like a cruel thing to do, but as I thought about it more I realized that it really wasn't. Babies are brought up eating their special baby food and drinking their bottles, while the rest of the family indulges in table food. It wasn't any different for Erik, who was still not able to eat "grown-up" food. It made me feel better knowing that this would not dampen Erik's fun..

The "party" turned out to be as special as we had hoped. Erik was the guest of honor in all respects. Used to a lot of attention being lavished on him, he didn't get over-excited or experience any setbacks on that day or the days that followed.

***

Life continued on an even keel. Erik's health was stable and he was developing as normally as the next child, though he seemed to feel a little unsure about walking without support. That was fine with me, because I knew that once he started walking on his own he would be leaving the baby stage, and I wasn't ready to let this period go just yet. He was such a joy to have around.

Harold and I going to our jobs each day, picking up Erik and taking him home with us each night put us in the routine of the rest of the world. It was a happy time: a time of mental relaxation as we became accustomed to the normalcy of life.

We were becoming addicts to the natural flow of each day. We began first thing by getting out of bed and putting the coffee pot on. Then while I prepared breakfast, Harold would take his shower and then go in and get Erik ready so we could all set down to eat breakfast together. Then once we were all ready, it would be time to leave. Erik would be dropped off at a neighbor's home and then Harold would drop me off at the bus stop before going on to his work. At the end of each day, whoever arrived back first would pick up Erik, we would eat dinner and the rest of the evening after dinner would be spent playing and talking together. Nothing unusual about the routine for most, but for us it was special.

Erik thought it fun to push, throw, and knock everything down. He'd give us a toy and then take it away over and over again. He also liked to put things in containers and dump them out again. He had one favorite cabinet in the kitchen: the one that held our pots and pans. I started putting the older ones in front for him to use and my good ones in the back. Erik loved to crawl over to the cabinet, open it and drag out the pots and pans. He seemed thrilled by the loud sounds he made when banging them together.

On weekends we would plan little family outings, visit with friends and family, or just sit around the house together watching TV or playing games with Erik until he began to rub his eyes: the signal that it was time for bed. Then we would sing a song to him while bathing him, and afterwards name each article of clothing as we put on his pajamas, until finally he was ready for sleep. Once tucked in we would read to him first and then, as we saw his heavy eyelids drop, put in a tape to play while he drifted off to sleep.

***

Erik's ability to form words and word-like sounds became a godsend. The development of the frontal lobes of his brain continued, as did his ability to reason and speak. We encouraged his interest in language and his understanding of two-way communication by being avid listeners and responding to his sounds. To polish his memory skills we played games like patty-cake and peek-a-boo with him. We cherished this brief but remarkable period when our baby's communication skills were emerging. As we were soon to discover, it was perhaps his most important skill.

***

The value of communication for Erik proved itself on January 2, when Erik pointed to his forehead and said, "It hurts!" He kept repeating those words, with tears rolling from his eyes.

It was nine months since he had been released from the hospital, and we had become comfortable in our simple everyday existence, letting go of all the commotion that had proceeded this time. Now it was all coming back.

Dr. Cotanch had told us that Erik might experience headaches, which often arise from increased pressure on the skull, and that we should contact him at the first sign of this happening. So we called Dr. Cotanch, though I tried to convince myself it was nothing to worry about—that he probably just had a little bug or something— but I knew it was time to worry when I had to respond affirmatively to Dr. Cotanch's question: "Does he seem tired and withdrawn?" I was then told to bring Erik to his office immediately.

I told myself to try and remain calm, but it seemed impossible to follow my own advice. I watched as the doctor examined Erik, reminding myself that hydrocephalus was not an uncommon pediatric disease and thus the neurosurgeons were quite efficient at the procedure and its complications. Hadn't Dr. Cotanch told us previously that shunt placement also had a very high complication rate? Consequently, patients with CSF shunts were frequently brought in for a wide spectrum of complaints. So, should I be worried? I thought about this for only a moment before telling myself, yes, you betcha; because the doctor had also said that shunt problems are potentially life-threatening. Any complaints consistent with a shunt malfunction should prompt urgent neurosurgical consultation. Wasn't that why I had reacted so swiftly in the first place? Of course it was. Unable to wait any longer, I asked the doctor, "What is the problem?"

As I continued to watch Dr. Cotanch examine Erik, he explained that the most common complication, which accounts for half of all shunt complications, is obstruction in the proximal portion of the tubing or at a valve. There also might be an infection or over drainage, but at this point he felt confident Erik had an obstruction and not an infection or a problem with over drainage. Headache, vomiting and lethargy are classic symptoms of increased intracranial pressure, pointing to a blockage. Since Erik did not have a fever, the chance that he had an infection was reduced. Dr. Cotanch wanted to run some test.

Erik was hospitalized and testing began immediately, with radiographic imaging and CSF evaluation. Dr. Cotanch explained that the radiograph imaging started with an evaluation of ventricular size compared to the previously recorded size. Plain radiographs of the shunt valve and tubing were also needed to assess the continuity of the system and to rule out kinking of the tube.

After the imaging studies, CSF analysis would be required, so Erik was given a shunt tap, which was preferred to a lumbar puncture since the latter procedure will occasionally miss infections. He explained that they would insert a needle attached to a manometer into the valve chamber while occluding the outlet valve. By occluding the outlet, the manometer would reflect the ventricular opening pressure. Inability to obtain fluid would signify an occlusion proximal to the valve. After the pressure was recorded, the outlet would be released and fluid drained into a distal catheter. Distal obstruction is present if the fluid will not drain from the manometer.

The testing began and as Dr. Cotanch had determined, Erik had a shunt obstruction and required urgent shunt revision.

On January 6, 1971, the obstruction surgery was performed successfully and shortly thereafter Erik was back home with us. On the day of his post-operative examination, Dr. Cotanch was pleased with Erik's recovery and our quick action in bringing the matter to his attention. He added that our quick observation and immediate contact had saved Erik's life.

We had saved Erik's life! I hadn't thought of it in that way, but now that it had been said by the doctor, I accepted it as fact. I had been so wrapped up with wanting to play a full-time role as a mother that I hadn't realized my role was substantial whether Erik was home with us or at the hospital. Our role was not only nurturing, but sounding the alarm. Harold and I were the ones who, yes, knew him better than anyone else and therefore knew when something was wrong. No bigger compliment could have been bestowed on us then that.

***

Erik was now only three months away from his 2nd birthday, when he would officially become a toddler. This major rite of passage happened when Erik ventured his first steps alone and began feeding himself with a spoon, though his aim wasn't the best. So along with having to watch for any shunt complications, we had to make sure he didn't run into a wall or fall on his head.

As each week passed, Erik demonstrated a complete recovery from the surgery, and his new mobility gave him an increased independence; though he still was so tiny, rushing here and there, getting into everything and laughing as he went. It was a time of sheer happiness for all of us.

This would be Erik's first full fledged birthday party and though I knew a two-year-old didn't understand much about birthdays— I did, and I needed to begin the ritual of birthday parties for our son. It started out simply enough—purchasing a package of Disney invitations and sending them to Erik's playmates in the apartment complex, outside friends and family members. I stuck with the Disney theme, decorating our apartment with colorful balloons and putting Goofy and Donald duck candles on the cake, so Erik could learn how to blow them out. I spent evenings wrapping lots of presents in colorful paper and making sure the camera was ready to take a massive amount of pictures. I had ordered a special cake made and had plenty of the Neapolitan ice cream blocks in the refrigerator. The closer it got to the date, the happier I became—so naïve was I about what I was getting myself into.

Finally the day arrived. All of his playmates came along with all of our family and friends. We were surrounded by ten, two-year-olds, all together in one apartment. Party favors for the little ones were everywhere. It was hard to organize much in the way of games for the toddlers, as they tended to prefer doing their own thing, so I just made sure there were a lot of toys out for them to play with. Just getting them to sit still to sing 'Happy Birthday' was enough to encourage putting off opening the presents until later—much later. From noon until two o'clock I felt as though my head was spinning, but I managed to remain calm until the last person was sent home. Then I sat down, surveyed the damage and decided the party was a success.

That evening, Harold and I had no trouble falling asleep when we were finally able to climb into bed. I can still remember his last words before sleep claimed his body: "Never again; never will I go through that again!" But at some stage during that restful night's sleep, he lost that thought totally.

***

Erik made sure that we had the opportunity to experience the "terrible twos". Having gained full mobility of his sturdy little legs, he moved through the house at a rapid pace. There was no keeping up with him, or figuring what he would do next. Even at that young age there were signs of his coping with his size. He had the ability to get in and out of a chair that most two-year-olds lacked.

It was like a gift with him figuring out how to do anything that he wanted to do, though he was so much smaller than the rest of the children. By now Erik was the height of a 9 month old which was quite small in comparison with his 2 year old playmates.

Nothing could be moved high enough to remain out of his reach. He would climb, crawl, or do whatever it took to get at something he wanted. It was a busy time to say the least. I would take him shopping with me and regret it before I had even managed to enter the store. He would want to touch everything he saw. I began to wonder why grocery stores displayed so many of their goodies within such easy reach of the little passenger's of a shopping cart. If Erik could reach it, he would get it. If he could not open it, he ate it paper and all. He would add those treats he wanted to deal with later to the conveyor belt to be rung up with all the other purchases.

It was even worse in department stores, where he would reach out and grab at the clothing or jewelry on display. He had also developed an uncanny liking for the feel of stockings. Whenever I had an attack of temporary insanity, I would make sure Erik was firmly holding on to my hand before venturing inside a store. He would continue his usual routine of inspection, only now he could do his favorite thing—rub the legs of every woman with stockings on who passed within his reach.

Slowly Harold and I learned how to gain some semblance of control over Erik. "No!" began to mean something to him. In the grocery cart, I would watch his little hands attentively, and at the first sign of exploration, I would try and turn his attention elsewhere.

He had become a little chatterbox and loved to talk. This could have quite an effect on the other shoppers; after a conversation with Erik, some of them ended up forgetting their purpose in coming to the grocery store in the first place. Here was this little boy: approaching three years of age and chattering away, but the other shoppers wouldn't have known this. In appearance, Erik still had a real "baby face", and his size was closer to that of a child of seven months, or nine months at the most. Fascinated shoppers would come up and talk to Erik directly. After a while I got tired of trying to explain that he was almost three when they would remark, "He's such a bright baby, and so friendly!" I would just say thank-you and continue shopping.

More and more, Erik drew people to him like a magnet. He had a large circle of friends his age, and just as many teenagers and adults wishing to join the circle. We constantly had people telling us, "There's just something special about him". Of course, his unique size would first attract the older members of the clan, but it was something else that held them there. In any case, watching our son grow during this period was a special time in our lives.

CHAPTER 5
1972

Just about everyone in the world has had at least one headache. Some people rarely get them, while others have them almost every day. Either way, we pay little attention to them and the headache is soon gone, but sometimes headaches become so painful or so frequent that we start to worry that it might be something more serious. All the time when a child or an adult has a shunt, a headache is never taken lightly, so I called his pediatrician.

Dr. Boettrich gave three year old Erik a thorough examination. She talked to him, asking if he could tell her where it hurt. She watched his facial expressions as she continued her examination and in an effort to soothe me she said, "The good news about headaches is that the majority of them are completely harmless. However, every once in a while a headache is a warning of some serious, so we can't be too cautious. We need to find what triggered the headache."

Dr. Boettrich talked, poked and probed and then announced that I should get Erik dressed and meet her in the office. As I dressed Erik, I tried to determine what she might say, but there was not a hint given throughout her exam. I didn't register any feelings that suggested whether I should be unconcerned or worried. So I gave up trying to second guess her findings.

In Dr. Boettrich's office she didn't offer a diagnosis, but instead told me she had placed a call to Dr. Cotanch and set up an appointment for Erik the following afternoon. She explained that she was not comfortable with us waiting any longer than necessary, but that I shouldn't worry as it might not be anything seriously wrong. I tried to be positive as I left the pediatricians office that day, but doubt surrounded me. Something was wrong.

At Dr. Cotanch's office the next day I watched as he examined Erik and before entering his office, I knew how this day would end. I could hear the words he spoke as I sat in his office, but they sounded distant as though coming down a tunnel and entering my head. I heard him as he explained that a shunt malfunction is one of the most common clinical problems in pediatric neurosurgery, but the diagnosis can be both difficult and perplexing. At this point Dr. Cotanch felt that Erik was experiencing a shunt dysfunction, but he needed to run tests to verify his findings.

It was his plan to admit Erik at Genesee Hospital and that took place immediately.

We knew the routine by now. With orders from Dr. Cotanch, Harold and I took Erik to the Admissions and Registration area at the main entrance of the hospital. We had our folder of information ready and rapidly produced Insurance identification card, social security number, noted that there were no current medications that Erik was taking and finally provided information on next of kin including name, address, phone number, and relationship. We were then asked to take a seat and within an hour we were taken up to pediatrics to get Erik settled in.

The clinical suspicion of shunt failure was enough to necessitate operative exploration. Erik had symptoms reminiscent of previous shunt dysfunction but the exact cause in this case had to be found. Testing began. It could be subgaleal fluid accumulation, cerebrospinal fluid (CSF) leak, a shunt disconnection which would show up on the radiographs, or an enlarging syrinx. With the uncertainty a shunt patency (nuclear medicine) study and Camino continuous intracranial pressure (ICP) monitoring finally demonstrated evidence of shunt failure. The determination was to perform surgery to remove the obstruction and then revamp the shunt and on February 10, 1972 the operation was performed. The original insertion path of Erik's shunt was realigned to one that the doctor felt would improve the shunt's operation, and thus came the successful conclusion to another medical episode in Erik's young life.

***

On May 29, 1972, Beulah, Harold's mother, passed away at the age of 58. In between the medical episodes in our son's life, we had managed to make occasional trips to Oklahoma so that Harold's family could see Erik. Beulah had come to Rochester to be with us after Erik's birth and on several other occasions in his young life. We had been programmed early on to not take anything for granted and, as the years went by, this had proved to be a wise path to follow.

The day started out normally for us: with no premonitions of anything amiss as we went off to work, returned home to an energetic three-year-old requiring attention, prepared our dinner and sat down to eat. Conversation was minimal during those days, as our attention was usually absorbed with watching little Erik's latest antics. After dinner I went about preparing Erik for bed, before handing over the reading of his nightly story to Harold.

One constant that had carried over from Erik's newborn days was his sleeping soundly through the night. At three years of age, Erik slept from between nine and thirteen hours a day, including an afternoon nap. If he didn't get this amount of sleep he became irritable and overtired. He knew that at a certain time each day he would change into his pajamas, brush his teeth, listen to a story and then take his favorite stuffed animal to bed. If we changed this routine he would have trouble getting to sleep. After having heard the problems other parents experienced trying to get their children to sleep, we had come to realize that, in terms of his sleeping patterns, Erik was a blessing. It may have been because we put him in a good frame of mind for sleep, by playing quietly with him or reading him a story before putting on soothing music until he passed out. No matter how tired or busy, we made sure to stick to the same pattern each night.

We sat up watching television for a while and then turned in for the evening. No sooner than the light had been switched off, we found ourselves drifting easily into sleep. We were sleeping soundly when the silence was broken by the ringing of the telephone. At first I was disoriented, not being used to receiving late night phone calls, but by the third ring I was out of bed and hurrying to the living room to answer the phone.

In a sleep-laden voice I said, "Hello?" Initially there was silence at the other end, then just as I was about to hang up I heard a faint voice coming across the wires. I listened intently, with the phone plastered up against my ear, until I finally recognized the voice as Beulah's.

There is a three-hour time difference between Rochester and Oklahoma, so at first I wasn't worried by the hour of the call; but then the whispering voice alerted to me that there was indeed something going on. After several attempts, Beulah finally managed to tell me that she had been in a car accident and was calling from the hospital in Tulsa.

I placed a hand over the mouthpiece and called out to Harold several times until he finally joined me in the living room. "It's your mother," I whispered. "She's been in a car accident." That was all he needed to hear; he went straight into the kitchen to pick up the extension.

Beulah told us she had sustained only minor injuries—just bumps and bruises—but there was something in her tone of voice that made me doubt her. I peeked into the kitchen and could tell by Harold's expression he wasn't convinced either. I remained silent and let Harold talk with her until a doctor who had just arrived in Beulah's room came on the line.

After a brief introduction the doctor explained that Beulah was jaundiced, which is often a precursor to more serious liver ailments, including liver failure. Harold asked the doctor what he meant by jaundiced, and he responded that jaundice is characterized by a yellowing of the skin caused by the liver's reduced ability to process a pigment known as bilirubin.

There was a moment of silence before Harold asked what needed to be done. The doctor replied that while the liver is unique in that it can regenerate itself if partially damaged, prolonged abuse or severe damage can doom its ability to perform its life-sustaining role. He then explained that he had yet to get back the test results but believed Beulah was experiencing liver failure, also known as hepatotoxicty, which typically only happens when a large part of the liver is damaged beyond repair. He then asked Harold to confirm his mother was a drinker, which Harold did; though he said he didn't consider her to drink excessively. Listening on the other line, I tended to disagree.

When we finally hung up, Harold mumbled, "She's yellow. Pains on her right side. Possible broken ribs." I knew he wasn't talking to me but more to himself, trying to sort it all out. Looking at me, but not really seeing me, he asked me to dial Nanny's phone number in Bartlesville. "I need to know what happened," he said.

I dialed the number and watched Harold return to the kitchen to pick up the extension. Soon Nanny came on the line. "Sister?" Harold's grandmother had always called her daughter Beulah 'Sister'. "No, Nan. It's me," Harold said, then quickly explained that he had just talked to his mother at the hospital and needed to know what had happened. Nanny told Harold that his brother Joe had come home from the Navy and he and Beulah had gone out for a drive to talk. She had later received a call telling her that they had been hit broadside by an approaching car. Their own car totaled, both Joe and Beulah had been taken to emergency by ambulance. Beulah had been admitted but Joe, uninjured, had been released. So far all they knew was that the doctors were waiting for test results. They were all worried.

As if this wasn't enough at one time, Nanny told Harold that Joe held himself totally responsible; he had gone off somewhere and nobody had been able to locate him. Harold could sense the extent of his grandmother's worry, so he stopped pressing for details. He instead told her that we would stay near the phone and she should call as soon as she heard anything about Joe or his mother.

We didn't go back to bed; instead we made a pot of coffee and sat up discussing what we should do. The decision was easy—we would leave for Bartlesville first thing in the morning.

We packed our things together in the early hours of the morning and I called my sister Mary to explain what had happened. She felt that we should make the trip and said she would be happy to mind Erik for us. With that arranged, we packed a suitcase for Erik and, as soon as it was possible, notified our employers that we had to go out of town for a few days. We decided we would drive straight through to Bartlesville, which would take about 18 hours.

We started out directly after dropping off Erik at my sister's, explaining we weren't sure how long we would be and requesting she notify Erik's sitter. Mary told us not to worry about anything: just to drive carefully and let her know when we got there.

Harold, who had been working as a driver for Nabisco, had been asked to stop by the plant before we left. We did and were surprised to be given a box full of snacks to take with us. Soon we were on I-490, heading toward the thruway which we would take us to the Pennsylvania border. We drove through Ohio, Indiana, and in Illinois pulled over so I could drive and Harold could get some sleep. At the Missouri border, Harold took over driving again and, with the sun coming up on a new day, we crossed the Oklahoma border.

We finally crossed the Bartlesville city limits on the afternoon of May 30. By then we were both beyond tired and in desperate need of a bath. We both opted to stop at a motel, where we made arrangements to use one of the rooms to take a shower and change our clothes. Then we got back into the car and drove straight to the home where Harold grew up.

Nanny met us at the door when we arrived. She had heard the car driving up and had waited nervously on the porch for us to join her. As we hurried up to her, we could see her face clearly. Her small frame shook as she tried to hold back the sobs that consumed her body and even before she had said anything, we knew we were too late. We stood on either side of her, supporting her frail frame and managing to move her inside, where Nanny informed us that Beulah had been very sick. Apparently the accident had triggered an illness that must have been latent within her for some time. It wasn't the injuries she had received from the accident that had killed her—they had been fairly minor. The cause of Beulah's death was toxic hepatitis.

Joe had finally come home and Harold talked with him, trying hard to convince him that he was not responsible for the accident, or for his mother's death. I spent my time with Nanny, taking on the job of contacting friends and family members. When Dot, Harold's only sister, arrived from California, where she had been living for some time, we went about checking bills, insurance policies, funeral arrangements: all the administrative details, so that everything would be in order for Nanny. There was a constant flurry of activity as friends and family dropped by to offer their condolences. And no one came empty-handed. There were flowers, cards, and so much food that we didn't have anywhere to place it all.

The day of the funeral arrived and we tearfully paid our last respects to the woman who had claimed such a large part of each of our hearts. It wasn't easy to say goodbye; to think of never seeing her or hearing her voice again. But life must go on; we had to turn our attention towards Nanny, who was now all alone. All the children had long since left home and begun their own lives, leaving Beulah and Nanny as the only residence of the house. Harold and I tried to convince her to leave Oklahoma and return with us to New York. When she declined, we suggested she consider moving to California with Dot, trying to make her understand that we didn't want her living in the house all by herself. But she wouldn't hear of it. Over and over again she said she had lived in that house so long it had become a part of her and no one was going to make her leave it. Nanny stood firm on this conviction. She was tough: very capable of taking care of herself, and we had to face the fact that there was no argument in the world that could change her mind. So we gave up trying.

Once all the details had been taken care of, we began the trip home; our heads filled with thoughts of Beulah. Harold was quite talkative for a change and told me stories of his childhood that I hadn't known before. He shared with me those personal intimate moments that we can have with our parents and tend to forget until something like this happen. She was a good woman who had passed away at an early age and we silently said our last goodbyes.

As we approached the city limits of Rochester we were comforted knowing we would soon be with Erik. We had been gone for two weeks.

***

With Erik walking, we needed more space and fewer stairs, so we began looking for a more suitable apartment. The apartment at Stowell Drive had three sets of stairs to climb to reach our apartment. Erik was now of an age when he should be allowed to play outside with his friends, but after running around, managing the stairs was a little too much. So we decided to make it easier for him.

Our resident address became 493 Stowell Drive: which was a newer apartment development with lots of children around Erik's age. There was one flight of carpeted stairs in the building, making it safer for Erik inside, but outside there was a sacrifice as the driveway ran in front of each building. We cautioned Erik about the dangers of the driveway and made him demonstrate he understood what he must do before he stepped off the sidewalk.

Erik, now almost 3 1/2 years old, had become a pro at making friends, so we didn't worry about him fitting into his new surroundings. One of the big plusses for Erik was that he would be around animals here. For some time now Erik had wanted a pet, but they were not allowed in the other apartment development. Here, across the drive from our new apartment there were townhouses where pets were allowed. The close proximity to dogs and cats would give us a chance to see how he reacted around animals, and would help us to decide, later, if we should get him one of his own.

One of the things I admired about Erik was that he listened and obeyed us without question—but this did not mean that he gave up. When he returned to the matter of having his own pet, he was prepared to meet the jury. Though dogs and cats were out of the question, birds, fish, gerbils, hamsters and other small pets were not. How could we say no? Harold was as enthusiastic as Erik about having a pet, so I gave in, even though I knew I would be the one voted to clean up after it until I had taught Erik, or conned Harold, to do it.

I stayed home when they went to the pet store, but wished I hadn't when they returned with "Charlie" the parakeet and "George" the gerbil. They proudly held up the tube cage and bird cage for my personal inspection; all I could see was the hours of cleaning ahead of me. At first I found George the gerbil repulsive. It didn't matter what species he was—he looked like a rat. But I soon learned to accept him. Charlie, on the other hand, I immediately liked.

CHAPTER 6
1973

Shortly after Erik's fourth birthday celebration, he again started having headaches. At his first words, "My head hurts," I immediately placed a call to Dr. Cotanch and was told to bring Erik in. This time was different and I could tell it once Dr. Cotanch was into his physical examination of Erik. I also sensed from my answers to his questions that this headache was nowhere near as severe as the previous ones that Erik experienced. I was beginning to think I might have jumped the gun.

Dr. Cotanch told me that he was quite sure that something else was causing Erik's headache as there didn't seem to be any problems with the shunt. I felt relief at his opinion, but was still concerned, but Dr. Cotanch was not about to just dismiss the matter. Instead he told me that in Erik's case I was right to consider that the headache was a sign of a more serious condition.

When I asked him what he thought it might be he added that most childhood headaches belong to one of two categories: tension headaches or migraine headaches and he was pretty sure Erik was not experiencing a migraine headache which usually run in families.

I couldn't imagine any tension in Erik's life, but then I was not thinking that a change of location, or desire for a pet could be a cause of tension. It could be. I mentioned this to Dr. Cotanch who stated that this might be a cause of tension, but he was thinking that it might more in line with a problem with Erik's vision, sinuses or teeth.

"What next?" I asked. Dr. Cotanch advised me to set up an appointment for another checkup with his pediatrician, Dr. Boettrich, which I did immediately.

On the day of Erik's appointment with Dr. Boettrich, I watched closely as she examined Erik, but her expression gave no clue as to how serious the problem might have been. Once she had finished, she told me to dress Erik and come into her office, where she informed me that she could not find anything wrong.

"So, what should we do now?" I asked. "His head hurts, I can tell that." Dr. Boettrich explained that she wasn't saying that he did not have headaches, only that she was not sure what was going on. She would contact Dr. Cotanch and would be in touch. Dr. Boettrich did just that and on May 16 Erik was again admitted into the Genesee Hospital. Since Erik had a shunt, they performed blood tests and x-rays in the hope of solving the problem, but no underlying cause was detected. Erik was released and the doctor recommended an acetaminophen, preferably children's Tylenol, be administered to see if it helped.

In a follow up visit with Dr. Boettrich she said it might be helpful if I kept a journal and wrote down what time the headache began and how long it lasted. I should keep track of the possible triggers: stressful situations, tiredness, certain foods, intense lights or noises, exercise or injury. Symptoms such as nausea, vomiting, changes in vision should be noted and if possible the exact location of the pain. Finally I should make note if the pain was relieved by the medication. This information would be helpful in pinpointing the problem. She then set up another appointment.

At the next appointment, Dr. Boettrich again examined Erik and I told her that apart from having headaches off and on, Erik seemed to be fine. Then I gave her the information I had written down at her request and she looked over it while I dressed Erik.

Later in her office, she informed me that she had an idea. She was beginning to feel that Erik's headaches may be related to a problem with his vision. Rather than just guessing at what might be wrong and hoping a suggestion would work, she preferred to try and rule out all possible causes. So she gave me the name and phone number of Dr. Hobart Lerner, telling me he was an excellent ophthalmologist.

Dr. Boettrich explained that children need to be screened for eye disease and have their vision tested by a pediatrician, an ophthalmologist, or another trained screener. This is a normal routine from birth on up. With Erik having these headaches, he required a thorough examination, which she was not equipped to perform in her office. I contacted Dr. Lerner and, with Dr. Boettrich's recommendation, was able to arrange for an appointment within a few weeks.

***

Dr. Lerner was not what I had expected. Wearing contacts myself, I had dealt with eye doctors before, but this doctor was very different from mine, who was relaxed and easy to talk to. In contrast, Dr. Lerner, a small man with a thick head of white hair and flawless skin, was easily excitable. He first sat down and explained what would happen during the eye examination, telling Erik he would need him to identify objects such as pictures, letters, or spots of light on the wall. He also said he may need to put drops in his eyes in order to assist with the examination, but that it would not hurt. Erik seemed quite content with this information as he climbed into the big black and silver chair when directed by Dr. Lerner.

Throughout the examination, Dr. Lerner told me everything he was doing and why. He was constantly doing two things at once, asking me various questions and then making comments based on my response into his tape recorder. He also recorded his observations as he examined Erik. He made me quite nervous, but I had been informed he was one of the best ophthalmologist in the area, so I didn't complain as I watched him in action.

151

He checked Erik for nearsightedness, farsightedness, astigmatism and eye movement ability; he checked to make sure his eyes were properly aligned, how his eyes reacted when exposed to different levels of light (red papillary light reflex), and for any other general problems. He informed me that an irregular light reflex may be a sign of abnormalities within the structure of the eye. These could include cataracts (clouding of the lens), problems with focusing light, or possibly tumors.

Since Erik couldn't read yet, Dr. Lerner's vision screening was done quite differently from the exams I had experienced, but I found it fascinating; especially the "tumbling E game". The tumbling E game, also called the Random E's Visual Acuity Test, is useful, Dr. Lerner explained, in determining visual acuity in children. Erik was asked to identify the direction that the open end of the letter "E" faced by holding out 4 fingers to mimic the letter "E." There were other games he incorporated that made the examination informative to the doctor, but also fun for Erik.

At the end of the examination, Dr. Lerner told me I would be contacted once he had the results. Erik and I were then ushered out.

Several weeks had past before we were contacted and an appointment was arranged. Dr. Lerner repeated most of the tests he'd performed at Erik's first examination. I sat feeling the sense of control that the doctor demonstrated with each movement and each word spoken. I felt intimidated and quite uncomfortable in his presence, as though I wasn't smart enough to question his actions, though he never said or did anything to warrant this feeling.

The examination was a lot quicker than the previous one, and I sensed that it had only been done to confirm the doctor's diagnosis. I was right. Later, in his office, Dr. Lerner informed me that Erik lacked binocular vision. Just as I was about to ask, he explained that this meant Erik's eyes didn't both operate simultaneously, causing problems with his depth perception. In order to maintain binocular vision, simultaneous binocular movement of both eyes is necessary. This movement requires the coordinated use of extra ocular muscles, and the eyes need to be properly aligned in order for corresponding retinal areas to be stimulated by the same object, allowing the cerebral synthesis of the two ocular pictures into a single mental image. When this process doesn't take place, the patient is said to have strabismus.

I could feel Dr. Lerner's eyes on me, waiting to see if I had understood what he had told me. I had a general idea but wasn't quite sure I understood completely. I decided to remain quiet and nod my head slightly, as if I had totally grasped what he had told me. Dr. Lerner then continued.

"Strabismus, which is Erik's diagnosis, is a deviation of his eye which he cannot overcome. The exact cause of pediatric strabismus is not fully understood. It can occur in healthy children without any known health problems. However, strabismus is common among children with disorders affecting the brain, such as hydrocephalus."

At this point Dr. Lerner signaled me to come over next to Erik. On closer observation, and now knowing what I was looking for, I could see the slight deviation of Erik's eyes when asked to look at a specific object.

Dr. Lerner continued, saying that the two most common types of childhood strabismus are esotropia and exotropia. Esotropia is the condition where the eye turns inward. Young children with esotropia do not use their eyes concurrently. Children with this condition, and farsightedness, are generally prescribed glasses to straighten the eyes. When this doesn't fix the problem, surgery is required to align the eyes. Exotropia is the condition where the eye turns outward; it is usually intermittent in children. Although glasses or prisms may help control the outward turning eye in children, surgery is often needed

After his little demonstration, this overly-hyped individual said that Erik's problem would require surgical correction, entailing the rotation of Erik's right eye to a different position. It would be a simple surgical procedure with little discomfort for Erik, outside of wearing a patch over the eye during the stage of post-operative healing. "Any questions?" he asked.

I wanted to ask if this could cause the headaches, but since I had a feeling that it could, I decided not to appear stupid since I did have another request. Hesitatingly, I told Dr. Lerner I got the general idea of what he was saying but could he explain it a little more clearly and in terms I could understand. The doctor thought for a moment and then said that Erik preferred the use of his left eye. His right eye was turned in slightly and was not being used to its full capacity. "Is that better?" he asked. "Yes, better," I replied.

I listened as Dr. Lerner again began talking into his tape recorder. The precise term for little Erik's eye problem is a right esotropia (convergent strabismus) of a mild degree for distance and slightly more for near range.

Again we were ushered out, and I received further instructions for the arrangement of Erik's hospitalization for the eye surgery procedure.

***

There was no doubt in my mind that this "strictly business" doctor knew what he was doing. From talking with medical people and acquaintances I had learned that Dr. Lerner was well-known, and not only in Rochester—he even had some patients who had traveled from Europe to be treated by him. Though he lacked the social amenities that I had become accustomed to, he made up for this in professional ability. I was determined to like the good doctor and overlook his shortcomings.

Erik was admitted into the hospital on October 11, with his surgery scheduled for the next day. Once I had settled Erik in his bed, I took him for a tour of the pediatric wing, giving me the opportunity to check out which patients were in for eye surgery and whether it was being performed by Dr. Lerner. I had learned this little trick from another parent, who had informed me that the hospital liked to have each patient think they were the only one the doctor would be operating on that particular day, but in actuality that doctor might be performing multiple operations in a single day. And in this case she was right. Though I had confidence in Dr. Lerner, it was with dismay that I learned he would be performing four eye operations on the day of Erik's surgery. I decided that a prayer was in order. So I prayed real hard that Erik would be the first one to go to surgery! My prayer didn't go totally unanswered—Erik turned out to be Dr. Lerner's second scheduled procedure.

Prior to the surgery, Dr. Lerner explained the surgical procedure, telling Harold and I that eye muscle surgery, or "strabismus surgery", involves either increasing or decreasing the tension of the small muscles on the surface of the eye which enable the eye to move in all directions, and that Erik would be given a general anesthetic. At no point during the surgery would the eye be removed, but a small incision would be made on the clear membrane covering the white part of the eye. The surgery would then be performed through this incision and not involve actually cutting into the eyeball. He added that the fact that the strabismus had been found early was in Erik's favor, because it usually improved the chances of restoring normal binocular vision.

Harold, not feeling that sense of ignorance I felt, said, "So, that takes care of the problem and it's over." Dr. Lerner stared in his direction for a moment then stated that even after having undergone the surgical procedure, some patients required further eye muscle surgery in the months or years following their initial operation, to further refine their ocular alignment.

All of this information occupied my mind the following day as I waited for Erik to return from surgery, which had been quicker than I anticipated and I took this as a good sign. I turned out to be right.

Dr. Lerner was satisfied with the results, though was not yet able to determine whether Erik would now be able to use both eyes to provide visual fusion. This would be made clear over time. He explained that the recovery from the surgery should be smooth and uneventful; however, there are postoperative issues that can be anticipated. Some mild sleepiness may persist after awakening from anesthesia. Temporary nausea or vomiting is possible; however, very effective medication was given during the surgery to prevent this. As for eating and drinking, it could be resumed as tolerated and if Erik felt any pain it should be mild and controlled with Tylenol.

"Thank you, Dr. Lerner," I said before asking what I needed to do once we were home. Dr. Lerner explained that in the days following the operation there may be mild crusting of the eyelids and blood-tinged tears may appear. He had prescribed an antibiotic ointment that I should use on the eye during the first week. As for restrictions, Erik could be as active as usually, but swimming should be avoided for two weeks. As for the final result of the operation, it may not be known for six weeks.

On October 13 Erik was discharged to our care once again. I was amazed at how quickly he recovered from the surgery, demonstrating none of the possible post-operative symptoms or requiring any special medication. During his follow-up appointment, Dr. Lerner prescribed glasses with base-out prisms for Erik, to facilitate further correction and to help Erik to learn to use both eyes simultaneously. He told us that his office would call when the glasses came in and we should schedule an appointment for the fitting.

***

When we arrived on the appointed day to pick up Erik's glasses, I again felt as though it was all a normal routine, and it scared me to think how accepting I had become. We were ushered into an examination room and, upon entering, Dr. Lerner asked Erik to sit down; only Erik wanted to stand, and acted as though he didn't know how to sit, or what the word 'sit' meant. Dr. Lerner asked him once more and when Erik made no effort to comply, the good doctor said, "Okay, suit yourself," and slipped the glasses on Erik.

The events that followed were almost cartoon-like. Dr. Lerner had explained that the prisms in the glasses would draw Erik's eyes into alignment, but I was unaware of how great the effect of the prisms would be. After placing the glasses on Erik, anticipating their effect, Dr. Lerner positioned himself behind Erik to break his fall. I was seated in front of Erik, watching as he kind of squinted up his nose, looked straight ahead and then just keeled over backward, falling into Dr. Lerner's waiting arms and laughing. The episode was so comical that I ended up laughing along with him, though Dr. Lerner's mood remained serious.

***

It was November 24 when Erik started having headaches again, and I thought it logical to assume they were somehow related to his eye surgery, considering it was so short a time after it had been performed. So I immediately contacted Dr. Lerner and again visited his office. After a thorough examination the doctor was convinced Erik's headaches were unrelated to the surgery or the glasses. Though there was a slight chance that eye strain resulting from adjustment to the glasses might cause headaches, the doctor didn't think this was the case. He therefore suggested Erik be examined by his pediatrician, who I contacted immediately and she in turn after talking with Dr. Lerner, set up an appointment with the neurosurgeon.

Erik was readmitted into the hospital and put through another battery of testing. At the completion of the testing on December 1, Erik was discharged, with Dr. Cotanch promising to get in touch as soon as he had reviewed all the test results.

***

This was not an easy time with so much going on all at once so I had to find a way to accept what I couldn't change so I turned to the Truth Game again.

Erik was being taken care of by us and by his doctors and this meant that the possibility of anything going unnoticed was very slim. The fact that Erik was allowed to come home meant that whatever was happening it was not life threatening to the point he needed to remain under constant surveillance. Finally, I had to appreciate the fact that Erik was home and I was able to take care of him.

That evening, Erik seemed to be in constant pain. Following instructions, I gave him Tylenol for his headache, but it seemed to persist right up until the time of the next dosage. In our home that evening no one ended up getting any rest.

The next morning, suffering from exhaustion and lack of sleep, we found that Erik seemed to be doing better, which made it easier for us to get through that day and those that followed.

***

We received a call from the neurosurgeon advising us to readmit Erik that day. As Harold had already gone to work, I phoned him to let him know where we'd be and then called my job to let them know I wouldn't be in. I was so thankful for the consideration I received from my job at Dollinger Corporation. They had been so understanding of the situation and only asked that I keep my work up to date and not that I try and make up the time. If I had to worry about my job, I don't think I could have made it through the ordeal.

I took Erik to the hospital, where we were soon taken to the pediatric ward. Dr. Cotanch came to see us, explaining that the shunt needed to be revised. He calmly informed us that Erik had to undergo surgery again. His shunt was not operating properly—the path would be revamped so that the shunt ran from the ventricles in the brain down to the abdominal cavity which was more than capable of handling any amount of CSF delivered by the shunt in all but the most unusual cases. How this worked was that the rhythmic contractions of the intestinal organs would tend to move the tip of the shunt catheter around the abdomen, thus minimizing the chances of it becoming sequestered in scar tissue and subsequently blocking.

I was exhausted and sure that it showed, but determined to listen to what Dr. Cotanch had to say. When I was finally left alone with Erik, I tried reading to him, but he fell asleep immediately. He had been given pain medication that made him quite drowsy so I was on my own.

I needed to sleep but I was too keyed up to do that and opted for watching television in the lounge. That is where Harold found me when he arrived, bringing dinner for us both. We ate in silence after I had told Harold all that Dr. Cotanch had said, and then we watched a little television before I encouraged Harold to go home and get some sleep. Shortly after he left me, I drifted off.

It must have been close to 5:00 o'clock in the morning when I awoke to the sound of motion going on in the hallway. Hesitantly, I got up, my whole body aching from the position I had slept in and taking some time to come back under my control. I went to the lounge door and looked out to see a bed being wheeled pass the doorway, with a small lump appearing under the sheet that was pulled up over the body that lay on the bed.

My breathe sucked in as I realized what I was witnessing and my heart went out to the man and woman who stood crying in the hallway. Quietly, I moved back into the lounge.

On December 5 Erik was taken to surgery and the shunt was revamped, with the connection made to his stomach instead of his heart.

The operation was successful. Now, as Erik grew, changes in the length of the torso would be accommodated by tubing being pulled out of the abdominal cavity as there was an extended length of tubing placed into his stomach cavity for that purpose.

The headache episodes came to an end. On December 8, 1973, Erik returned home with us—one more mountain had been climbed.

The year really went out with a bang! We toasted the arrival of the New Year, asking that it please, please not be as eventful as 1973 had been. All we could hope for was that our pleas be heard. We had to believe that it would be better if we were to face it sanely. But like the song says, "What will be, will be". We can't control our destiny; but we can hope, can't we?

CHAPTER 7
1974

Control comes from all around us. We are born into this controlled existence and will continue under its influence until the day we die. Everyone, at some point in their life, will demonstrate discontent, depression, anger. Everyone will have the limits of their endurance tried at least once in their life. The degree to which they can "spring back" is a major part of what keeps them sane. What perpetuates this "drawing back" to sanity? I often wonder about this when caught up in a situation that cries for mental release. In any case, it allows us to return to become a healthy, active part of society.

Consider that we are told it takes approximately nine months of nurturing within the womb to prepare the human animal for the first traumatic thrust into the world we live in. Following on the heels of this realization, we learn that after five years of family nurturing we are expected to present our child for conditioning: school, the institutional change that is our prearranged destiny. In the confines of this learning institution, tailored to prepare the child for society, we are presented with experiences, facts, beliefs and values. We are constantly reminded that only those determined "fit" will survive. The manifold importance of preparing our young for their presentation to this controlled environment plays a major role in our early parenting years. We were no different.

Harold and I started with the intangibles of developing strength, intelligence, endurance and adaptability. We tried to embed the principle of what is "right" and what is "wrong" into Erik. We then moved on to the educational concepts of the alphabet, numbers and colors. We purchased the Walt Disney "First Learning Games" and talked with other parents, reading the books they recommended. But we still weren't 100% sure about what we were doing.

In between the preparations for Erik's schooling, the medical issues continued. At Erik's next eye appointment I was determined to ask a question. Dr. Lerner had earlier mentioned that Erik might need further eye surgery. He had not made further mention of it since then, but I wanted to make sure that if there was to be another surgical procedure that it was done before Erik entered school. I waited for an opportune moment to broach the subject, but finding none, I just took the plunge.

"Dr. Lerner, Erik will be entering kindergarten in June." I then explained that I didn't want to interrupt Erik's schooling and thought that maybe, if there was evidence of Erik needing further eye surgery, that it could be done before he was due to enter school. Once I'd gotten it all out, I sat back in my chair, trying to not look too overbearing.

"Mrs. Saxton, I am aware that Erik is four. I know that after four you turn five and enter school." That was the extent of his reply. I felt like a child myself as I sat there, though I hadn't really been shocked by his response. This was a "no-nonsense" type person who I had come to know and respect, even if I didn't fully agree with his straightforwardness at times like this.

Once I had stopped feeling stupid for having asked my question and presuming to know "his" business, he favored me with more detail. Dr. Lerner said that he had been watching Erik's progress closely and felt confident that the initial surgery and the corrective lenses would do the job. Therefore, for the time being, he saw no need for any further operations.

In September of 1974 Erik entered kindergarten.

Along with the usual adjustments that parents face, with Erik there were also special considerations that had to be dealt with. First there was his size. Having become accustomed to his being so small, I tended to forget how it affected people who were seeing him for the first time. Erik was five years old and about to be thrust into a schoolroom full of other children the same age, which would make his smaller stature stand out even more. Added to this was the fact he also had the features of a younger child. Seeing this cute little boy standing in front of you for the first time, it was hard to believe that he was of kindergarten age. Even though he was walking as well as any five-year-old, and talked better than most because of the circumstances that had forced him to deal with adults on a continuing basis, in looks, size and stature he resembled a child of two, or possibly three. I soon realized that my worrying about his ability to fit in with his peers had been premature.

Though small in height, Erik had fine-tuned his ability to charm and befriend. I somehow learned along the way that in order to prepare Erik for his future I had to be an assertive parent, which is not to be confused with an aggressive parent. I felt that if Erik could see how sensitive I was to his feelings, he would learn to be sensitive to the feelings of others. Assertive parenting also means being firm and not being afraid to disagree, set limits and provide appropriate negative consequences such as time out, grounding, and so on. I believed that to help Erik face the future I needed him to demonstrate affection and respect for others, and from his birth I tried to make it clear that he was his own person, and not just an extension of us, his parents; hopefully, this would set him firmly on his own feet. I wanted him to feel confident that his individual life was important and that it was not his responsibility to gratify the needs of his parents. In other words, he was not to see himself as the fulfillment of a father's unfulfilled dreams or a mother's never-realized wishes. Hopefully, with this attitude instilled, he would concentrate on himself and the world that developed around him. When you step back and think about it, this was no different from what other parents wanted for their children.

At this point in his life, Erik's size benefits him where girls are concerned, as they want to mother him; while boys his age become his friends and willing protectors. All of this is good in helping him with the transition to school, but in other ways it could present problems. I can recall one instance that involved his two special friends, Holly and Toni Marie, from our apartment complex. The girls where three years older than Erik but had been his constant companions even prior to school, looking after him and introducing him to the other children in the neighborhood. Holly was a cute light skinned blonde with big blue eyes, and an outgoing personality while Toni Marie was an olive skinned, shiny black haired beauty with spunk. Both were only children and this may have been what attracted the three of them to each other.

When Erik began kindergarten it was only natural for them to be the ones to walk him to the bus stop and make sure he got to his class on time. After the first week, when I insisted on being at the bus stop to see Erik off, I allowed them to take charge since they had proven to me how responsible they could be. Holly and Toni Marie would take him to the bus stop each morning. This continued through the school year, the three of them inseparable as they took the bus together each day. When they were out of school, the two girls would then go to Erik's sitter's townhouse, which was in front of the apartment building, and play with Erik until I arrived home.

On the day in question, it was well into winter and I had bundled Erik up in his snow suit, hat, gloves and boots. The boots were the biggest problem, as they came quite a distance up his little legs, making it hard for him to walk. This, as well as the extra layer of clothing, made it difficult for him so the girls offered to come and take Erik to the bus stop earlier than usual. I was at my desk at work when the telephone rang. It was the school calling to ask why, on such a cold winter day, had I allowed Erik to come to school without a snow suit or coat.

The call took me by surprise, and I was unable to reply right away. I could picture Erik that morning: all dressed in his winter clothing as I kissed him goodbye. Finally I relayed this information into the phone; I was told they would find out what happened and get back to me. They called me back at around 12:30 p.m. They had found Erik's snowsuit, and asked me to stop by after school on my way home. "Yes, of course," I replied.

I wasn't really too concerned by the whole event; perhaps because his snowsuit had been found, or because I had faced so many problems that something as relatively trivial as a lost snowsuit had no effect on me. After informing my boss that I had a situation to take care of, I left the office and drove to the Parkland-Brookside Elementary School, on English Road. I parked out in front and entered through the double doors of the front entrance, trying to walk softly down the long hallway but the sound of my high heels on the tiled floor announced my approach.

The door to the office was open so I walked in and announced myself. I was soon seated in front of the principal's desk, listening as she told me the story.

On this morning, Erik had arrived at his classroom on time, but without a snowsuit or boots, so of course his teacher had questioned him as to where his winter clothing was. Erik had answered her by saying, "I don't know." When asked if he had worn his snowsuit and boots to school, he replied, "Yes." This confused the teacher even more so, making one more attempt to figure out the puzzle, she asked him who had his snowsuit and boots, to which Erik had replied, "My sisters."

The teacher, pretty sure that Erik was an only child, had her assistant take care of the class while she went to the office to verify whether or not this was the case. Erik's records were pulled out and they revealed he had no sisters or brothers. Now they needed to find out who Erik considered to be his 'sisters'. So, at the end of the school day, the teacher waited near the door as Erik left the room and, in a few minutes, saw two girls come to gather up Erik and take him down the hall to the girls' bathroom. The teacher followed and stood out of sight as she watched the girls produce Erik's snowsuit, boots, hat and gloves, which they immediately put on him. When they reached the door, the teacher surprised them and took all three to the office.

Holly and Tony Marie were scared and nervous at being summoned to the principal's office but Erik remained calm as he sat between them, listening as they told the story of how he had fallen in the ditch by the side of the road at the bus stop and had been covered in mud. Not knowing what else to do, as soon as they got to the school they had taken off his snowsuit, hat, gloves and boots and, in the girls room, had washed off the mud and laid the clothing on the heating vent to dry. They stressed that they had been careful, checking on his clothing to make sure it was still there, not burning and that the heater ideal was actually working and drying the clothing. Apparently it worked. The clothing was dry and clean at the end of the school day.

Erik was questioned as to why he hadn't told them this and he replied, "They were going to give it back". The principal and teacher had to concentrate to keep from laughing and once they found themselves in control, questioned Erik on why he had said these girls were his sisters. To this Erik simply replied, "Because they are my sisters." Both adults looked at Holly, and Toni Marie, who looked as unrelated to each other as they did to Erik. It was not necessary for the principal to ask for further explanations since the records had verified they were not siblings. The three did not share the same surname and the records revealed that they resided at three different addresses, though in the same complex.

At the conclusion of the matter, both the principal and the teacher understood that to the children they were close enough to be brothers and sisters in their minds. As for the incident, though done in the best intentions and no one had been hurt guidelines needed to be established. The children were told that if something like this happened again, one of them must tell the teacher or the principal and let them handle the matter.

***

Of course there were other problems, but they were all small and easily corrected. All in all, Erik had a successful kindergarten experience. He made friends easily, liked learning new things and seemed to catch on quickly. He was seen as a very sociable child who got along well with his peers, and his attentiveness in the classroom was appreciated by his teacher. At the elementary level, Erik's progress was commendable and I happily turned the page on this chapter in our life and moved forward.

For our family unit, 1974 was indeed a good year, though outside of our family unit it would be argued differently. The scandals revealed by the Watergate affair continued to cripple the Nixon presidency and the economy slid into crisis. Inflation hit 10.3% and unemployment soared to 7.2% by the end of the year. But the economic depression feared by many did not take place so it could be argued that it was a good year all the way around.

CHAPTER 8
1975

Change is an inevitable part of life, and we experienced many new and exciting changes during this period.

Erik wanted a dog: a conviction supported by his father, who said that every boy needed a dog. A pattern had begun to form where, more and more, I seemed to be outnumbered when there was a family vote to be had, but I usually gave in willingly. In this case we knew that we would have to move into one of the townhouses if Erik had a dog, but the waiting list was extremely long. As much as I wanted to stay put, I knew that we needed to start looking around for either a house or townhouse before the next school year began.

The whole matter was extremely important now as we needed to be settled permanently in a school district, so our new home would have to be in an area where we wished Erik to continue with his schooling. The kindergarten that Erik attended was wonderful, but after checking into the different school districts, we found that the Henrietta system was more to our liking, so we began looking around this area.

We searched long and hard for a house, checking out several townhouse developments as we went along, and as it got closer to the start of the next school year, we had to make a decision. A townhouse was a great choice for us, since we needed a little more space and privacy than an apartment provided, and most of the ones we looked at allowed pets. The benefit of not having to mow the lawn or take care of repairs made the prospect of a townhouse even more enticing.

We found the whole business of house-hunting quite a chore. First, to get an idea of the type of home we would be happy with, we went out on evenings and weekends to look at homes in different areas; we looked at all styles and shapes of house until we had become more confused than ever. We did, however, agree on one point—we liked the Henrietta area. Though considered a suburban area of Rochester, it resembles more of a country setting with the conveniences of suburban life.

We needed to consider the responsibilities that went with owning a home. There would be yard work, maintenance and repairs, especially if we bought an older house. We needed to find a real estate agent who knew the ins and outs of the area in which we were interested. Deciding on the style of home we wanted, such as ranch, colonial, etc, would also narrow the search. With so many considerations, we would find that though one house met our criteria in certain respects, it was way out of the ballpark in others. So when time ran out, it wasn't hard for us settle on a townhouse for the interim. We moved to the Country Hill Estates Townhouses on August 1, 1975.

While searching for our new home, Harold and Erik also found time to search for a dog—and this search proved to be much quicker. They procured a black Labrador retriever puppy that was the last in a litter of thoroughbreds. The puppy came with his papers, and a reasonable price tag, so they made the purchase on the spot. This could have presented a problem but luckily Erik's babysitter and her family were willing to keep the dog at their place until we were able to move.

With each day bringing us closer to the move, the expressions on Holly, Toni Marie and Erik's faces became sadder. To them the separation meant they would not see each other again, though we explained that they would, only not every day. As grown-ups we understood that temporary housing meant there would be moves to new locations, but friendships would continue to go on. For the children this was still a lesson to be learned..

***

At lot of thought had gone into the change of residence. With medical expenses and the costs associated with an expanding family, our financial burden was increasing. Harold had been through a succession of different jobs in a quest to accumulate more money for the purchase of our home. Even with me working full time as a secretary we seemed to be always coming up short, so Harold continued his search for a better paying job. He worked for Kodak during the day and at night undertook a training course in investigative science to help him find a lucrative part-time job on the side.

Not cut out for factory work, Harold left Kodak and returned to sales during the day and security work at night. The family unit suffered from this arrangement so we sat down and tried to figure out what to do. As a teenager, Harold had dappled in the electrical field, working for an uncle who owned an electrical contracting company in Oklahoma. He had enjoyed this type of work and it paid well. If he could follow this path he would only need to work one job. This would mean that Harold would have to go back to school, but we agreed that training to be an electrician was profitable.

During the day, he worked eight hours as an electrical trainee, and attended school every evening. It paid off and by the time of our move into the townhouse Harold was a registered electrician with the Electrical Union, Local 86. We were financially stable.

***

With us moved George the gerbil and Charlie the parakeet. Charlie's cage was placed in the living room, while George's tube cage went into Erik's bedroom. This arrangement worked well for all concerned.

For some time it had been apparent that Erik wanted to have a brother or a sister, so it didn't come as a shock when he asked us about this. We had avoided discussing the subject for quite some time, but now our son had brought the matter to the surface. We needed to talk about it and decide what we wanted to do. Did we want another child? Yes, in truth we had always thought of having more than one child. Could we afford another child? Yes. With Harold's income we could comfortably afford to have another child. Then what was stopping us?

This is where we ran into complications. We could go ahead and have another child, but what if Erik ran into medical complications and had to be hospitalized? Would we have time for another child? Then there was the issue of his physical problems. What if the next child had the same medical problems? Could we deal with "square one" all over again? The topic involved too many 'what ifs', and not wanting to think about them made it hard to reach a solid decision on expanding our family unit, so we stopped discussing it or even considering it. We told Erik that we needed to wait until the time was right. Eventually, Erik stopped asking and we put the matter to rest, turning instead to exploring the area around our new home.

About forty miles from our townhouse we discovered Conesus Lake. Long considered the "jewel" of Livingston County, Conesus Lake is the western-most Finger Lake in Upstate New York, located south of Rochester along Route 390. It is a year-round sporting and recreation center: fishing, water skiing, sailing, boating and swimming in the summer; duck hunting in the fall: and ice fishing, ice boating, ice skating and snowmobiling in the winter.

The Lake also serves as the water supply for the Village of Avon and the Village of Geneseo. The eight mile long lake is barely a mile wide and covers an area of about five square miles, its depth being only 66 feet, making it one of the more shallow Finger Lakes. The shore area we liked most was accessed through a grove of trees that almost reached the water's edge. Here we would set up camp before heading down to the water, where Erik's dog, who he had named Lassie, would romp in the water while we waded on the shore watching the water-skiers and boaters, yelling at Lassie each time she tried to swim out and retrieve one or the other. Harold would build a fire and I would cook over the open flame while Erik and his dad fished and Lassie ran about, until it grew dark and we needed to make our way home again. The times we spent at Conesus Late were among my most precious memories for many reasons. There was the joy of packing a picnic lunch, cooking over an open flame and watching as Harold introduced his son to the joys of fishing, and Lassie demonstrated to Erik why it is that Labrador retrievers have webbed feet.

We usually drove to Conesus Lake in our 1973 Maverick, but one day Harold decided to make the trip in his red 1968 Firebird. The car, purchased for $500, had required a further investment of thousand of dollars just to get it on the road. The Pontiac firebird was a bold and beautiful thing to Harold. From the first model in mid-'67, the Firebird turned heads and got people talking big time and Harold wanted one, even if it was 7 years old and in need of repair. It was a 'man's' car and I had no desire to drive anywhere in it, but to preserve the peace I went along with his decision.

It was to be an eventful day all around. Erik caught his first fish, and Lassie almost succeeded in retrieving his first canoe. We stayed longer than usual and it was dark when we finally packed up for the return trip home. Ten, possibly fifteen, miles away from home we heard a strange noise, which we later realized, when one of the car's wheels came flying off, must have been the sound of the wheel nuts disintegrating. Harold managed to expertly control the three-wheeled car off the highway and onto the shoulder, bringing it to a safe stop. We sat there trying to catch our breath while Erik laughed in the back seat. We could have been killed. I wanted to stress the point but knew that Harold was already feeling responsible, since he knew the car wasn't totally ready for a long distance run. I turned around on the car seat to make sure that Erik and Lassie were indeed unharmed, and finding that they were fine, I turned again and waited quietly for Harold to decide what to do next.

It was late and dark out now, and this was not a high traffic road even during the day. As for houses, they were few and far between and, as it so happened, none were visible where we sat. There was no one traveling on the road to ask for help, but we had passed houses at some point so Harold decided to hike back, and taking the flash light from the glove compartment he gave orders for us to lock the doors and keep the windows rolled up.

To pass the time I turned around and played a game with Erik until he wanted to just play with Lassie, then I leaned back against the head rest and waited. At least a half hour later Harold returned alone, which wasn't too much of a surprise. At night, a 6'3" black man built like a football player is not likely to have many doors opened up to him. I hadn't thought about it until then so I suggested that I try next and, having no other choice, Harold reluctantly agreed.

I took the flashlight and got out of the car with Harold explaining to me that there was a house a quarter of a mile up the road on the left hand side that he had stopped at. There were cars in the driveway and lights upstairs so he was pretty sure there was someone in the house. He told me to be careful and if permitted to enter the house I should call triple A or someone to come get us. As luck would have it, the homeowners let me in and I arranged for triple A to come out, thanked the homeowners and then made my way back to our disabled vehicle.

Harold was waiting outside the car and I could tell he was worried about sending me off in the dark. He had found the car wheel in the field next to where we had pulled off and had put it in the trunk. There was quite a bit of damage to the car and the only way it was moving was if it were towed, so Harold was glad to hear that triple A was on its way.

We climbed back into the car to wait. It was quite warm inside and Erik asked if he could open his window. Not seeing any reason why not, I said, "Yes." The minute the window was down, Lassie, becoming irritable in the confines of the car, jumped out the window. She was still only a puppy, a little over a year old and not obedient as Harold and I climbed out and called her to come to us. Lassie ran in the opposite direction of our voices. She stopped on the shoulder of the other side of the road from us and stood there like a naughty child defying our authority.

I'm not sure who heard the truck approaching first, but at the same time we stopped calling for Lassie, hoping she would stay where she was and not run across the road to us. But it was not to be. Lassie began running across the road just as the semi truck sped passed us and we knew she hadn't made it.

Erik had watched from the car as his puppy disappeared from sight. I ran back to the car when I heard him crying uncontrollably, barely conscious of the truck braking or aware of the driver getting out and bending over the form at the side of the road before he ran back toward us.

The truck driver was talking to Harold and soon they were walking towards the form by the side of the road. When Harold and the truck driver returned, they reported that Lassie was still alive but quite badly hurt. We all needed to decide what to do. Harold told the truck driver what had happened and that we needed to wait for the tow truck. The truck driver, wishing to help, offered to take the dog to the vet. He and Harold walked back to where Lassie lay, and I watched as they carefully lifted her into the truck and then drove off.

When Harold returned he explained that he had given the driver the information he needed to take Lassie to our vet. Then, we tried to console Erik. When triple A arrived, we were given a ride home.

Lassie died from internal injuries later that night: what had started out as a wonderful family outing ended in tragedy.

***

Erik had been truly upset by the lose of his beloved puppy but, as little children have a way of doing, he recovered quickly. It was only a month after Lassie's passing that he raised the subject of getting a new dog. Happy to see him smiling again, we all went out and picked out another dog—a Labrador retriever, from the same breeder as Lassie but from a mixed litter. Erik called him Joe. He was part black lab and golden retriever, but Erik didn't care about his mixed breed. He fell in love with Joe immediately.

Joe wasn't at all like Lassie. He was bigger, more defiant and more destructive. Each morning after his walk we would tie him to the rail on the back deck so that he could enjoy the warm weather, but he soon lost the privilege as he constantly was breaking his leash and roaming the development. Wanting to keep tradition and make Joe apart of it, we took him, but only once to our spot at Conesus Lake.

I remember it was a hot day as we made that trip we enjoyed so much down the lonely, sparsely populated roads. We were singing when all of a sudden I noticed an atrocious smell coming from the back seat of the car. I asked Erik what had happened and he said Joe had been sick. I forced myself to turn around and was immediately sorry that I had. One whole side of the car was covered in dog vomit that was spreading around with the movement of the car.

There was nothing in the car to wipe it up, and we knew there would be no place ahead where we could stop and clean the car, so Harold turned off the road and headed toward the nearest town, pulling in at a small corner store where we were able to purchase paper towels and disinfectant. The smell was overbearing in the heat, but we managed to clean up the mess without adding to it. We stored the remaining supplies in the trunk, and then made a decision on what we should do. Since we were closer to the lake than we were to home, we decided we might as well continue on.

We only stayed at the lake for a short while. No one felt like eating, the fish weren't biting and we were worried about Joe being in the car again. We decided it would be best to make a few stops along the way home to give Joe a break and some fresh air. This seemed to work, and we finally made it home safely without another mishap. Erik and his father put Joe down for the night while I fixed something for us to eat. Our appetites had returned along with our humor once we had made it safely home and we were able to laugh about the whole ordeal.

***

Since moving to the new location, we had found a daycare for Erik to attend while we were at work, only it distanced him from the townhouse and did not allow him to become acquainted with the children in the development who would be attending school with him. Along with this problem having to rush to the day care after work to get him on time was not working out well. So we decided to hire a babysitter to come to our home to watch him. We wanted someone who was willing to come in the morning to see that Erik got on the bus and one who was able to be there when Erik arrived home from school.

We interviewed several before finding Pam Ruggeri, who possessed all the qualities we wanted in a sitter. She was in her early twenties, able to be there early each morning and stay late without a problem; but more importantly, she had the time and energy to do things with Erik. After several months the relationship grew strong and it was obvious that Erik loved Pam and she loved him. Pam became part of our small family and Erik part of hers. There were days when Pam's parents would come and take Erik out for the day, either to the park or to a farm where he and Pam would ride horses together. She was responsible yet able to play with Erik at his level and she made his time with her memorable.

***

Erik was faced again with death. One day, on our return from work, we entered Erik's room to find a Kleenex lying over an area of George the gerbil's tube cage. Pam took us aside and explained that

177

she had gone into Erik's room and found his gerbil just lying in one spot. She thought it odd but assumed he was sleeping. But when she returned later and he still hadn't moved, she was sure he was dead so had covered him up with the tissue. Pam had taken it upon herself to explain to Erik that George had gotten tired and had fallen into a deep sleep. Erik didn't express any grief when we told him how sorry we were. Instead, he asked if he could have another gerbil.

At first I was concerned by his lack of emotion, thinking he might have been keeping his feelings inside. But after thinking about it a little longer, I realized the death of a gerbil is not the same as the death of a dog. There were no words that could alleviate the emptiness he had felt after the loss of that special "friend" who had shared his heart and life, even if only for such a short time. Though Erik had loved George, being only a gerbil he hadn't been capable of showing the same love in return, which made the effects of the loss less traumatic.

There were more replacements. After George the gerbil's passing, two more came to occupy his former home. They ended up being not as friendly as George and we soon had to get rid of them. Then Charlie the parakeet died, to be replaced by Tweetie. Tweetie was a good little parakeet and ended up being the only replacement pet that met our expectations.

As for Joe, we eventually had to give him to another family. He was friendly enough but caused a lot of trouble with the neighbors and was constantly getting into mischief around the house. There was the time he opened and ate a tackle box full of fishhooks, costing us a fortune in medical treatment; and when my husband purchased an expensive pair of work boots only to find that Joe had eaten one of them down to the sole by the next morning, we knew something had to be done. As much as we hated to, we had to find Joe another home where he would be free to run around and unable to get into trouble. It took some time to convince him but eventually Erik understood why he couldn't keep Joe. After that we stuck to fish and birds.

On April 10, 1975, Erik turned seven years old. He had adjusted to his surroundings and, as expected, had made many friends, who were invited to his birthday parties each year, along with his other friends, making for a large group of children. We loved children and we loved putting on the parties, which we put a lot of planning and thought into, usually arranging them at least a couple of months in advance. At the end of each party, when we had to clean up the mess, I would have to calm Harold down as he said he couldn't go through that again. Sure they were noisy, even messy, but the point of the parties was for Erik and his friends to have fun—and that they did. So when Harold would ask me to cut down the list for next year, I would say, "Sure," with my fingers crossed behind my back.

Our most recent move, to the townhouse development, represented our fourth address, and therefore friends made in the four different locations needed to be invited to Erik's birthday parties. The development was situated in a wooded area at a distance from the road, with our townhouse being the farthest back from the entrance off the main highway; plus it was on a dead end street. This made it a safe place for a child's birthday party and the children looked forward to it each year. After Erik's sixth birthday we were educated enough to plan the parties in the basement, which was the first floor of our three-story townhouse dwelling. This made it easier to clean up afterwards, and I was young enough to make the many trips up and down required to prepare the party room for the guests. I would begin by bringing down snacks from the first floor, then once these had been eaten or thrown about, I would bring down the cake. After the party food had been exhausted we led the children in different games until the time came to move the party out to the back yard, where the children would entertain themselves under our watchful eyes.

Rochester's unpredictable April weather sometimes ruled out this last part of the plan, but for most years it was on our side and the party moved along without any major problems; that was, until Erik's sixth birthday. When it was finally time to send the children home, just as in previous years, some parents came to pick up their children, while those who lived in the development had been instructed by their parents to return straight home afterwards.

I had made sure that each child had their property and their favors before they left, then went about the cleaning up regimen. Harold had returned home in time for dinner but after everything had been cleaned up, so I put him on kitchen duty. I was relaxing in the living room with Erik, watching television, when the phone rang. It was a parent of one of the children in the development who had come to the party. The little boy, Danny, had not returned home.

I could remember having said goodbye to Danny as he left for home. I even reminded him to go straight home; but knowing how upset his mother was, I told her not to worry and that we should start first by calling the parents in the area to see if anyone had seen Danny. No one had, and without being asked, the parents formed a search party. Armed with flashlights, we started searching around the open areas and then through the woods, but with no success. Danny's parents decided to call the police while the rest of us continued our search.

While on my way to again check under the back porches to see if the child had crawled under one and fallen asleep, someone touched me on the shoulder, making me jump in surprise and hit my head hard on the edge of the deck. Turning around sharply, I managed to knock my assailant's flashlight out of her hand, along with the breath in her lungs. It was one of the other parents. After we had both recovered, she said, "We've called off the search." I was puzzled at first, then fear took over when she said they had found the little boy. In a shaky voice I asked if Danny was all right. She then smiled. "Seems Danny left the party with my daughter and all this time they have been playing together upstairs in her room while we've been out searching."

***

After that scare, you would think I would have second thoughts about having another party. I did, but gave in when Erik asked to have one. Erik's seventh birthday held no such surprises and passed successfully. Afterwards, I realized that each year the children grew older and wiser, which some parents might not agree with, but it is true. This wisdom helped in making the children understand the ways of the world which meant that if they enjoyed doing something, they knew they had to obey the adult rules for that something to happen again.

***

It was seven o'clock on a Thursday evening in October. It had been a chilly but bright autumn day and most had taken advantage of the weather to put out their Halloween decorations. There were cobwebs covering the shrubbery, ghosts and skeletons hanging on front doors, and glowing carved pumpkins on doorsteps. After finishing dinner, Erik and I saw Harold off to night school. He was still working during the day and attending electrical classes in the evening, but his enjoyment of the classes meant that it wasn't too much of a hardship.

Erik waited impatiently for me to finish in the kitchen and join him to watch one of his favorite television programs, 'The Jeffersons'. He had been feeling fine most of the day, though earlier in the month he had started having headaches again. I had taken him to see his neurosurgeon, then his eye doctor, but neither could find anything wrong. They just advised me to watch him closely. To be on the safe side, I had scheduled an appointment with Erik's pediatrician for early the following month.

Lately I had noticed the headaches increasing in frequency and lingering for longer periods of time. As instructed, I gave Erik Tylenol and sat for hours rubbing his forehead until the headache had run its course; but from Erik's pained expressions I could surmise that the headaches were causing him agony even though he received some comfort from my manipulations. I would continue to knead his forehead, thinking that whether or not it helped the pain, the closeness counted.

It was close to seven o'clock that evening, while Erik was stretched out on the couch and I was sitting in a chair across from

181

him, that it all began. Erik said something, and as I couldn't hear what he said, I got up from the chair and moved over to the couch next to him. I was taken aback and, as I looked down at my child, was in total confusion. The blood began to race through my veins and I started feeling dizzy. All I could do was stare at him. Erik hadn't spoken to me; he couldn't have, as I could now see that his mouth was moving uncontrollably, and his eyes seemed to be staring blindly.

"Erik?" I called out timidly. When there was no answer, I frantically cried out his name, as though this might help elicit a response. I had no idea what to do as I leaned over him, kissing him on his cheek and rubbing his head to try and make him respond to me. I needed to hear him say, "I'm okay, mommy". But as I continued to call out his name over and over, while choking and sobbing uncontrollably, I realized this wasn't going to happen. Then my ears perked up and I stopped for a moment, listening closely for the sound that had distracted me. It came again. It was a sort of clicking sound, similar to that made when the tongue momentarily hooks to the roof of the mouth. I leaned in further and noticed Erik's tongue flitting up and down in his mouth.

Not knowing what to do or what was happening to my son, my sobbing resumed. Erik wasn't responding to my frantic calls because he could not hear me.

"You must be calm; you must do something!" I told myself.

Not yet in full control of my faculties, I found myself analyzing the situation. It must have something to do with the headaches, I reasoned, as though this realization could help me get it together. I found myself standing by the couch and admitting I didn't know what to do—I just didn't.

Then a little voice in my head, as clear as a bell, told me that Erik was counting on me to be strong and in charge. I sensed more than felt my feet moving me toward the kitchen, where I picked up the phone book and flipped through the pages. Then, as though I was in control of what I was doing, I watched my hand as it reached down and grabbed hold of the receiver and my fingers began dialing the number. The ring tone sounded in my ear: once, twice and then a third time, before the call was answered by Dr. Cotanch. I had called his home number, just as I had been instructed to do in the case of an emergency. No doubt, this was an emergency!

When I heard Dr. Cotanch's familiar voice saying, "Hello", I crumbled slightly in relief at the sound of the voice that to me signified HELP. Incoherently I began blurting out details of what was happening.

"Slow down, Mrs. Saxton," Dr. Cotanch said. "I can't understand you, so please get a hold of yourself and slow down. Is it Erik?"

I knew I had to obey, so I took a gulping breath to center myself and repeated what I had witnessed that evening. I told him in detail what had happened from the time I first thought I had heard Erik say something to the moment I had dialed his number. Dr. Cotanch remained silent throughout my explanation, and once I had finished, I waited for him to respond, silently praying I had explained things in a way that he could understand and that he could now take control of the situation. I was not to be disappointed.

In an authoritative voice, he said, "It sounds like Erik is having convulsions. So listen carefully, Mrs. Saxton," he instructed me. "You need to get Erik to the closest hospital. I will meet you there. Do you understand?"

I nodded, then remembering he couldn't see me, said, "Yes." The line was then disconnected.

I quickly gathered up our coats. Erik, still lying on the couch, had become very still, which scared me even more. I leaned down to see if he was still breathing, gratefully giving thanks when I found that he still was. As I put on his coat, over and over again I said, "Please let him be all right, please."

When I was almost done preparing Erik for his ride, I stopped short and turned in his direction, certain I heard him say something. I went back to him, leaned in close and heard his tiny voice say, "I'm okay, mommy." The relief those words provided gave me the strength I needed. I hurriedly put on my coat and jotted a quick note for Harold to let him know we were on our way to Strong Hospital. "Are we ready," I said, not expecting an answer, as I swung my purse over my shoulder and checked to make sure I had my keys. I then picked up my son and carried him to the waiting car, locking the door behind me.

It was cold inside the car as I stretched Erik out across the back seat and then climbed behind the wheel, starting the car and cranking up the heater, which blew out cold air as we commenced our journey to the hospital. The heater soon began to warm up the car and I felt an urge to hear words spoken aloud, even if they had to be my own. I heard myself pray again, "Please, oh please don't let my baby die." At first it shocked me to say such a thing because, though I may have thought this, I hadn't let it come out until now. I began to wonder what I would do if I lost Erik, but the thought was too much to bear so I tried to remain focused on driving.

From the silence of the car's interior, I heard a weak, barely audible voice say, "Don't worry, mommy, I'm all right."

"Oh my god," I said, realizing Erik must have heard me, and feeling ashamed to have given into my weakness. I turned around to look at my son lying on the back seat, and with little effort but with firm belief, I said, "I know, baby, I know." But it was too late: Erik had given me words of comfort but was unable to hear mine. One look at him let me know that he was once again beyond hearing my words.

I turned around and with renewed determination continued to drive, trying to ignore the odd clicking sound that came from the back seat, because if I acknowledged it I would only panic.

I drove right up to the front doors once we had arrived at the emergency entrance, then turned off the car and jumped out. I opened the backseat door and reached in, gathering Erik's precious form and carrying him into the building, trying to ignore the hospital personnel who attempted to take him from me. I made it to the desk before finally being forced to hand Erik over to one of the white-uniformed attendants that had been pursuing me. I then watched as my son was taken from my view while I was guided in the opposite direction.

The emergency staff then took control of things. With the precision of a wind-up doll, a nurse pumped me for the information necessary to complete her forms. I answered distractedly while they constantly assured me Erik was being taken care of and that I would be taken to him as soon as they had all the required information. With this incentive, I provided the details as quickly as possible. Then, with all the information in place, I was ushered to the examination cubical currently occupied by Erik.

A doctor was with him when I entered, and I stood silently as he went through his paces, with Erik laying there vacantly staring up at the ceiling. An IV had already been placed in his arm and the doctor was making repeated attempts to get Erik to respond. When he realized I was in the room, he began to ask me questions. I replied to his probing in the hope he would tell me Erik was all right.

Time passed; I don't know how much, but it did pass—in extended periods of silence. Then the doctor finally had some success. "Can you hear me?" he asked Erik. Very faintly, I heard him reply, "Ahuh." The doctor appeared satisfied, and I could tell he was just as happy as I was with that one little word. We continued to stand there, apparently waiting for something, but I was not informed exactly what, when finally the doctor broke the silence. He informed me that he believed Erik was having convulsions, which are different from seizures in that they are a phenomenon rather than a disease. Seizures, on the other hand, are sudden attacks that result from a disease such as epilepsy. He continued, stating that Erik's movements were muscle contractions and that even though he could hear us he was unable to respond. He then asked me if I understood. I nodded my head to indicate I did now.

When Erik began to have another convulsion, the doctor examined him again, apparently unsure of his original diagnosis. I found myself repeating Erik's medical history for his benefit and then let him know that Erik had never had a seizure or a convulsion before, adding that all his records were kept at Genesee Hospital. The doctor seemed puzzled for a moment, then, satisfied that Erik's condition was stable, he turned to me and said that he was going to make arrangements for Erik to be transferred.

Looking at Erik, I wondered if this was wise. Sure, this guy was a doctor and knew what he was doing, but still I was worried. It was then that it occurred to me that I had yet to see Dr. Cotanch, though he had told me he would meet us there. I turned to the doctor and told him that it was okay if he wanted to transfer Erik, if that's what he felt was best, but shouldn't he wait until Dr. Cotanch had arrived. I then let him know that I had called Dr. Cotanch and that he was to meet us at the hospital. The doctor excused himself before returning to tell me not to worry: they would take care of contacting the doctor for me but in the meantime it was best that they prepare Erik for transport.

The ambulance was waiting as the attendants wheeled Erik through the emergency doors. I looked at him and kissed his cheek, realizing he had become non-responsive again. In the midst of such experiences I tend not to question the voice of authority; instead, I accept the role of being a provider of information, and make myself available to perform anything that is asked of me. And this was the way I reacted in this situation, trying to convince myself that the hospital was making the right decision and that I must comply. I even accepted their instruction that I must drive myself as I would be in the way if the attendants needed to work on Erik. I told myself I would be able to maneuver the car one more time.

***

I rushed to my car and climbed in. The interior had become cold again so I put on my gloves, wiping the tears from my eyes so I could see better. I gripped the steering wheel tightly and made all the right turns towards the hospital as my mind churned over the details of what had happened. My heart was hurting from the pressure of having to face something totally foreign and not knowing what to do. As I was deep in thought, at first I didn't hear the car horns blaring. But when I eventually did, I looked up and around me and noticed that something wasn't right. It wasn't until I looked to my left and noticed the line of trees separating me from the other traffic that I realized I was driving on the sidewalk. Trying desperately not to panic, I managed to make it to an opening and steer the car back onto the road. The horns stopped blowing and I finally pulled into yet another hospital emergency entrance.

The familiar structure of the Genesee Hospital released some of the tension that had been building within my body; but it all surfaced again once I entered. My nerves were frazzled and my mind weary as I tried to respond to the questions. I knew the questions—an unwelcome necessity—had to be asked and had to be answered, but it was only with great effort that I was able to restrain myself long enough to supply all the answers.

Then finally I was allowed to see Erik. Dr. Cotanch soon joined us. Before I had time to ask, he informed me that he had been waiting for us at Highland Hospital. When we hadn't arrived in a reasonable amount of time, he called Genesee Hospital to alert them and advised them to contact him if I brought Erik there. Highland was the closest to our residence, but I had been so confused that I had gone elsewhere. But all of this was no longer of any consequence. Erik was receiving proper care under the direction of Dr. Cotanch. The medication Erik has been administered slowly began to take effect, and he was soon able to sleep. Feeling safe and secure, I finally broke away and called my sister, Mary. I briefly filled her in on what had happened and where we were, adding that I had left a note for Harold but that it now listed the wrong hospital. A glance at the clock verified that Harold should be on his way home. Mary told me not to worry; that she would let Harold know. With this matter taken care of, I felt more relaxed and returned to Erik's side, to find another doctor with him. He explained that Dr. Cotanch had to leave for a while and that he had been assigned to stay with Erik. He introduced himself as Dr. Wendell and said that though Erik's records had been sent for, it would be helpful if I could tell him all that I knew.

I wasn't sure if this was for real, as I sensed that Dr. Wendell had spoken with Dr. Cotanch and was now just trying to occupy me so that I wouldn't get all hysterical on him. On the other hand, I knew that Erik's hospital files were quite extensive and couldn't all be carried down in one pair of arms, so I complied.

I mentally tried to sort out all the details and present them in a coherent and orderly fashion. I told Dr. Wendell that Erik was six weeks old when he was first admitted to this hospital. Several admissions had followed before the operation to put in a shunt was performed in 1970. At that point Erik had been diagnosed as being hydrocephalic and was also found to have a cartilage disease which was medically termed achondroplasia, meaning Erik was an achondroplasic dwarf. I then added that revamping of Erik's shunt was required following the initial operation to relieve the pressure on his brain as a result of the fluid buildup. Following these procedures there had been eye surgery for strabismus in 1973 and a further procedure to revise the shunt in that same year.

I purposely avoided going into too much detail, mainly because right then I couldn't deal with too much detail, and I was certain Dr. Cotanch would have passed on the most important aspects of Erik's condition before leaving. I gathered I had been correct in this assumption, as the doctor seemed satisfied with the extent of the information I shared. He did, however, ask one further question: when was the last time Erik had been hospitalized? To this I tearfully replied, "It's been almost two years!"

I heard the sound of heavy footsteps quickly progressing up to the cubicle occupied by Erik and I. The draped entranceway then opened to reveal a worried Harold. I quickly introduced him to the doctor, who was then in the process of examining Erik. Satisfied that he was doing as well as could be expected, the doctor then left Harold and me alone with our son.

I could have painted him a visible picture of what I had experienced that evening, but one of us having to see this was enough. Instead, I presented Harold with a more sterile vision of what happened as he was already worried enough. After sharing with Harold what had happened, we waited together silently.

It was one o'clock in the morning when it was finally decided that Erik was stable enough to be transferred to the pediatric floor. Still under the influence of the medication, he continued to sleep peacefully. Harold and I were told to go home and get some sleep. Dawn was quickly approaching, and the day ahead of us was anticipated to be a busy one. A little hesitant but confident that Erik was in good hands, we took our leave, checking in at the pediatric desk to let them know we would be returning early in the morning.

It turned out to be one of Erik's longer hospital stays. On the morning of the twenty-fourth of October, continuing on to Friday the thirtieth, Erik underwent diagnostic procedures to uncover the "foe" responsible for his convulsions and present medical state. There were a series of x-rays, tomagrams for horizontal and vertical layered exposures and a cerebral angiography for visualization of the blood vessels after injecting a radiopaque substance.

The fluid was injected into Erik's neck, with x-rays of his head taken as the fluid circulated through the cerebral vessels. By visualizing the cerebral veins and arteries, it was explained that it would be possible to localize lesions which are of sufficient size to distort the normal pattern of cerebral vascular flow. Several films are taken at rapid intervals from various angles.

An electroencephalogram (EEG) was done to measure Erik's brain electrical activity. For this procedure Erik lay in a darkened room with his eyes closed. Movement, interruptions and external distractions of any kind had to be kept minimal.

Along with all of these diagnostic procedures there was yet another. Erik was given a lumbar puncture—better known as a spinal tap. This involves inserting a needle into the lumbar space of the spine and removing cerebrospinal fluid (CSF). Aside from being an uncomfortable procedure, it is also not without its hazards. That is why, though at the time it was considered the most accurate procedure for establishing the existence of intracranial pressure, it is more of a "last resort".

***

On October 30, Dr. Cotanch called us in for a final consultation. He had reviewed some of the tests and found nothing abnormal taking place to account for the convulsions. He assured us that he would be going over the remaining results and reminded us that it was not unusual for the cause of a convulsion to not be found. The good news was that Erik was now stable and there was no need to keep him in the hospital. We could therefore take him home and wait for the results there. There was one changed and that was that Erik had to take medication to eliminate this happening again.

I couldn't help thinking that we were about to embark upon an episode of history repeating itself. I tried to keep this thought at bay and not let it lessen the joy of having Erik home with us. Even though I thought about it, I was comforted by the knowledge that Dr. Cotanch had never failed us before and that I had no reason to doubt that he would come through for us again.

Erik was home, but things were a little different now that he had to continue to take Dilantin as prescribed by his doctor. Dilantin is basically used in cases of epilepsy, and we were told that it was very effective against partial seizures and primary generalized tonic-clonic seizures in people of all ages. Dr. Cotanch explained that the brain cells need to work at a certain rate to function normally, but during a seizure brain cells are forced to work much more rapidly than normal. The Dilantin helps prevent brain cells from working as fast as a seizure requires them to, and thus the cells are prevented from all firing together in an uncontrolled surge, thereby stopping seizures just as they are beginning.

I was a little confused by the prescribing of seizure medication when it was thought that Erik had a convulsion and not a seizure. So I asked the doctor if this meant that Erik had had a seizure. Dr. Cotanch explained that at the present time there was nothing conclusive as to the cause of Erik's medical emergency, so therefore it was safer to prevent this episode from happening again, which was what Dilantin would do. He then told me that we should watch Erik carefully. The first sign of an allergic reaction to Dilantin is a rash, so if we saw any skin problems, we were to call him immediately. The most common side effect in children was jerky movements of the eyes, called nystagmus. These movements often do not interfere with a child's vision but can be upsetting. He went on to tell us that in a few children Dilantin causes problems with thinking or behavior, mood change, slow or clumsy movements, or a loss of energy, and that we should be sure to let him know if we saw any of these side effects.

The Dilantin made Erik sleepy, which could be demonstrative of a loss of energy, but he didn't seem to lack energy when he was awake. Even the doctor agreed that there was nothing to worry about for now; and as November progressed, the medication seemed to be doing a good job, as Erik had no headaches or reoccurring convulsions.

***

Erik went back to school, though I had been hesitant to allow him to return, but Erik's insistence that he wanted to go to school and the doctor's verification that he could see no reason why he shouldn't go to school overruled me. Outside of demonstrating exhaustion when he returned at the end of the school day, Erik was doing fine. He had missed a month of classes, but with our help and that of his friends he managed to slowly start catching up.

It was then that I realized it was not just Erik's young age that helped him put the past behind and go on with the present. It was determination and a need to do what he wanted to do. I had wanted to put a stop to the cause of the problem only that was out of my control, so I began to train myself to not concentrate on the problems that I had to put in another's hand to manage. Instead I had to find a way to control my emotions so that I could continue to enjoy each moment. I found the strength to do just that in watching Erik.

I couldn't help but marvel at Erik's determined spirit, which allowed him to pick up where he left off, unencumbered by the dilemma that had transpired. As usual, he didn't seek any special consideration. And, adopting his mindset, I was able to fully enjoy the moment and not dwell on the past.

When the final reports were read, Dr. Cotanch called and explained that it looked like Erik had had a convulsion and though it might be a one time thing, he wanted to keep him on the medication.

***

On the morning of December 15th, Erik awoke with a headache. After giving him his medication, I sat on the side of his bed, rubbing his forehead in the darkened room. I talked to him, noticing that his speech seemed sluggish. On my way to get a wet washcloth to apply to his forehead, I decided to put in a call to his pediatrician's exchange so that she would know to contact me as soon as she got in. Then I returned to sit with Erik. I tried not to appear too anxious and frighten my child. Once the episode had finally passed, I started busying myself with getting out Erik's clothes while telling him I didn't want him to go to school that day but instead felt we should go to Dr. Boettrich's office.

Erik, who had been watching me move about the room as I talked to him, replied, "Okay, mommy, but I feel all right now."

I let him know that I understood, but informed him that maybe Dr. Boettrich had something that might eliminate him from having to go through another 'headache', and this seemed to satisfy Erik, at least for the time being.

I was doing a superb job of hiding my anxiety until I heard Erik say, "Mommy, can you dress me?"

This was totally out of character for my child. Not that I don't enjoy helping him dress, but he never asked for help and always seemed to want to do it himself. Dressing himself was one of the things he prided himself on doing alone. So at that instant I knew something was wrong. Though not apparent in his voice, I could sense something definitely wasn't right. I turned around and looked at Erik, still laying motionless on the bed, and asked, "What is it?"

Matter-of-factly, Erik said, "My left arm isn't working right. Will you help me?"

What could I do? There was only one thing that I could do at that point, so I simply replied, "Yes, mommy will help you, Erik."

Throughout the process of getting him dressed, I watched Erik closely. The weakness on his left side was not only apparent in his arm but in his leg as well. I recalled the side effects of Dilantin but couldn't remember this being one of them. I tried to conceal my concerns, as I didn't want to worry Erik. He was being so brave while I was crumbling on the inside with the wonder of it: what is wrong?

I not only finished dressing Erik, but helped him downstairs and fixed his breakfast. While he was still eating I received a call from Dr. Boettrich, who told me to bring Erik in first thing that morning. As Harold had already left for work, it was my responsibility alone to put on a cheerful face for Erik. I could not allow myself the luxury of confused thoughts or actions as I drove Erik to his pediatrician's office as soon as he had finished his breakfast.

I remained calm in the doctor's waiting room, though I was a little troubled by the fact that Erik didn't want to play with the toys, preferring to sit and wait beside me instead. Each time I looked at him he gave me a big smile, which I immediately returned. We sat for only a few moments before being ushered into one of the examination rooms. Dr. Boettrich had joined us before I had even had time to help Erik get undressed. She examined him attentively, carefully probing and observing his movement, or lack of movement. While I was dressing Erik after the examination, Dr. Boettrich re-entered the room to tell me that she had made an appointment for us to go to Dr. Cotanch's office next.

There were several questions I wanted to ask but realized it wasn't the time. All Dr. Boettrich told me was that she thought Erik needed to be seen by his neurosurgeon right away, and that she had called ahead to let them know we were coming. So I helped Erik get ready and we were soon on our way to Dr. Cotanch's office, where, having been expected, we were attended to immediately.

After Dr. Cotanch's examination, arrangements were made for Erik to be re-admitted into Genesee Hospital. Exactly what was happening I would not learn for some time.

***

From the 15th until the 19th of December, Erik was put through a series of tests similar to those performed previously, but nothing showed up that explained Erik's headaches or this weakness on his left side. Finally Dr. Cotanch presented us with another alternative: they wanted to inject a nuclear dye through an artery in Erik's leg.

By now our confidence in Dr. Cotanch was at a level where we tended not to question his decisions. Harold and I both agreed to this process as readily as we had the earlier procedures, but then Dr. Cotanch educated us on the pros and cons. The forceful pro was that the results obtained from the procedure may lead to a positive identification of Erik's obvious problem. The forceful con was that, as a result of the procedure, Erik's leg may be damaged by the injected dye! We were given time to make our decision.

What a decision to make! What if this ...? What if that ...? Once we had gone through all the possibilities, we were faced with the fact that we really had no other recourse. Delaying the discovery of the cause of Erik's problem was even less attractive than the possibility of something happening to his leg. So we gave our consent, only hoping that we had made the right decision. With that, the procedure was performed.

Erik was moved to a room closer to the nurses' station in the pediatric wing. He would have to be under constant observation. As for me and Harold, we waited and waited for word that Erik was out of danger. When we were informed that no damage had resulted from the test, we were elated; though discovering the test had not revealed anything quickly brought us back down again. We were no closer than before in determining the cause of Erik's brief partial paralysis.

What now? I wondered. Everything that could be done had been done for Erik, so maybe he had just slept the wrong way or banged a nerve that caused him to temporarily lose the use of his left arm.

I tried to convince myself that may have been the cause, but deep down I knew it was more serious. It was a paralysis of his left arm and leg that I was seeing, not some bruised nerve that would heal and make the paralysis disappear. I refused to admit that it could be permanent; only that there was something causing it.

We didn't know; the doctors didn't know, but we were certain they wouldn't give up until they had found the cause. So when we were summoned for a consultation; I was sure that Dr. Cotanch would tell us we could take Erik home, watch him closely, and wait for him to contact us. I was almost right … but there was more.

Dr. Cotanch told us that he was going to schedule an appointment for us to take Erik to Buffalo, New York, where a new type of machine had proved itself successful, in a number of cases, finding physical problems that previous testing methods had been unable to reveal. At the time that this information was being shared I was too numb to ask any questions, but once home I wished I had asked for more information. Then I thought about it and realized this was again something that was out of my control and what was important now was that Dr. Cotanch had found another alternative to find out what was or had happened to Erik. So now we needed to wait and while we waited for the call from Dr. Cotanch live must go on.

I took the next few weeks off work and stayed with Erik. Erik was already learning how to cope with the weakness on his left side and asking to go back to school. I wanted to keep him home with me, but knew better so I contacted Dr. Cotanch, who told me that it was okay with him if Erik wanted to go to school.

That first day was so much like the first day he climbed on the bus to go to kindergarten. I filled his head with words of comfort and reminders to be careful, and I watched Erik get on the bus and when he had found a seat he waved from the window as he went on his way to school.

***

Erik was only afforded the opportunity of attending one day of school before we were to take him to the Millard Fillmore Hospital in Buffalo. The appointment was set for December 23, 1975.

Not one to sit back and wait for something to happen, or for that matter leave all the research up to the doctors, I had gotten into the habit of cutting out any information I found in newspapers and magazines that dealt with surgical procedures, cures and the like. I started going through the papers at the library and learned about the CATT machine. An article printed in the *Buffalo News* on Tuesday December 16, 1975 was encouraging. The article was headlined "Revolutionizing Treatment at Millard Fillmore". The story told of the savings in terms of hospital costs and time with the use of a new Brain Scanner, received at the Dent Neurologic Institute of the Millard Fillmore Hospital in December, 1973. The "newness" of the technique, as well as the success, was apparent once I read that there had only been 10 institutions in the world with such a device back then; but at the time of the writing of the article the number was exceeding 100 as the demand for the scanners by hospitals across the country increased in the wake of continuing reports about the value of the technique. Viewed by one doctor as the frontier to an entire new epoch of brain research, the CATT machine which stood for Computerized Axial Transverse Tomography, basically put, used a fine x-ray beam and a computer to map brain structures in a narrow slice of the brain through which the beam has passed. The computer printout indicated the density of structures encountered, allowing trained personnel to interpret the readings. The scanner itself could handle up to 24 patients per 12-hour day.

The Millard Fillmore Hospital was receiving requests for the use of the machine from more than 24 hospitals as far away as Puerto Rico and Las Vegas. The machine had reduced the number of routine skull x-rays and reduced or replaced drastically the use of traditional radioactive brain scans. The traditional tests, such as Erik had been going through during his observation periods, were still being used in many cases, such as aneurysms and other vascular problems, and with lesions at the base of the brain. These were seen as limitations of the CATT machine scanner. On only three occasions had the

CATT machine been reported to have missed things it should have picked up; and with such a record of success, it was leading to the development of whole-body scanners based on the same principles.

On December 23, Harold, Erik and I witnessed this amazing advancement in the field of medicine. A radiological technologist operated the scanner. The machine was huge, making Erik, who was laid on a table with his head inside the large structure, look so small and helpless.

Harold and I were informed that the CATT scan would show the detailed anatomy of Erik's brain and nearby structures. Tumors, blood clots, cysts, as well as many other abnormalities, would be recognizable in the x-rays. The intensity would be measured by a very sensitive detector and the readings would then be analyzed by a computer that would calibrate the picture, making it visible on a TV-like monitor screen. The results would appear as three-dimensional pictures giving a clear view of brain tissue.

These pictures would be studied and photographs taken of each scan. Next the radiologist's interpretations would be discussed with the physician, who in this case would be Dr. Cotanch, and the photographs would be sent for comparison with other x-rays and laboratory tests.

Seeing our reaction to the size of the machine, we were informed that the scanning process would be quick and painless. The only discomfort to Erik would be the injection of a special chemical into his blood stream before the scan was taken. The chemical would change the density of some tissues, thereby causing the amount of x-ray absorption to change. The whole procedure would be completed in approximately thirty minutes.

***

We stood before a glass wall and watched the tiny form of our son being scanned by this huge machine. I tried not to think about anything except watching what was happening in front of me and once the scan was completed, the radiologist asked that we wait while she looked over the resulting pictures. When she was satisfied with their quality, we were allowed to go.

As we walked away from the hospital, I became hopeful again. The CATT machine had a phenomenal success rate, so I was sure that we would soon learn what was wrong. Erik, who had gone through so many different tests, was happy when I assured him that I was confident they were done with the testing.

Over the following days, I often wondered why Erik never asked about the weakness on his left side. Here was a little boy that was able to walk, run and kick a ball without a problem, yet now his movements were limited and he accepted that. What was it about him that he could overcome so much so easily?

***

Another matter that was making news around this same time caught my interest. On November 29, 1975, President Ford signed into law the Education for All Handicapped Children Act. The legislation contained extensive amendments to the Education of the Handicapped Act that was already in place. The role of the federal government in the education of the handicapped would be increased to include provisions designed to ensure that free and appropriate public education was available to all handicapped children, to ensure their rights and those of their parents. The law would allow for the government to assist states and localities in providing the education, and assess and ensure the effectiveness of efforts to educate these children in a free, appropriate public education system that would offer special education classifications and related services at public expense.

I was unsure of what all this meant. Erik was already in a public school, not in an institution for handicapped children. Our experience with such an educational arrangement was having taken Erik to the Al Sigl Center (a local facility) when he was four. Here

Erik was checked for his educational level, his physical limitations and dexterity, along with many other areas of disabilities. Once the results were reviewed, it was determined that Erik did not need this type of facility. I had hoped that the presence of other children with various handicaps would be beneficial to Erik in accepting his "specialness". In any case, he was refused entrance. Later, after having thought about it in depth, I realized that no matter where he was educated, he would eventually have to fit into the world around him. What better way for this to happen than to be apart of the "normal" society from the beginning. Besides, I had observed that Erik did accept himself and seemed to be proud of who he was.

Reading the articles that appeared in the paper introduced me to a new word: "Mainstreaming". Handicapped children would attend special education classes within the public school system and become a part of the student body, having lunch and some of their classes with the regular class groupings. This would allow the students the opportunity to be in contact with non-handicapped peers. It was felt that the experience would benefit both groups. It would increase the self-confidence of the handicapped student and lead to a deeper understanding within the non-handicapped students. The education provided within the public environment would result in better education.

There were problems being realized with the law. Regular-classroom teachers were complaining that they hadn't received additional teaching aides, training or special materials to deal with the handicapped children. But it was reported that this matter was being looked into and appropriate steps would be taken.

I learned from yet another article that there were workshops being set up to help parents in understanding the process. I decided to check into this. At this point I was unconcerned. Erik was not part of any special classes in the Rush-Henrietta School District, nor had there been any problem with his schooling. But it may be something that might come up later on. I filed the information away to review again later.

Right now there was Christmas to contend with and then the celebration of yet another New Year. All of this kept me busy while waiting for the results of the CATT scan.

CHAPTER 9
1976

When we were contacted by Dr. Cotanch, the news was not good. Harold and I had earlier been informed that if the data received from the CATT scan was negative, Erik would not be readmitted. But if there was proof of a disorder, the reverse would be true. So It was with a sense of apprehension that we received the instructions to readmit Erik into the Genesee Hospital on January 5, 1976. Soon after arriving in pediatrics we were summoned to meet with the neurosurgeon.

Dr. Cotanch seated himself in close proximity to Harold and I. We were prepared for the worst but were hopeful it wouldn't be too hard to take and that we would manage to adjust. But there was no way we could have prepared ourselves for what Dr. Cotanch informed us: it was beyond anything we could have imagined. We were told that, theoretically, Erik had a very dense, large mass in his head; which meant we were dealing with a possible cyst, a possible tumor, or a tumor within a cyst.

I tried to concentrate only on what the doctor was saying, and not on the matters surfacing in my mind. I had an overpowering urge to scream out the unfairness of it all. The miracle CATT machine had let us down. I had thought that the result would be definite, not one of choice! I forced myself to listen as Dr. Cotanch said that the CATT scanner had revealed a large mass in the right cerebellar hemisphere. This explained why Erik had developed the weakness of the left side, and why he had experienced the headaches and the resultant convulsions. The cerebellum relays movements, and the mass was located in this vital area. Dr. Cotanch continued, explaining that the cerebellum rests against the brainstem, which is the most important part of the brain as far as vital processes are concerned. The doctor paused after he presented each piece of information, either to allow us to activate our coping mechanisms or to give us time to ask questions. Either way, it didn't matter—both Harold and I were too shocked to do anything more than listen.

I wanted to think positive right now, but it was too hard to think that way. Erik wasn't yet seven and what the doctor was saying was not even fair to face for a young child.

Dr. Cotanch explained that if the growth was a cyst, which he had every reason to believe it was, it would require surgical drainage or removal, which because of the apparent size of the cyst was a dangerous procedure. On the other hand, a tumor could be disastrous.

This was how I interpreted his words: whether Erik had a cyst or a tumor, in both cases surgery was imperative. If it was a tumor we were dealing with, it could grow. Without surgery, even if it was only a cyst, death was imminent. This growth, this large mass, was already trying to immobilize Erik. Before we were told, I had already accepted the necessity of surgery, which Dr. Cotanch had scheduled for January 9.

The pre-surgical procedures began immediately. Erik had been through it all before. Some of the tests were painless and simple; others more complex, causing pain and discomfort. The whole process involved a general physical examination and systematic examinations of cranial nerves, the sensory system, motor system, and autonomic functions.

I was there every day with Erik. He wanted to go to school, he wanted to see his friends, and he wanted to go home. Though these were all the things I wanted for him, I had to keep his spirits up by not allowing him to think about school, friends or home right now. What was important now was that he get well again. And so I pretended interest in the smallest of things, the safest of things, from his food to brushing his teeth and taking a bath.

Our faith rested in the hospital and its staff; and though concern made us wary, our confidence and trust was not shaken. Each day that passed with Erik unable to use the left side of his body was proof of the need to place our faith in the hands of the doctor to make this right.

***

After a total of four days of consultations and procedures, still we didn't have that one answer: that one finding to deal with. Harold and I talked together endlessly. What did we do now? What was best for Erik? We were unable to answer these questions. We were not the authorities—they were. They were the ones who would determine Erik's destiny. So there was no other alternative but to let the hospital follow the guidance of Dr. Cotanch. We believed in him; we had to. He must make the decisions and be allowed to carry them through. Erik's life was at stake and surgery had to be performed no matter what they found.

We knew from past experience that when a specific diagnosis was not possible using noninvasive or simple biopsy techniques, it might be necessary to surgically explore the area in question. So it was no surprise when we were told Erik would first undergo exploratory surgery and that we would be notified as soon as the doctor knew what we were dealing with and what the actual surgery would entail.

They came for Erik at eleven o'clock on January 9. I struggled inwardly to keep my strength firm and to keep all negative thoughts about the outcome at bay. Silently I prayed, "Let it be a cyst, let it be a cyst!" Such a gruesome prayer but in this case the best possible result.

Even though I took no note of the time, the waiting seemed to last an eternity. I felt as though I had spent enough of my life waiting and wondering why all this was happening. The waiting alone was hard enough, but the barrage of questions I couldn't prevent my mind from asking made it almost unbearable. Yet, inbred in each of us is the desire to find out why things happen as they do. Though well aware of how dangerous such thoughts can be to one's psyche, I couldn't help it. I knew it was pointless to ask why. There was no answer to that question. Yet there were so many mysteries to deal with that, finding myself unable to do anything else, all I could do was repeatedly ask why this was happening.

Harold arrived at the hospital and joined me in waiting for the outcome, and though we were there together, our minds were not. Harold was silently thinking his thoughts and I my own.

Finally I saw the neurosurgeon approaching. I felt myself becoming tense; partly to appear strong and partly to be prepared for the news. I stared into his face, trying to read his thoughts, but I got no premonition. When he was directly in front of us, Dr. Cotanch did not keep us waiting or wondering a moment longer as he immediately told us that it was indeed a cyst.

I felt Harold squeeze my hand and I turned briefly to smile at him. Dr. Cotanch gave us our moment and then when we were back with him, explained that he didn't want to alarm us, but that though it was a cyst, it was of an incredible size, covering the right hemisphere of Erik's brain.

All we could do was stare at him and Dr. Cotanch's features were imbued with compassion, knowing how difficult it was for us to hear how critical Erik's condition was but that he had to tell us.

We listened to his medical terms, explaining that what we were dealing with was a large porencephalic cyst—a gap in the brain that should have contained healthy brain tissue had been replaced, rather than displaced, by the cyst. He explained the impending surgical procedures and the time period involved.

I was now listening, but more involved in looking at the doctor closely I saw something more than just sympathy in his eyes: it was a deeper feeling of a more personal nature. I could tell he cared about us and about Erik in more than just a detached, medical way and this gave me the strength I needed to accept his words.

Before returning to surgery, Dr. Cotanch encouraged us to not lose sight of hope and to try to not worry, though I was sure he knew we couldn't help worrying. Right now I felt it was important that he felt the trust we had in him and that he understood that trust was what gave us hope.

***

"A desire accompanied by expectations of, or belief in, fulfillment"—the dictionary definition of the word 'hope'. Could I survive without hope? Would I act any differently if I did not believe there was hope? Who knows?

Harold and I were alone again—I mean really alone. We didn't even talk with each other as we sat and waited for news. We couldn't talk right then; we each needed to deal with the situation internally before we could confidently put our thoughts and feelings into words. Eventually we were able to again turn to each other; but only tentatively, so that we wouldn't betray our inner feelings.

Once we were beyond this point, we lay it aside and talked idly about unimportant matters to try and fill in the time. George and Nancy joined us, and family members came to help us through the waiting period. These visits helped raise our spirits above the gloomy atmosphere of the hospital.

Finally, news arrived. We were approached by the anesthesiologist, who introduced himself and immediately told us that the operation had gone well and that the neurosurgeon was on his way up to talk with us further. Harold and I turned to each other, both of us overwhelmed by the same thought—Erik was alive! He was going to be all right.

A verbal celebration began as we shared our joy at the news with our family and friends. Moments later we were talking with Dr. Cotanch who related what he had told us before. The cyst had been opened and made to freely communicate with the ventricles, and the Pudenz shunt to the peritoneum. In simple language, the cyst was being drained through Erik's existing shunt.

Knowing that Erik was safely out of surgery gave me an overpowering sense of relief, and I was confident the worst was over. While my mind went through the process of accepting this news, Dr. Cotanch told us we would soon be able to see Erik in the recovery room. I paid no heed as I heard him caution us at to what to expect in terms of Erik's physical appearance, as I had seen Erik after surgery before. At that moment, nothing could have dispelled my feeling of relief, knowing it was all behind us know. I was bathing in an aura of happiness—my son was doing fine.

I paid for this complacent attitude later when looking down at Erik's face in the recovery room. It was a face I couldn't recognize. His whole head was swollen beyond recognition. As if to accentuate the change, his head was encased in a turban of bandages. As my legs started to give way I felt hands hold me on either side. Slowly I was helped into a chair that had been placed near Erik's side. It was far worse than I had expected.

***

Rituals, I know, play a major role in hospital procedures. An average hospital stay for Erik began with activities such as laboratory tests early in the morning, with the rest of the day consisting of treatments or scheduled surgeries, visiting hours and rest periods. Then there was the regular observation conducted by the nurses, which included monitoring and charting his vital signs—pulse, blood pressure, temperature, urine output—on a frequent basis; as well as evaluating his physical and emotional needs. From experience I have learned that a good nurse is worth her weight in gold!

Doctors' rounds might occur at various times during the day, and the resident doctor or assistant would often visit Erik early in the morning. Dr. Cotanch's visits were often the high point of the day for Erik and myself; but towards the end of Erik's stay, unfortunately the neurosurgeon was often in and out of the room so fast that I didn't get a chance to clarify any questions or doubts unless I asked him to sit down so that I could talk to him; and when I did, I made sure I was prepared with a list of any questions I needed answers to.

Erik was now being administered medication before breakfast, and throughout the day and night as prescribed by the doctor. Being attached to an IV meant that he received frequent visits from the nurses to check the drip and the contents of the IV bag. His meals were normally brought by orderlies three times daily, and at night I would usually get him a drink or a snack.

Along with the rituals there were timetables that had to be adhered to, and I viewed them regularly. The timetables seemed to be formulated without consideration to the comfort of the patient. Erik would be hungry by seven-thirty each morning, so I would try to help him forget his discomfort by encouraging him to sleep. Then, without fail, the door would burst open and a towel and washcloth would be presented. Half an hour later a breakfast tray would arrive. At eight-thirty the breakfast tray would be taken away, without enough time in between or before to perform the morning rituals of brushing teeth and washing up, which would have to take place afterwards. Dinner would arrive early, usually around 4:30 p.m. It took Erik some time to adapt to this regimen, and I as well, only after so many years we began to get comfortable and that comfort encouraged us to feel as though we knew what was best for our child.

***

Now though, I would have welcomed all this and appreciated it as a part of the standard procedure. Because this time the routine was not to be the case: I was to learn about a whole new, frightening procedure. This time I was to see a different area of the hospital— one that I had no interest in familiarizing myself with. I would find myself playing the role of helpless bystander as the drama unfolded. This time Erik left the recovery room to be taken to the ICU.

The Genesee Hospital Intensive Care Unit is a self-contained unit of thirteen individual modules located around a central nurse's station. Monitoring of the patients is accomplished with the latest technology available and by specially-trained Critical Care Nurses. The Intensive Care Unit blends combined state-of-the-art monitoring and diagnostic equipment with the compassion and understanding of a professional nursing staff. It is essential to have fully-equipped and prepared support units for critically ill or injured patients, so there are blood analyzers which measure biochemical factors; ventilators which help patients breathe; haemofiltration and other life support machinery; defibrillators and monitors which measure vital body functions such as heart rate, blood pressure and brain activity; and infusion pumps and syringe drivers which deliver drugs to patients.

Due to Erik's need for rest, and the limited space, only two visitors were allowed in the room at any one time, and food or drink were prohibited in Erik's cubicle. The ICU staff seems to understand our anxiety at knowing our child requires critical care. We are told that the visiting hours in ICU are flexible and designed to respond to the specific needs of the ICU patient and family.

So there I was: Erik had been moved from Recovery to the ICU. Evening had descended and I was alone, after having convinced Harold to go home and get some sleep. I had arranged to stay with our son day and night, simply because I couldn't leave.

Erik was unconscious and unable to talk with me. No other patient's family member wanted to talk with me either. It felt as though grief and worry filled the empty spaces and this feeling entered every pore.

It was so quiet, with not a word spoken above a whisper. It was also cold, in a depressing, intemperate way. There were no windows through which to survey the outside world; no other world existed apart from that which surrounded me. I looked around noticing the decor was drab, with no focal points; and, as if all this wasn't gloomy and depressing enough, it was even too dark to read! There was nothing to look at and nothing to do: nothing to help facilitate my desperate need to escape. I didn't seek anything permanent, just a way of temporarily removing myself from this reality.

White clad figures hovered about everywhere. One proposed that I endeavor to try to get some sleep. How could I sleep now when it wasn't really over. This was not the place that I was use to expecting after Erik had surgery and thus as far as my head and my heart was concerned, this was a nightmare and I didn't want to close my eyes. And there was no chance of it happening since under the influence of stress and frustration, I had become an insomniac.

Trying to convince me that sleep was what I really needed, the ghostly figure told me my perception would be dulled even further if I didn't sleep; my judgment would be impaired, which would cause my feelings of depression to grow beyond endurance.

The nurses were convincing as it seemed, from what I had been told, that only sleep could make everything better. Soon another nurse, in her sparkling white uniform, dragged in a recliner and placed it beside Erik's bed. I was not expected to say anything, just accept her offering and follow the instructions—sleep!

There was limited space within Erik's cubicle, but enough to recline the chair while still leaving a pathway to and from his bedside. I threw my coat over me and told myself that all I had to do was close my eyes and relax.

But it didn't work. When I closed my eyes, frightening visions were projected across my eyelids. If I were to look at them a moment longer I would totally lose control. If I allowed myself to unleash my thoughts they would only become distorted into these nightmarish visions. I could therefore not allow myself to succumb to sleep.

Another nurse suggested that I leave the ward. Seeing my look of horror upon hearing this remark, she quickly added that she meant only temporarily, to pacify myself. I considered this offer and finally accepted that it may be beneficial in helping me maintain my sanity. Before leaving, I was given a cup of coffee to take with me.

A sign confronted me while walking down the hallway: 'We also ask, for your protection, please do not stand in the halls. Wheelchairs, beds, and other equipment must go through this hallway.' This influenced my decision to move to the waiting area just outside of the ICU where I found more to read.

The walls were plastered with all kinds of information. One sign read: 'We recognize that this is a stressful time for family members; the nursing staff will make an effort to keep the family updated on the patient's condition.' I walked around sipping my coffee and reading the signs, until I came upon one that read: 'All Members of the Clergy are always welcome. If your minister or priest is not available, the Unit staff will contact the hospital chaplain for you. A meditation room for quiet and prayer is located in the main lobby. You may visit the meditation room at any time.'

If I had any doubt of the seriousness of this place, it was now forgotten. From the first sign to this last it was obvious that anyone placed in the ICU was not considered to be out of danger. This was something I didn't want to think about as I sat down an surveyed the room.

Here there were metal chairs, a well-worn couch, several ash trays, and bland walls. As I took all this in I realized there was something missing. Though almost all the beds in the ICU were occupied, there was not another human being around. At first I didn't understand how this could be. ICU is essentially a section of the hospital for those patients who are considered to be in critical condition and need 24-hour surveillance. Where were the people? Where were the relatives? Someone had to be close to these patients, so where were their loved ones.

I then remembered that my purpose was to relax, not worry about what should be. Now alone in the waiting room, with the closed door shutting me off from the immediate situation, I found that I could. Slowly the tension receded as I sipped my coffee, having to admit that it felt good to forget.

This feeling was short-lived. As I lifted my gaze to the window of the door before me, I could see an acceleration of activity taking place just outside. This was sufficient to pull away my cloak of tranquility and replace it with anxiety. I rose from my chair, feeling my body turn cold. My heartbeat automatically quickened and for an instant I couldn't move from where I stood, having to summon the strength to force my shaking legs to carry me toward the door, which I barely had the energy to push open.

I immediately proceeded toward Erik's cubicle, but a few steps from my destination I ran into an obstacle. A nurse purposely blocked my way and gently took hold of my arm. She guided me to a chair, saying, "You can't go in there just yet. You will be in the way." She then added, "Please, don't worry, Erik will be all right."

Unable to see anything from the chair, I had no idea what was going on inside the room. Then, having reached the point where I could no longer bottle up my emotions, all my pent-up anger, frustration and feelings of helplessness poured out in the single demand, "I'm his mother, let me go to him now!"

What a waste of energy that turned out to be. "I'm sorry, but I can't let you go in there," the nurse replied. My desperate words had obviously fallen on deaf ears.

With difficulty, I managed to restrain myself from bolting from the chair; but like an animal poised to pounce on its prey, I waited for the right moment to make my move. The opportunity came when my self-appointed guardian was temporarily interrupted by another nurse, who required her assistance across the room. I quickly made my way through the entrance doors to find two doctors laboring over the form of my small son. And Erik, oh my God, Erik was shaking all over. I stood just inside the cubicle, immobilized with terror, and stared, stupefied. Upon noticing me, one of the doctors' shouted, "Get her out of here!" I was totally submissive when the nurse came and maneuvered me back to the corridor outside the ward.

She stayed with me and tried to console me, but now her words fell on my deaf ears. Her speech was incomprehensible to me. I kept saying, "Why can't you understand? I need to be with Erik. He needs me!" I had seen my son—his hands clenched, arms and legs jerking as his muscles twitched, and unintelligible sounds coming from his mouth. In a terror-stricken voice, I said, "He's dying; he needs me!"

We repeated this performance over and over again, with neither of us understanding each other, until finally a doctor emerged from Erik's room and sat down beside me. He calmly told me that Erik's high fever and the shock of the extensive surgery had culminated in his convulsing. Touching my arm, he said that Erik was now resting comfortably and the danger had passed. When I asked if it would happen again, the doctor simply replied, "Yes, it might."

Finally, I was allowed to return to Erik, though on two conditions. One was that I must rest if I wanted to help Erik. Though I had trouble accepting this, I knew I must comply. Second, I was to remove myself and call a nurse, if one was not present, if Erik showed any signs of convulsing again. This I could accept, and agreed to follow their instructions.

Once inside Erik's room, I watched the movements within the ICU through the drapes. I watched the nurses, attendants and doctors come and go as they kept close observation over my son and the other patients in ICU. I sat there until I couldn't stand it any longer, then got up and stood by Erik's bedside. I gazed down at my son. I loved him so much. There was an IV needle in one of his small arms, as well as a loose-fitting blood pressure cuff, and he was receiving blood through another puncture in his arm. This, along with the swelling and bandages, made him look incredibly uncomfortable. But Erik showed no sign of his discomfort. I reached down and gently caressed one of his swollen cheeks. There was no response. I spoke soothingly to him. There was no movement. Erik was unconscious.

I needed to talk to someone and so I choose the only person I could talk to at that moment. "God, please let Erik embrace life once again," I prayed and then feeling that he would hear me, I said, "Erik, I don't know if you can hear me, but please know that I love you so very much."

I told Erik that day that my love filled me with a need to protect him and touch him. I wanted to talk to him and laugh with him again. There was a need for me to continue to explain away his sadness and kiss away the hurt. He was my life and I could not let him go.

I began to feel motion beneath the hand that was still resting on Erik's cheek. I had been staring out beyond the walls of the hospital, my mind displaced in my effort to subconsciously reach Erik. This sudden motion drew me back and with misconstrued hope I looked down at my son once more. My mind registered the exact same jerking movements I had witnessed earlier. I knew what I must do, and remained in control as I summoned the nurse. Once I was sure Erik was again in competent hands, I moved to the corridor to allow the doctors and nurses freedom to move about in the cubicle. My role was to master my fears in solitude.

I was unable to sleep throughout the rest of the evening, as I was constantly having to get out of my chair and make room each time the nursing staff needed to attend to Erik. During the wee hours of dawn, however, I must have finally dozed off, because I noted a change in the faces of the staff as I slowly regained my senses. The day shift must have arrived. I got up and looked at Erik. He was still unconscious, but I leaned over and kissed his cheek, telling him I was there and saying good morning to him. I then stood up and stretched my arms. The movement immediately brought a nurse over to Erik's cubicle.

"You're awake." It was more of a statement than a question so I didn't feel obliged to respond. I was offered a towel, soap, washcloth and toothpaste: everything I required for my morning preparation. I felt a little better afterwards, and returned to Erik's room, where someone handed me a cup of coffee. I seemed to be given an awful lot of attention without having to say a word. It must have been because I looked like I needed it. I began to appreciate the ICU staff.

The days at the hospital seemed easier to face than the nights. I had no assigned duty except to stay out of everyone's way. I watched as Erik's temperature and blood pressure were taken, before being asked to move from the cubicle while two nurses went about changing his bed and his clothing. Eventually I was allowed to help a little with this process. By the time the doctors arrived, Erik was clean and the bed made once again.

Erik's vital signs were taken and the doctor tried to get him to respond to his voice, but without success. Next, Erik was pricked with a pin to see if he would respond to pain. There was no movement: nothing that said he had felt or heard anything. With a nurse's assistance, the doctor began changing the bandages on Erik's head,

213

neck and stomach. The bandages were soiled with the drainage from the cyst. I didn't have to be asked to leave; I knew this would be too much for me to handle so left the cubicle on my own volition.

Erik showed no signs of reaction throughout the whole day. All the necessities relating to his care were performed by hands other than my own; I drank coffee and tried to absorb myself in magazines. Silence permeated the whole ICU area; different from the night, when there were the sounds of the flutter of the staff entering and exiting cubicles where something had gone wrong or medical observations or record updates were due. Most of the daytime activity was of a settling nature, with few unexpected interruptions to this relatively placid routine. It was during this time that I made phone calls to keep everyone informed of Erik's progress. Yes, for them it was presented as progress while for me it had to be accepted in a different light. Erik was in a holding pattern, awaiting the verdict, but only his father and I needed to know this.

Family came and went throughout the day; but most often in the evening they hid out in the patient's cubicle, with no one seeing much of each other or speaking a word.

I tried to appreciate the quiet but couldn't—it was still a period of waiting: a period of wondering when the sounds and episodes of the previous night would start again with Erik or another patient.

I kept getting up to take a closer peek at Erik. It was during one of these times that a nurse came over, pulling shut the curtain that had been left open most of the day. I then heard drapes being drawn down the line of cubicles. More out of curiosity than anything else, I wanted to know what was going on. I peeked through a small opening in Erik's curtain and saw what appeared to be a patient being wheeled out of ICU. The sheet covering the still form had been drawn up to cover the head. I didn't have to be told what this sight meant.

Even though I didn't know this person or their family, I felt an attachment. I tried not to analyze the precise nature of this attachment because it scared me. I stood there crying for this person, or maybe I cried for myself and for Erik. Erik had shown no sign that he had any hold on life. None of the patients in ICU seemed to have that capacity. Anyone could have been next. Erik could have been next! I pulled myself away and sat back down on my chair. I wanted all of these people to have many more tomorrows and so I said a little prayer.

The drapes were reopened and a nurse asked if I would like some food. I told her I was not hungry but she persisted, only giving up when I insisted that I really couldn't eat anything.

Harold had been checking with the hospital all day, and when I saw him approaching me in the ICU, I realized that it must be later than I thought. The hours had been passing without me knowing.

He was tired from work and the strain of the situation but had thought to bring me a change of clothes, which I gratefully accepted. After getting changed, I updated him on Erik's progress, softening the corners of the episodes that had required me to leave the room. I didn't conceal the fact that Erik was still quite ill, but I didn't think it necessary to put him through the mental anguish I had experienced.

I knew it was hard for him to have to leave and go to work, but there really was nothing either one of us could do at the hospital, so my being there was really enough. I asked questions, though the explanations I received were not always to my liking, and the space in the cubicle was quite limited, making it a little uncomfortable. Besides, they wanted Erik to get as much rest as possible, to aid his recovery, and though they would usually call to notify us of a change in his condition, with me having been almost constantly by his bedside, this hadn't been necessary. I had made sure Harold knew I would contact him immediately if anything were to happen.

I sensed his reluctance to leave that evening, but I reminded him that as an electrician he must get proper rest or I would have both of them to worry about, and I didn't think I could take that. Harold understood.

***

Throughout the following day and night, Erik again suffered convulsions. I was terrified each time they occurred, as by then I was aware they could be fatal or at least result in permanent brain damage. Each time Erik began to convulse I would alert the ICU staff, if they were not already with us, and forces to take care of the situation were immediately put into motion.

One day, as a way of filling in the time, or perhaps out of curiosity, I asked one of the nurses how the ICU personnel were chosen. I also asked if they liked working in this area. The nurse gave me a general run down, saying that most of the nurses and doctors chose to work in the unit, not only for the benefit of the experience but also because of the internal feeling of accomplishment obtained by helping those who really need their help and they had a need to provide medical assistance to a diversity of patients. In the midst of our conversation, the nurse was summoned and excused herself. I stood there for a moment, contemplating her remarks, before returning to Erik. What type of person wanted to deal with the threat of death at any given moment.

The nurses were kept quite busy. So were the doctors, being summoned over and over again for one patient or another who needed special attending. I tried to keep out of their way as they bustled about from cubicle to cubicle in their soundless shoes. I occupied myself by trying to appear outwardly calm, while inside my heart pumped blood in time with their footsteps, and I regularly checked to see if Erik required their attention.

Each night I was unable to sleep for any significant length of time, and each morning I would try to refresh myself by washing up and changing my clothes. When I looked in the mirror I saw the torment of fear etched across my face. There was nothing I could do to conceal it. There was always a stream of new patients and families joining us in the ICU, and the faces of most of the other family members looked much the same as mine.

Sometimes upon my return to Erik's room I would find a doctor examining him to try and get some kind of reaction. It was during one of these moments that I was told that there had been some improvement in Erik's vital signs. His fever was down and his coloring had improved. I was drained of energy, and my ability to think rationally was limited to understanding that these were meant to be words of encouragement, but the only words I wanted to hear was that Erik no longer needed to stay in ICU.

Dr. Cotanch visited Erik at least twice a day and each time he gave me his honest opinion which was that we had to wait it out now, while Erik's body began to heal itself.

I was now mentally exhausted and it only took one look at me to see that all I had gone through had turned me into a nervous wreck. I couldn't even help change Erik's bed anymore; I could hardly walk to and from the bathroom. I grew weak from lack of sleep and lack of nutrition, though I tried to participate in both.

I was becoming all too familiar with the procedures in ICU. Each time the staff changed-over, the incoming doctors and nurses were given verbal instructions regarding each patient. There were also charts, but these weren't their sole source of information. The instructions they received covered the routine for patient checks, the prescription of medication, and hygiene requirements. I sat watching and listening, paying particular attention when a nurse or doctor tried to reach Erik by voice or the inducement of pain. I studied their face each time they were unsuccessful.

And so it was that during this process, as the doctor leaned closer to Erik and said something, I sat bolt upright—I heard Erik speak. I had heard it!. I don't remember actually getting out of the recliner and approaching Erik's side, and I sensed rather than felt the shifting of the hospital personnel to allow me space by his side. I don't even remember what I said. All I remember is the feeling of life that returned to my body as I called out to Erik and heard Erik respond to my voice, and the sense that he knew who I was and that I was there with him.

Erik didn't say much and the effort it took for him to speak was apparent in the weakness of his voice; but I overlooked all that. I was so happy just to hear his voice again; just to know that he then knew that I was with him. I held his hand and felt the slight pressure as he gave my hand a weak squeeze. I could feel the tears welling in my eyes as I looked at my child. Joy filled my heart as I heard the doctor say, "The worst is over now." We had entered a turning point.

By the time my husband arrived that evening, Erik had been talking off and on all day. He had even opened his eyes, though because of the swelling it was more of a peek. And his voice was still only very weak. Yet, as though he understood his father's need to hear him, Erik managed to say a few words for his dad. The joy of hearing his son's voice again was written clearly across Harold's face.

The days following were relatively uneventful, but in the best sort of way. Erik continued to improve, staying awake for longer periods of time and becoming quite coherent. He was taken off the critical list and was considered to be in 'satisfactory condition'. I remained with him in ICU. My strength started to return as I ate now and I was able to sleep more during the evenings and wake up really refreshed in the morning.

Erik's improvement was clearly noticeable. Color returned to his face and he no longer required blood transfusions. He began taking nourishment orally along with the IV. He was returning to us. And then the most eventful day came. It was the day I had been waiting for: the day that marked the start of Erik's recovery after surgery. On January 19, 1976, Erik was finally moved from ICU to the pediatric wing of the hospital.

***

The day Erik was transferred to pediatrics was a bright day indeed. Nurses and interns alike openly displayed their pleasure at having Erik with them again. He was becoming well-known and well-liked in pediatrics. At the age of six, he had spent almost as much time in the hospital as he had with us at home. It was like we shared Erik. And you know, I did not mind. I did not mind sharing my child, Harold's child, with them.

Upon returning to pediatrics, Erik still needed to be under close observation. For that reason he was placed in a private room across from the nurses' station. Confined to his bed, this could have been a lonely time for our son, but he never was alone. Erik, unable to go to them, had the children and even the parents coming in to see him.

At first Erik was allowed to sleep as often as he wished, but gradually he was urged to stay awake for longer periods of time. The nurses and doctors were instructed to talk with him and make notes of how he responded to questions and conversation. Unaware this "experimentation" was going on, I was a little surprised when informed that Erik had been found to be communicative. To the pediatrics' staff and his doctor, the results meant that Erik had not suffered brain damage as a result of the cysts or the operation.

I had been so involved in watching my son recover, and so preoccupied with joy that he was no longer in pain, that I hadn't even considered the possibility of further consequences. So it was like having someone give you a present that turns out to be what you wanted most—I had good news and no worry!

Erik continued to improve, and progressed to the next step—it was time to get him into a sitting position. Each day his bed was cranked up a little higher and remained there for longer periods. It turned out to be a long process but Erik gave it his best shot.

The first time the bed was adjusted in this way, Erik pleaded, in a frightened voice, "Catch me, mommy! I'm falling, mommy!" His cries were so sincere that it was hard to believe the nurse's explanation that being in that position made him dizzy, resulting in Erik feeling as if he was going to fall. Gradually the sensation passed, and Erik even began asking for his bed to be cranked up. Erik's condition was upgraded to "satisfactory".

Erik was an exceptional child. His development was accelerated by all that had taken place, and he was growing up to be a caring and friendly person. Other frequent visitors to the pediatric wing shared their special feelings for our son with the pediatrics' staff. Harold and I were constantly being told something "nice" about Erik. He would willingly share, or even relinquish his claim on a toy that another child showed interest in. He was quick to smile and a joy to have around. As for his intelligence, well, fortunately there was no doubt that he was bright. On one of my returns to pediatrics, I had gone to his room and found he was being entertained by a boy who appeared to be around eleven or twelve years of age. The boy was sitting on the edge of Erik's bed and they were engrossed in a conversation about baseball. Erik interrupted the conversation long enough to say, "Hi, mommy," and then returned to talking with his friend. After giving Erik a hug I sat down in a chair and listened to the two of them. They would get excited and then sad as they discussed the ups and down of their favorite team. Finally the visitor said, "Well, I better go now so you can talk with your mom. I'll come back later." Then the boy turned to me and said, "He really knows his baseball!" I had to smile. Like most of the older children that would find their way into Erik's room, they left thinking that Erik was around their own age! He could talk about anything and appear to be knowledgeable on the subject. He had developed an uncanny talent for absorbing information, which allowed the children to overlook his size and see him in a different way than the way he was seen by adults.

When Erik was not listening, he was asking questions about one thing or another. He wanted to know about everything in life and would store the information and retrieve it the next time he had occasion to converse on the matter. The result was that he could fit in with most people, most of the time.

Harold and I were changing too. Our interests were expanding, and though our "tastes" were different, we were able to find new avenues of interest on the same topic. On a more personal level, we had developed a deeper sense of loving and caring. For us friends were a necessity of life, and once we had made a friend, we maintained a close relationship with them. A change of house or job did not push a friend out of our circle once our life intermingled with theirs. We had become highly sensitive to all aspects of life and as a result, it was a happy time—we began to find it easy to laugh and have fun. Like Erik, we had found life to be highly enjoyable

The time came for me to return to work; which meant I had to call the hospital during the day to find out about Erik's condition and to hear what he had been up to. It was hard, and not at all the same as experiencing it with him. I couldn't help resenting the fact that I had been with Erik each time he was in a serious condition but was pulled away whenever he began climbing toward recovery. If I had to choose, I would have wanted to be with him during his worst experiences, yet I wished I could haven been with him through both. But I resigned myself to the fact that I had to work.

***

The trauma Erik experienced during his hospital stay resulted in a few surprises for me. Along with not even considering the possibility of brain damage, I had forgotten about the weakness on Erik's left side. It was not until Harold and I were called into conference with the doctor that the matter surfaced. We were informed that Erik was paralyzed on his left side; the paralysis being evident along the full extent of Erik's left side, including the muscles of his face, his side, and the length of his extremities.

The doctor then went on to say that Erik would need to be examined by a specialist in the field of paralysis. There was hope that the paralysis was only temporary but this was something that would have to be determined by the specialist. We were made aware the adjustment to paralysis could be an extremely difficult process both physically and psychologically. Sudden paralysis of a previously healthy, active child could pose psychological problems for not only the patient but also the parents. For this reason, both Harold and I would be meeting with the psychologist along with Erik.

How did I feel about this? I could not find an answer within myself. I talked with Harold and he seemed to be in the same frame of mind. We should be devastated, hurt, mad—something.

The concept of paralysis was difficult for us to comprehend. It was something we knew very little about and had no personal experience with. Added to this was the fact that, because Erik was confined to his bed, the paralysis was not actually evident, nor did it seem to be causing any unusual problems or discomfort. Harold and I seemed to be more concerned with his progress, and that was going well.

Erik was assigned a tutor to help him with his studies. He was still taking medication and had experienced no further episodes. His incisions were healing properly and the drainage of the cyst was meeting with the doctor's approval. Each day the swelling was less noticeable and the face of our son was returning.

Dr. Cotanch introduced us to the Physical therapist, the assistants and aides who would perform components of the physical therapy procedures and related tasks. These individuals would assist the physical therapists in providing services that would help improve mobility, relieve any pain, and prevent or limit permanent physical disabilities. It was explained that Erik would now be given exercises, massages, possibly electrical stimulation, special baths, and even hot and cold packs. The physical therapist would report Erik's responses to treatment to Dr. Cotanch and to us. As to the hours and days that Erik would be taken for physical therapy that would be left up to the physical therapist after he had time to evaluate Erik.

This seemed like something I could participate in and so I asked if there was anything I could do. The Physical therapist gently explained that there was a proper method they needed to follow and it required a moderate degree of strength in assisting Erik with their treatment. In some situations Erik would need to be lifted and because of his surgery this was best left in the hands of the professionals. As much as I wanted to be part of this, I was able to understand their reasoning.

A few days later, I was informed that Erik's PT exercises would be conducted on a daily basis by a therapist who would also teach Harold and I how to do the exercises with Erik. It was explained that the exercises would strengthen the muscles and help familiarize Erik once again with the feeling of manipulating his left side.

At first we watched, then guided by the therapist, we participated with their assistance. Each time Erik concentrated throughout the exercises and tried to make the movements, but he couldn't. Harold and I took turns doing the exercises alongside him, each of us encouraging him to concentrate on the feel of the movement. We encouraged him to move the right side and then try to repeat the movement on the left side. We tried to keep his spirits up by telling him that he must be patient and it would happen.

The physical therapy invaded all parts of Erik's waking hours. When Erik ate, we were to remind him to use both sides of his mouth. When he spoke, we were to remind him to again use both sides to form the words. There were few activities Erik could do that we hadn't received rules and regulations on how he should do it. But that was okay, as it meant we were finally able to play an active role in Erik's rehabilitation.

Once Erik had overcome the sensation of dizziness when in a sitting position, we were allowed to take him out of his room in pediatrics. At first these trips were made in a wagon with pillows to support him, as he was unable to sit well on his own. But Erik improved and moved up to being mobilized in a wheelchair with pillows stuffed into the sides. Each stage of improvement was brought to Erik's attention so that he was aware of his achievements step-by-step.

Erik enjoyed his "outings". He enjoyed being in contact with the other children in pediatrics, who at first stared at him, but once he had become familiar to them would run up to him each time they saw him. Erik patiently responded to their questions about his swollen face, his bandages and his weak side. I was amazed at how well he handled the questions and supplied the answers. The curiosity of his peers did not seem to bother him.

More often than not, the children would ask when Erik would be able to play with them. With all the extra activity in addition to his recovery routine, Erik tired easily but somehow managed to keep himself going. He would not give up. He gave full concentration to his studies, his exercises and his outings.

He was a part of a family at the hospital. Children walked alongside his wheelchair, talking and laughing with him. The nurses would not have to interrupt their duties to take Erik for a ride: the older children willingly offered to do this for them. All the attention seemed to aid Erik's recovery in all areas.

Erik's appetite returned and he started to look stronger as he gained back some of the weight he had lost throughout the ordeal. The doctors were quite pleased with the rapid rate of progress he was demonstrating. Each day we could see a change as Erik mastered one more feat. Without having been forewarned, Harold and I knew it wouldn't be long before we were told we could take Erik home.

On February 3, 1976, Erik was reported as being in "good" condition. He no longer required close monitoring, he was taking all of his nourishment orally and he was allowed to spend more time outside the confines of his room. He was moved from the private room to a double occupancy room in pediatrics.

Erik now had a companion to live with, and the relationship seemed very important to him and his new room-mate. They became close friends as they shared their private thoughts about their illness and their parents, for starters, and then other topics that are not to be shared with outsiders. The friendship expanded beyond the boundaries of the room and they formed a special bond, becoming like brothers. Erik's room-mate cheered from the sidelines during his therapy sessions. They helped prepare each other for their school lessons each day and boosted their spirits by offering words of encouragement. Upon our arrival at the hospital each evening, the staff gave us a review of the details of Erik's day, and mentioned how impressed they were by a child his age being able to understand so much. It was hard for most to believe that Erik, who wasn't quite yet seven, knew the value of compassion and understanding.

Then a major event took place: Erik started laughing. Yes, he had talked and smiled, but not laughed aloud. Laughter, to coin an old phrase, is the best medicine. You can smile even though you are sad, but it takes a real deep-felt joy to cause you to once again enjoy laughter. Hearing Erik's laughter washed away all doubts, all worries. I could feel a wave of peace wash over me, and I realized it was my son helping me instead of me helping him.

Erik became known as the "attention getter". He seemed to have an ability to draw people of any age to him. His friendliness and the need for people to be with him seemed to come from a feeling he projected. This feeling could roughly be translated as: "I'm happy being me." Like an expert fisherman he cast the line and reeled in the unsuspecting bystander with his charm. And the victim of the moment became fascinated by the capturer, with Erik bringing out the best in them.

***

The time for Erik to return home was drawing near, as we were advised that arrangements had been put in place for the therapy to continue at our home, and a nurse had been assigned for outside visiting care. The tutor had also advised us of the days she would be visiting to continue Erik's schoolwork. Dr. Cotanch met with us and provided instructions on the medication and gave us a prescription for the Dilantin. Once all the arrangements were in place, all we had to do was wait for a release date.

More tests and examinations were required before Erik was allowed to depart. We were instructed that Erik's doctors would be in contact to set up an office visit, but this would be based on reports given by the visiting nurse and therapist. Soon all the preparations were completed and all the reports and papers filed. On February 7, 1976, Erik was released from the hospital.

Erik's return home was also different from previous releases from the hospital. This time instead of having Erik relinquished to our personal care, we were taking a little of the hospital home with us. Harold and I would be involved in the recovery process but professionals would be continuing their regimental routines—but none of this diminished the joy of taking Erik home.

When we finally arrived home, the neighbors were waiting to welcome Erik, and though tired, Erik remained sociable—and we followed suit. Parents joined us for coffee while the children gathered around Erik and filled him in on what had been happening. Pam, Erik's sitter, came over to welcome him home and eagerly accepted the added responsibilities of Erik's care, which would be extensive; but Pam considered Erik part of her family now.

Erik's schedule of activities was put into place. His tutor was not to resume Erik's studies until three weeks after his return home, but in the meantime his classmates tried to bring him up to date, and Pam also worked with him when she could. When the tutor came she was aware that Erik had missed quite a bit of school, but felt confident that with the extra help he had received he would be able to rejoin his class in second grade. Though Erik looked forward to school, he wouldn't be able to return until the beginning of the next school year in September.

***

Throughout this period Erik remained happy, affectionate and optimistic; and Harold and I felt much the same. We tried to make the atmosphere for his school lessons similar to that of his class room. It wasn't long, however, before changes to his schedule needed to be put in place, as Erik was heavily involved in hospital procedures, school lessons, and spending time with friends and family. Though rearranging the schedules didn't seem to help much, we found having classes in the morning and therapy in the afternoon to be the best arrangement.

Erik's friends were allotted times when they could come and visit, and there were times when he needed to be left alone. I began to notice physical signs of fatigue on his face. He forced himself to stay awake through the evening meal and he forced himself to spend time with us. It hurt to see him so weary from trying to do his best to meet the demands of everyone around him. He wanted to be a good student, a good patient, a good friend, and a good son.

Somehow Harold and I knew that we had to let him control these areas of his life. We couldn't interfere any more than we already had. And we were confident that Erik would find the right way to find a happy balance in his life.

***

Everyone wanted to help, which in most cases came in the form or advice, or as I began to see it, expressions of concern. I realized that no matter how old you are, you never have all the right answers; and no matter how experienced you have become, there is always someone who is smarter than you.

Harold and I have found ourselves listening to professionals in the medical field. We have found ourselves obtaining excellent advice from parents who have not personally experienced what we have gone through. And we have found ourselves learning from the children.

The best advice is to listen to all the advice that comes your way. To learn to remain open and capable of hearing and using all that is given to you from all avenues of life will result in success. This I have come to know as a truth.

***

In exactly thirty days Erik would be turning seven years old, and he had made a silent pact with himself—he would be walking by then. This was not quite what a seven-year-old should be looking forward to on his birthday, but circumstances had changed our son. There was no time to think about what he should want on his birthday; more important was what he *did* want. And Erik wanted to walk.

So the process of Erik beginning to learn to walk all over again began. The therapist, Erik, his friends, and the whole family pitched in with encouragement and enthusiasm to help him achieve this goal.

At first he was like a toddler experiencing his first steps as he kept close to walls and furniture to give him something to hold onto. But there was a key difference. The toddler finally seeks mobility on two legs rather than his hands and knees. Eventually the toddler walks, with all his parts taking direction and being coordinated from the brain. But this was not the case for Erik; at least as far as having full coordination of his limbs was concerned. His left leg continually gave out and refused to cooperate.

The weight of the paralyzed left side of his body threw him off balance each time he tried to take a step. But once up, Erik would not give in. He tried over and over again until he was exhausted from the effort. But even when he was forced to lie down and rest he kept talking about how he was going to accomplish the feat of walking. And so he would try again.

The therapy helped strengthen his left side as the days went by, but it took a lot of concentration and the melding of mind over matter to achieve this success. Erik had to learn how to "feel" the movements mentally as well as physically in order to be able to make the movement on his own. Yet we noticed that even when he was able to concentrate and mimic the movement, his knee would bend so far back that it looked like his leg was going to snap in two.

The wheels were put in motion to correct this situation, and in the meantime Erik was limited in the amount of time he was allowed to practice. Instead, the physical therapy was stepped up to continue the strengthening of the left side of his body. At first Erik did not want to cooperate with us. He wanted to keep trying to walk, so we had to watch him closely to make sure that he didn't keep trying when he thought no one was watching. Eventually we had to explain why it was so important for him to be careful—if he continued to try and walk for longer periods than was felt to be safe, he would injure the knee and walking would be put off even longer. Only then did Erik allow himself to be controlled by the experts.

But as the days passed, Erik did achieve some success. The feeling on his left side started to show signs of returning. His left arm had feeling and mobility to the elbow, and his left leg had feeling and mobility to the knee; and feeling returned completely to his trunk, face and neck. Erik was more than halfway there.

He was able to talk effortlessly, with full control of his facial muscles. He reacted to a prick or a tickle on his left side, and his neck totally supported the motion of his head. But this was not the miracle. The miracle was in Erik's uplifted spirits and his smile, as he saw the accomplishments as confirmation that he would reach his goal to walk again.

At Dr. Boettrich's request, we took Erik to a bone specialist to discuss the problem with his knee. The bone specialist talked with us first and then asked Erik tried to walk for him. As Erik made his way across the room, the doctor watched closely and made notes during his progress.

Then we were shown to a room where Erik was asked to undress and he was given a thorough examination. Harold and I were asked questions as to his mobility prior to the surgery and our thoughts on what we considered his progress to be. We knew he had the opinions of the doctors already and appreciated being asked for our view. Then Erik was asked questions to which he responded.

Once the mental and physical examination was completed, the doctor invited us all back to his office where he gave us his medical opinion of Erik's condition and needs. As he determined, whether or not Erik regained control of his left side, he needed support for his leg or he would sustain further damage to the muscles and nerves. Erik needed a leg brace to help him walk. He described the type of apparatus that Erik would be required to wear. It was not to be a full leg brace, but should reach his mid-thigh, offering support at the knee and the upper calf to stop the leg from going back so far.

I listened to the doctor and agreed with what he was saying. He wrote up a prescription and handed it to me and that's when I realized I had no idea what I was to do at this point. I had to ask him what I was supposed to do with the prescription. At least I knew that I couldn't possibly have it filled at the drugstore, but beyond that I had no idea. The doctor explained that I had to take Erik to the Rochester Orthopedic Laboratory to have the brace designed to the specifications of the prescription. He assured me that his dealings with them had been more than satisfactory and, if we liked, he would be happy to call and arrange the appointment for us.

I wanted to accept, not knowing exactly what we would need to say or do, but I also wanted to gain more insight which meant I needed to handle this myself. I declined the offer and told the doctor that I would make the arrangements myself. Later as we prepared to leave the doctor asked that we schedule another appointment with him.

As soon as I arrived home from the bone specialist's I placed a call to the Rochester Orthopedic Lab to schedule an appointment. On the day of the appointment we met with the orthopedic specialist who would be designing the leg brace, and the technician responsible for producing the finished product. Again Erik was observed while walking, and we were asked various questions, even where we purchased Erik's shoes. "Altiers," I told them. The orthopedic specialist explained that Erik would require special shoes for his brace and that the shoe store I had mentioned would be able to order the type of orthopedic shoes he required. I was then advised that I would be given a prescription for the shoes and that they must be ordered as soon as possible, since the left shoe would be permanently attached to his brace.

After the consultation, we were taken to a room where measurements of Erik were taken and then Erik was asked to remove his pants and lay down on the examination table.

I was as baffled as my son seemed to be. We talked quietly until we were joined by a member of the staff who came in and introduced himself before explaining that he needed to make a cast of Erik's left leg.

He worked quickly, explaining as he went along exactly what he was doing. When he was done and the cast had set, it was removed from Erik's leg and we were told Erik could get dressed. Later in the office I was told to we would be called when the leg brace was ready. Erik complained that his leg was itching. I was given a lotion and told to first wash Erik's leg and then put the lotion on. This should relieve the itching.

In the orthopedic specialist's office we were told that the brace would be lightweight, with just one steel bar going up the back of Erik's leg. Attached to the top of this bar, just below the knee, a leather strap would support the knee. The base of the metal bar would be hooked into the heel of Erik's left shoe, and the heel of Erik's shoe would be built up in a lateral position; with the thickest part being the back of the heel where the brace would connect.

I tried to visualize the finished product but couldn't. It really didn't seem to matter, anyway. All that mattered was that it would help Erik walk. From the orthopedic lab I took Erik to Altiers to be fitted for the shoes. The order was written out and the salesman told us that it would be approximately four weeks before we could pick up the shoes. Erik and I then climbed into the car to start back home.

Erik was quiet, not saying anything the whole way home. I was quiet too, thinking about the time schedule given by the shoe store and hoping it would coincide with that of the orthopedic lab. Once inside our house I settled Erik down and finally made reference to how quiet he had been. "Erik, what's wrong," I asked. "You haven't said a word all day to me." Then, trying to make light of the matter, I said, "Well, that's not entirely true. You did say 'yes' and 'ahuh'. Oh yes, and you told the man at the orthopedic lab that you thought it (the brace) would be okay."

I waited patiently for Erik to respond. Watching him sitting there, I realized he had a problem with the brace—he wasn't happy about it at all. He didn't have to say anything, as I could read it on his face. Instead of waiting for him to speak, I began to let him know that the brace didn't sound too pleasant but it would help him to walk, and that was what he should concentrate on for the moment. I asked if he understood this and Erik nodded. I then said that I could understand him not wanting to wear it, or being a little frightened by it, but to remember that it was going to help him walk better and for longer periods of time without him tiring out.

I could see he understood all of this but was still a little hesitant, so I was thankful that it would take some time for the brace to be ready. Erik needed time to come to terms with it. Whether or not he wanted to wear it, he had to; and I didn't want to have to force the brace on him before he had time to adjust to the idea.

***

The weeks went by and Harold and I continued to encourage Erik to be more optimistic about the brace. We had him walk in front of a full-length mirror so he could see how his knee bent back and threw him off balance. We carefully pointed out how tired he got after walking around a bit, stressing how much easier the brace would make this for him: he wouldn't find his leg aching after he had been on it for a while and it would help him balance himself better as he walked. In other words, without specifically saying it, we kept the idea of the brace alive in his mind as something that he should look forward to.

I received a call from the shoe store notifying me that the shoes were ready to be picked up. Before leaving to collect them, I called the orthopedic lab to tell them that I would be dropping by later with the shoes. Once there, I was given an appointment date to bring Erik in for a fitting. That evening I told Harold we had only one more week to help Erik accept having to wear the leg brace.

So we increased our "pro brace" conversations so much that we seemed to be referring to the brace at every opportunity; as a result, the first appointment went quite well. Erik was shown the brace for the first time and was able to try it on. I tried to read the expression on his face but couldn't tell whether it was one of acceptance or rejection. He had never seen a brace up close before, let alone worn one. I continued to watch Erik as the orthopedic specialist checked the fit to see if they needed to make any adjustments. Finally he was satisfied with the brace and asked Erik to walk for him. Erik complied and the difference in his stride was immediately apparent. The support was excellent: it not only controlled the knee but also made his foot point straight ahead with each step.

Erik walked slowly, holding on to the walking bars as he proceeded; yet still his face was expressionless as he answered the questions asked of him. Erik was such a well-mannered child that I knew he would not say if he didn't like the brace, only if it hurt him or was uncomfortable.

Erik finally said, "It's okay." The brace was removed for some minor adjustments and then put back on again. Erik walked even better. I glanced at the shoes: they were not the type that a seven-year-old would get ecstatic over wearing, but they were really not that bad.

Once we were out of the orthopedic lab and settled in the car, I glanced over at my son before starting the engine. I sat quietly for a minute then said, "How does the brace feel, Erik? Is it comfortable?" Erik replied, "It's all right."

I started up the car and began the drive home, turning to Erik again on the way and saying, "It's not at all what I expected. It's so simply made. It probably won't be noticeable under your pants!" To this Erik responded, "Ahuh."

I continued to sneak glances over at my son as we drove home, wondering what he was thinking and was refusing to say even to me. I wondered if I should say more, or if I would be invading his privacy. Perhaps he needed to work out how to accept this foreign object on his own. When Erik finally opened up, he said, "Mom, this brace isn't that bad! It's not bad at all!"

Once home, Erik tried to get out of the car by himself. He was a little shaky as he felt the brace force him to walk correctly by offering the support he needed. He grabbed hold of the side of the car and used it to support himself while he tried to get used to the new feeling of walking. Then, with determination, he reached the end of the car's support and walked on his own toward the front door of our house.

I followed close by his side but restrained myself from reaching out for a hand to hold. He had to do this on his own. Step by step he went until reaching the door with a smile on his face. But he wasn't done yet. I unlocked the door and he proceeded to master the flight of stairs ahead of him. He took careful, precise steps, using the wall and handrail as he went. And then he paused before taking the last step, while I waited patiently behind him. I watched the leg go up and then it was over—we were home. While I fixed him something to eat in the kitchen, it was obvious how happy he was with himself just by looking at his face.

***

Every day Erik was up walking around the living room, using the wall, the chairs, and the coffee table for support. Determination was stamped on his face as he urged himself to go on until he finally needed to rest. He continued this strenuous routine until the day Harold and I returned home from work to find that he had a surprise for us. Pam, his sitter, didn't say anything except that we were to go into the living room, which Harold and I did willingly. Once there, Erik told us to sit down. We looked at our son, who was sitting in the middle of the living room floor waiting for us to carry out his instructions. And then, gradually, Erik got up from the floor. Slowly he took a step, and then another, and another. Without holding on to anything, he made his way across the living room floor. His stride was steady and his body didn't waver as he approached us with a smile of accomplishment on his dear face. He had done it: he had mastered the brace and was able to make it on his own once again.

It didn't matter that he'd missed his target—it was three weeks after his birthday—our son was walking again!

***

We were always being confronted with change: changes that had to be analyzed and decided upon before they could be accepted. I had never given much thought to change in my life before. Most changes are those that we have no control over and therefore must accept. These are the easy ones. Then there are changes that force you to make a decision. These changes can be frightening.

234

At the end of June, 1976, the tutor gave us a copy of her final report on Erik. She was happy to inform us that Erik would be able to progress to the second grade with the rest of his class. At the same time, the therapist concluded her home visits with Erik. She felt that Erik's recovery had reached a limit that was more than satisfactory. We were instructed to encourage Erik, as well as help him, to continue his PT exercises.

Though I felt I should have been happy with the two reports, I wasn't. I spoke to Harold about this and he also expressed some misgivings, yet he felt that the professionals must have known what they were doing. Why did I feel like this? There was time enough for me to find out why, so I decided to tuck the matter away in the interim.

Night after night, when all was quiet and the day's responsibilities had been taken care of, I would think about what I should do. I wanted to share the problem with Harold, but I was the one who had been closer to the center of all that Erik had been going through in therapy. I was the one who had relayed the information to Harold when he could not be with us. I was the one who had to understand and decide before bringing the matter up once again. And so I found myself awake most nights just thinking. It finally paid off and I was able to make my decision.

The first step was to take Erik in to see his pediatrician. I explained to her, once she had shared her report with me, what had been bothering me for some time. I told her that if Erik had regained the use of his arm and leg to the first joints, couldn't it be possible that further therapy may result in even better results.

Her answer was simple: this was definitely a possibility and if we continued with the PT exercises at home, just like we were told, we may see this happen. At this point, whether the exercises were done by the therapist or by us, any further improvement would be the same. We had been taught how to do the exercises and Erik knew what he should do. In conclusion, she agreed that a PT therapist was no longer required.

After thinking about what she said, I had to agree also. We did the exercises just as well as the therapist did; and though I had no doubt that we could continue to do them as well, I needed to have this second opinion.

With that matter resolved, I then went on to the second problem that had been bothering me. I told the pediatrician that I had been thinking seriously about holding Erik back in first grade, even though the tutor felt that he was ready for second grade. First grade was a very important phase of Erik's education and, though I had tried, I felt that the school environment could not be adequately captured in a home situation. I also felt that Erik's size, his young facial characteristics and his unique ability to "fit in" could work to his advantage both physically and mentally if held back in first grade. To stress the point further, I stated that Erik had attended class for a period of no more than 30 days, spread throughout the year. He had been tutored for less than four months. Any child missing this much school could not possibly have experienced all there is in first grade. I then waited to see what Dr. Boettrich had to say.

While I was talking, the pediatrician had been listening closely. She said that she agreed with me and would write a letter to the school saying that she also felt Erik should remain in first grade for another school year. With this settled, she then went on to say that I should check with the school about transportation for Erik. Because of his condition, he would now be unable to take the regular bus to school. This was news to me! I hadn't even thought about the school bus. She gave me as much information as she could about this so that I would be better prepared.

I contacted the school administration concerning Erik and finally a decision was made. Erik would repeat first grade, as the school felt that our reasons, along with those of his doctor, were justified. Children need the experience of working and learning together with their peers, and the extent of Erik's experience in this area was limited. Further, being so well-known in the school, they were aware of his ability to "fit in" with the next first grade class. It all boiled down to him being mentally capable of handling the scholastic atmosphere of second grade yet not physically prepared. There was the added plus that in dealing with the questions from his peers that inevitably arose, it would be beneficial for Erik to have a slight educational lead over his classmates.

Harold was initially against holding Erik back, but once he had considered the advantages he fully concurred and supported me in the decision. We were then informed that the arrangements would be handled by the school for Erik to be transported by what was called a BOCES bus. This school bus is equipped for children who have physical handicaps and provides safe mobility for the student. Once the matter was settled, Harold and I sat down and discussed it with Erik.

Erik didn't seem to mind being held back, but at first he didn't like the idea of having to take a different bus than his other classmates; but even this he soon accepted. Then he moved ahead to the more important things, such as whether he could have a new lunch box and if I would make him a lot of new clothes. To both points I said yes.

It turned out to be much easier than I anticipated. I had been worried about Erik's reaction to not moving on with his class, when in fact this was minor. Erik hadn't really been with the class that long and, anyway, his friends in second grade would still be his friends.

***

My thoughts turned to Erik's clothes. Because of his size it had already become impossible to find clothes for him. Things in the store that would fit him were made for a much younger child. Anything that was appropriate for a child of his age to wear started at a size that would take him many years to grow into. So, from the time he was two years old, I had begun sewing all of his clothes. I was getting real good at it, and though I found it hard to get started, by the time the first outfit was completed, I was enjoying it immensely.

I made him pants, jackets, vests, shirts and even t-shirts that were age appropriate and suitable in style. This time I decided to use special hooks on his pants for ease of opening with one hand; a hidden left leg zipper so that he could easily get out of his pants by himself; and maybe Velcro closures with fake buttons on his shirts and vests. I also had to make sure the left pant leg was larger than the right.

***

By this time the new handicapped law had been passed that would require Erik to attend special classes, which would disrupt the school routine as he knew it. It was agreed that instead of putting the change in place immediately, Erik would be evaluated and any special services required would be introduced without too much disruption.

As a result of careful planning and open conversations, the school year went better than expected. All concerned were satisfied with Erik's progress. The school successfully kept Erik in the mainstream of activity, and Erik was able to show his peers that he could perform quite capably at their level. Harold and I continued to offer him parental guidance, though of course the ordeal required a period of adjustment for everyone concerned. Most importantly of all, there had to be open communication and respect for Erik's concerns.

There were questions that we had to help Erik answer when an inquiring student asked why he was like he was. There was also some name calling that he had to respond to in a positive manner and we all learned that his appearance was changing and that he must learn to react in a different way than most children. He had to seek a level of acceptance first before walking away from a peer. But he made it. It was a challenge at times but he managed to find a way to overcome the hurt and seek understanding. He not only overcame his own personal handicaps, but also the handicaps of others as a result of their lack of understanding.

Erik demonstrated superiority and was a source of education for his peers. We also found that Erik was helping us to grow as he grew, while helping the school and the students to grow as well.

This was quite an accomplishment for a child who had just passed his eighth birthday.

CHAPTER 10
1977

The world was changing around us and most of the changes were good. For so long beyond the walls of the hospital and doctors offices, I felt like I was on an island that kept me apart from everyday people. Though so many were willing to help, it was not easy for them to find ways of offering support, but they did their best.

Keeping my ears open, reading the newspapers and questioning those in authority about what I considered a necessity keep me abreast of the latest development one of which was the Rehabilitation Act of 1973.

I began to really understand the value of Section 504 of the Rehabilitation Act of 1973, which states: "No otherwise qualified handicapped individual in the United States ... shall, solely by reason of ... handicap, be excluded from participation in, be denied the benefits of, or be subjected to discrimination under any program or activity receiving federal financial assistance". By handicapped the law means any person who has a physical or mental impairment which substantially limits his or her major life activities.

I read and researched the parts that I could not comprehend until I could almost cite them verbatim, all the time looking for the section that would help Erik. In total, the law protects the civil rights of individuals who are qualified to participate and have disabilities such as blindness or visual impairment; cerebral palsy; chronic illnesses such as arthritis, cancer, cardiac disease, diabetes, multiple sclerosis and muscular dystrophy; a psychiatric disorder; deafness or hearing impairment; drug or alcohol addiction (Section 504 covers former users and those in recovery programs and not currently using drugs or alcohol); epilepsy or seizure disorders; mental retardation; an orthopedic handicap; a specific learning disability; a speech disorder; and spinal cord or traumatic brain injury.

Now I knew that the law encompassed many, and wondered how many people, like me, had not really understood the extent of inclusion and the benefits available. When I thought of how many people there were out there with a child, grandchild, sibling, nephew or niece with a disability, who were as ignorant of this law as I was, I wanted to find a way to help.

From experience I new parents of these children were experiencing a range of emotions, including guilt, anger, frustration and helplessness, as they struggle to raise this child while also working to improve the child's chances of becoming an independent, self-sufficient member of society. The laws regarding services for such children are diverse and complicated. Making the public aware of the needs of disabled children, and encouraging them to adjust in order to accommodate those needs, I was sure, would make people want to become involved.

Having never been through the experience of having my child shut away from the environment that he would someday have to live in, I can sympathize with parents who have. Before, I felt cheated in a way, as I did not get the benefit of using the various handicapped facilities, since Erik did not fully qualify. I no longer felt that way, and I was glad other children with special needs would be part of the general school system, where they could all benefit together with their peers.

One service that does accommodate special needs children is the Rotary Sunshine Camp, run by the Rochester Rotary Club. The Rochester Rotary Sunshine Campus was established in 1922 to meet the needs of children with physical disabilities. This state-of-the-art facility is situated in a natural, wooded environment. The building projects a warm, residential look and feel while providing high-tech amenities including the Medical Clinic and Arts and Crafts Center. Interior highlights include exam rooms, clinical support spaces, children's work and quiet areas, nurses' sleeping quarters and a nurse/staff station. Over a two week period, the children experience summer camp with other children with physical disabilities; and for that week they can put the world behind them and get a chance to just be kids, enjoying different activities such as swimming, camping, sports, and socializing. The camp is staffed by doctors and nurses, and the children sleep in cabins that have live-in staff. No disability is seen as too severe to prevent children from being children, whether they visit during Rochester Rotary's summer camping program, known as Sunshine Camp, or at other times throughout the year. I saw this as a way of introducing Erik to the reality that there were other children who required special care, and as an opportunity for him to experience the joy of physically helping someone else. What better way to realize his own abilities.

The experience was one that Erik cherished and looked forward to, as he asked when it would be time for fun in the woods. He earned merit awards for swimming: something that I would have been a little hesitant about him doing, but he proved to be an excellent swimmer and enjoyed the water. But it was not all play—he learned responsibility, too. He had to take his turn on the work crew assigned to clean up the cabins, as well as learn how to make his bed and rise on his own each day.

Harold and I went through a period of adjustment with our son away for two whole weeks. He came home only on weekends, and parents were not allowed to contact the children during the week except by mail. Knowing that Erik would be exposed to a world of experiences that we wouldn't be able to offer made it easier to accept his absence.

We were surprised by the way Erik spoke of his fellow campers, some of whom we met during check-in. There were children in wheelchairs, without arms or legs, yet Erik didn't mention any of this when he described them to us. He seemed to be able to see only the child and not the handicap. While I must admit I hadn't reached that stage yet, I knew that this was the only way to realize full acceptance of not only individuals with special needs but anyone who appeared different to us.

***

Another wonderful thing also happened around this time. While Harold and I continued to play our part in Erik's PT exercises, it was Erik's efforts alone that really claimed the rewards. He would sit in front of the TV or in his room playing while working at his exercises over and over again. He had made the exercises such an integral part of his daily routine that sometimes I don't think he even realized he was doing them. Nine months after the surgery, Erik had regained the use of his arm muscles to the wrist and his leg muscles to the ankle.

At only eight years of age, Erik had already gone through so much. Yet, even when considering the paralysis after the last operation, no one who knew him considered him a victim. He continued to keep climbing up, always overcoming the impossible. Each time he slid down one step, he picked himself up once again and took another step forward. I wondered what power he possessed to make him so strong at such a young age. I wasn't that strong. He was definitely not a victim of a tragedy, but more like a beneficiary of a miracle.

We were having the time of our life with Erik. Outside of doctor visits, Erik was ours to love and care for. It was like it must feel for parents who adopt a child that they have come to love. You take the child home and the waiting process begins. You enjoy the child immensely but in the back of your mind you have a fear that this much happiness can't be so easy to obtain. Until the final adoption papers are signed, the court hearing is held, and you are legally, completely sure that no one can take the child away from you, you must suffer along with the enjoyment of being with the child. And even then when you are alone you will still fear that some unforeseen obstacle will surface to snatch the child away once again.

That was how I felt as I watched and spent time with Erik. I enjoyed my time with him immensely, but when he was put down for the night and sleeping peacefully in his bed, I found myself thinking, wondering and hoping that everything that had happened to tear him away from us was now finally over. As the months ticked by it became easier to believe that that chapter of our lives had closed, and so the defenses against hurt and sorrow slowly lowered until I felt I no longer needed them.

Allowing myself to get "comfortable" turned out to be a wrong move on my part. It made me less capable of being able to deal with even the smallest problems. But what did I know? In any case, when I mentioned to the bone specialist that Erik had been recently experiencing problems walking, I immediately assumed his brace to be the cause, and that it just needed an adjustment, or perhaps a new one was required. Not for a minute did I think that surgery would be needed to correct the problem.

The doctor examined Erik in the same way he did during each visit. Afterwards, Erik and I were summoned for a consultation in his office, where I was informed that Erik's Achilles tendon was tightening. I begged to differ with the doctor, telling him that Harold, Erik and I had been faithfully doing the PT exercises, which involved a number of manipulations designed to prevent this from occurring. I found myself searching around for other ways to correct this problem before finally resigning myself to accept the "professional" diagnosis. Erik required an operation to lengthen the tendon itself in order to enable him to place the foot flat on the ground. I watched as the doctor had Erik walk around, and I could see that he was right. With the shoe built up at the heel, Erik wasn't allowing the toe area to come in contact with the floor.

As if to compensate for taking my son away from me once more, the bone specialist said it would only be a minor operation, requiring Erik to only be in hospital for a few days. He would then need to wear a leg cast until the tendon had healed. But this didn't really matter to me. What mattered was that Erik was going to have to go into the hospital once again, and I was unable to stop that from happening. Again I was to become the bystander and not the provider.

245

On February 20 Erik was admitted into the hospital, with the surgery being performed on the 21st. On the 22nd he was discharged—cast and all. The cast covered his leg up to the knee, with his entire foot also encased, apart from an opening at his toes. Erik thought it was neat having a cast on his leg, and he made sure plenty of people signed their autograph on it. We also had to learn how to bathe him without getting the cast wet—this was no easy feat to master, but we eventually managed. Each day, Erik was pushed down the school halls to his class in a wheelchair surrounded by children who also thought the cast was neat.

On March 19, to Erik's dismay, the cast was removed. Having really enjoyed the experience, he wanted to keep the cast on. Though it wasn't obvious to me right away, I slowly realized that for him the cast was something that the children saw as 'normal', whereas the leg brace had a totally different meaning to him and his peers.

Once the cast had been removed, a new prescription was written for Erik's orthopedic shoe. The heel would now have to be wider, to encourage Erik to begin walking correctly. With his new shoes fitted, he began his period of adjustment and learned how to walk on his own once again.

***

I found myself looking at Erik more and more, noticing each bump, bruise and scar, and recalling the story behind them. The latest scar of his was a long incision on the back of his heel which would forever remain as a reminder of the surgery to lengthen his tendon. The hook-shaped scar on the left side of his head and the incision on the left side of his neck and chest were reminders of the shunt that he had implanted within him. Though most of the scars have somewhat faded, their memory remains vividly clear.

I took consolation in the thought that nothing could happen that we hadn't already experienced. Our family of three had covered the medical spectrum—there couldn't be anything new in store for us outside of measles, mumps or chicken pox. I was also positive that I had met my last new doctor. Erik had a pediatrician, an eye surgeon, a pediatric dentist, a bone specialist, and a neurosurgeon—what else could we need! Well, I was soon to find out.

In January of 1977 an allergy doctor was contacted, and in March Erik went for his first appointment. During one of Erik's visits to his pediatrician, Dr. Boettrich had felt that Erik was experiencing allergic reactions rather than just colds. As it turned out, Erik was found to be allergic to just about everything and had to take two allergy shots a week along with medication. I found the testing for allergy-related properties to be most disturbing. After the initial visit to obtain medical history and a checkup with the allergy doctor, Erik was scheduled for two sets of tests: the first being on April 1 and the second on April 15. The test used to determine what Erik was allergic to is called the intracutaneous test. The allergen is diluted and then injected into, but not through, the epidermis. It is similar to the scratch test method where there is a test site and a control site area. The allergen is injected into the test site area and only diluent is injected into the control site areas. After ten minutes, both sites are checked for a reaction. Areas of positive reactions will have a whelp and redness.

Erik's back was used as the testing ground, and each injection was circled until every inch of his back was covered. Once the results had been tabulated, Erik was found to be allergic to everything that walks, crawls or blows in the breeze. As a consequence, Erik was to receive injections of a special serum for desensitization. The theory of desensitization is that the more Erik was exposed to the allergen, the more he would be able to develop what is called a blocking antibody.

When Erik commenced having his two allergy shots per week, Harold and I started scouting the house to remove any properties that he was allergic to. Though of course we couldn't control the conditions outdoors, we did warn Erik to keep out of the grass as much as possible and to not stand under trees. During the visit with the allergy doctor we were warned that sinus problems may result from allergies. The doctor also pointed out that Erik, who does not have a nasal bridge, may require reconstructive surgery on his nose at a later date.

Like Scarlett O'Hara, my reaction was to say that I'd deal with it when I had to, but I was not going to subject myself to having to think about it now.

***

During the summer of 1977 we finally made the trip to Oklahoma so that Harold's family could be reunited with Erik. Shortly after we returned to Rochester, Erik went on his annual two-week summer camp. The rest of the summer we spent at home, going on weekend outings together.

I remember the day being quite warm and humid, with the sun shining brightly and the sky clear and blue. Erik, Harold and I had decided to visit the Buffalo zoo that weekend, if the pleasant weather continued, and we were all looking forward to the trip. The workday went by with the usual problems and I looked forward to being home with my family. As it was quite hot, we indulged in only a light supper that evening and turned on the air conditioner while relaxing in front of the television. I must have drifted off to sleep on the couch, because when I finally responded to Harold he told me that he had been trying to wake me for quite a while. He wanted to know if I wanted to watch a movie or a sitcom. I told him to turn on the movie and then went to the kitchen for a drink of water to revive me.

I remember my legs feeling like they were loaded with lead as I headed toward the kitchen. I must have called out, or Harold heard me fall. When I awoke I was lying on the kitchen floor, with a worried husband looking down at me. Beside him was Erik, wearing the exact same expression. I had passed out. Harold helped me upstairs and into bed. When he asked if he could do anything else, I told him I would be fine.

I lay back on my pillow and tried to relax, but my head was spinning and a strange numbness had taken over my arms and legs, spreading through my body as my heart beat faster and faster until I was unable to move. Telling myself to calm down, I desperately tried to clear my mind, and took deep breaths in the hope of calming my racing heart. After what seemed like an eternity, my heat began beating normally again and I was able to relax. I fell asleep, not hearing Harold when he came up to bed.

The next morning I felt no better. My heart was palpitating and my arms and legs were still numb, with a prickly sensation going through them. Harold decided to go down and fix breakfast and let me rest. He brought up a tray and sat on the side of the bed while I ate. He asked what we should do and, after thinking about it, I told him we should call Erik's neurosurgeon. Harold placed the call and was told to bring me to Dr. Cotanch's office. On the way there I remembered we were supposed to be going to the zoo that day—I had spoiled our plans, and the thought made me feel even worse.

Harold practically had to carry me into Dr. Cotanch's office and, after I had been examined, help me get dressed again. Later, in his office, Dr. Cotanch explained that after having examined me he could not find anything neurologically wrong with me. He suggested I see my MD and have a complete checkup.

All plans were cancelled. Once we were back home, I called Dr. Douglas, my medical doctor, and scheduled an appointment for the following week, allowing Dr. Cotanch to have time to forward the results of his tests. Until then there was nothing for me to do except lay around the house. Whether it was weakness or paralysis I was suffering from, I certainly felt paralyzed—and it was spreading. By the time I was due to see the doctor, I could no longer walk, so Harold had to carry me. Dr. Douglas asked if I had any neck pain, neck tenderness or palpation; any history of loss of consciousness; or any changes in mental state resulting from trauma, alcohol, drugs, etc.

After the checkup he informed me that my symptoms seemed to indicate a neck injury, but he was unable to locate any injury. He wondered if there could be any nerve damage, but Dr. Cotanch had already checked for this and found nothing.

Cautiously, knowing the extent of the problems faced with Erik's medical history, Dr. Douglas added that some disorders have a physical cause alone, while some disorders are purely mental in origin. Where the physical and the mental meet is the realm of what is called a psychosomatic disorder. In such a disorder a physical illness has an underlying (or subconscious) emotional dynamic that maintains the physical symptoms. This may have been the condition I was faced with, or at least it couldn't be ruled out.

I had to ask the obvious, and that was if I was going crazy! The answer was "no".

Dr. Douglas said he would let me know when the tests were back but in the meantime I should go home, try to relax, and call him if there was any change.

I continued to feel as though I was paralyzed, and was unable to get up and move around. When the doctor called and informed me the test results were negative, I had trouble believing it. If these results were negative then there must have been something else wrong. The doctor explained that I had been under a lot of pressure and that this may have been the basis of my problem.

I knew he was referring to hysterical paralysis, which is a psychosomatic numbness of the arms or legs. He was saying that it was all in my head. When I came right out and asked him, Dr. Douglas replied that psychosomatic refers to physical signs or symptoms that can be caused by psychological distress; so, in a sense, it could be considered real. I had a feeling he was trying to soften the blow.

I was told that though it may be hard, I was to rest and take it easy, as the symptoms would only intensify if I continued to worry; and again I was told to call if there was any change.

I followed the doctor's orders and took the next week off from work. I lay around each day watching television and not doing much else. Harold and Erik took good care of me, and by the following weekend I felt like my old self again. As previously planned, I decided that we should go to Marineland and Game Farm in Canada for the day. Having already been responsible for one weekend trip being rescheduled, I didn't want to be the cause of another, so I insisted that I felt fine; and I really did.

But on the way there, just outside Buffalo, the feeling of paralysis reoccurred. Harold took the exit off the expressway and we soon found ourselves in the Emergency department of a Buffalo hospital, where I was again subjected to tests and asked to supply the names of my regular doctors. We then had to wait for the final report, which basically repeated what my own doctors had already told me, though in different words—it was all in my head!

***

I felt like an idiot, even more than before, as we drove home again. There was now a consensus among three doctors that the problem was in my head; yet the symptoms continued for three more weeks. Then, miraculously, the numbness or paralysis was gone.

This was when I started writing. I wrote about everything that had happened. I pulled out all the information concerning Erik that I had accumulated in files, and wrote everything up in my own words. This was the only therapy that I could think of at the time to encourage me to face the pitfalls put before me. If I wrote it then I had to face it and facing it meant that eventually I was accepting what had happened on the outside as well as on the inside. You can't write and not think about what you are writing.

I began to see my condition of mental paralysis as a gift from God. It was time for me to not only accept what had happened but to also not shy away from dealing with any further developments. It was imperative that I accept that which I could not change, totally and truthfully, or else face the consequences. I vowed to do just that.

CHAPTER 11
1978

Christmas of 1978 was upon us and I was determined to enjoy every minute of the festivities. I was quickly learning how to sit back and wait for an expected outcome without experiencing anxiety, tension or frustration. I was also able to let go of my need for immediate gratification or answers. All that I had gone through had taught me something very useful—I could display tolerance, compassion, understanding and acceptance, which made me feel fulfilled no matter what came to be.

I had come to terms with the fact that personal experiences, recovery, and change were lifelong pursuits to be approached in realistic increments. Such an outlook would prevent any inevitable setbacks and reversals from becoming overpowering. It was with this new attitude that I took Erik to his allergy doctor on December 14.

As was often the case in Rochester, there were several inches of snow already on the ground and the cold was so intense no one had to be reminded to wear their winter clothing. I accomplished quite a bit of my Christmas shopping that morning before picking Erik up for the appointment, which I had set earlier as Erik had complained he was having trouble breathing through his nose. I watched him closely and was able to see he indeed wasn't breathing through his nose. I knew it could just be congestion, but wanted to be sure. With my new attitude I refused to contemplate a worst-case scenario. Once we were in the doctor's office, a nose culture was taken and the problem was deemed to be a result of Erik's allergies. The doctor explained that Erik had what is called a perennial rhinitis. Perennial rhinitis can be allergic in origin, but in some people the cause is not known. He pointed out the indentation on Erik's right nostril, then blocked the left nostril so that he was forced to breathe through the right one. I watched as Erik tried to breathe but couldn't. When the left nostril was released, Erik was able to breathe again.

The doctor explained that he would first prescribe medication to try and correct the problem. He gave me a prescription for Keflex, an antibiotic used to treat many different types of bacterial infection, such as bronchitis, tonsillitis, ear infections, skin infections and urinary tract infections. For a period of ten days Erik would have to take 250 mg of Keflex four times daily; he would then have to return to the allergy clinic on December 28, to see if the Keflex had indeed cleared up the infection. If not, further x-rays would be required. Therefore, the matter was closed for the time being.

***

Rochester was getting ready for Christmas, with an action-packed Christmas lights switch-on event at Midtown, where the windows of the Sibley building displayed mechanical Christmas scenes. There were elves gathering packages for Santa and Mrs. Santa banking Christmas cookies. There were children sitting around Christmas trees, opening their presents, and there was a scene of Santa and the elves in the workshop making the tools for all the girls and boys.

Inside the mall was a monorail, running above the heads of the shoppers with metal stairs leading up to the track that was always lined with passengers waiting to board. And the main attraction was Santa's village sitting atop a mountain of fake snow with a winding path leading from the floor to Santa who occupied a chair in front of the village.

As if all this was not enough, the stores inside the mall had their own Christmas displays to attract the attention of the shoppers.

Even at 9, Erik enjoyed going to Midtown plaza and seeing Santa Claus and we enjoyed going ourselves. The festive mood made you feel all warm and cozy inside and the little elves that took the children up to sit on Santa's lap, always asked for input from the parents to make the moment special for the children. If ever there was a winter wonderland to be enjoyed by all, it was Midtown Plaza during the Christmas Holiday.

Once the Christmas tree lights were turned on for the first time, there was still the clock to draw the attention of the crowd. The "Clock of Nations" delights the young-at-heart. The clock is the center of interest in the 7 1/2-acre downtown shopping and business complex, opening on the hour and half-hour to present marionettes dancing to the music of twelve nations. When the clock struck the hour, the door of the appropriate dome opens and figurines dance to the music of their country. We never left Midtown Mall without seeing at least one nation open its dome.

***

I worked on getting spiritually and emotionally ready for the holidays.

Evenings were spent addressing the Christmas cards. Erik was responsible for putting the cards into each envelope, while Harold affixed the stamps and sealed the backs. Once the cards were done, it was time for the three of us to go out and get a Christmas tree. We would scour the neighborhood for the Christmas tree sales of local Boy Scout troops until we found one to our liking. Erik enjoyed the tree search tradition as much as the visit to Midtown Plaza, so we took our time and extended his fun until we were so cold we had to get home. Then, though he knew the routine of waiting a day for the tree to rest before putting it up, he would beg us to start putting on the decorations, but we stuck to our guns.

I took Erik out to buy his gifts for his father and friends, and then Harold took Erik to purchase his gift for me. In between it all, I made the extensive purchases for the family members and for Erik and his father. Each one of us had been given a special location for putting their packages and the other family members were forewarned not to go there. The space assigned for each of our packages was also the private space for wrapping the gifts, so every now and them one of us would disappear, only to return to find someone else missing. It became like a game, with each of us vying to be the one to get all their packages wrapped and ready to go under the tree.

In between times we managed to decorate the tree and the house and make it glitter from room to room. There were garlands and bows, candles and miniature figures adorning every space available. Even the table was transformed by a Christmas tablecloth and centerpiece. And, of course, there was mistletoe at each doorway entrance. When all was ready it was time for the get-togethers with friends and neighbors for dinner, gift exchanging or cookie baking.

Christmas always means "a time of renewal" for me, as I get especially excited about the end of one year and the beginning of another. Though it had been a bittersweet year, I was still excited, since each new year holds promises. When the whole family gathered together that year, I was the Christmas dinner planner. I cooked the perfect turkey, baked dozens of Christmas cookies, stirred-up a delicious Christmas pudding, and designated food assignments to other family members, which would include my sister Barbara's traditional sweet potato pies and one of my sister Mary's famous Carrot cakes. We had all the ingredients to please the palate and the heart, and as we saw every one to the door we stopped and listened to the Christmas carolers who showed up on our doorstep.

***

The day that Erik was due to return to his allergy doctor turned out to be a trying one. First, to start us out right, we had run into a water pressure problem the day before: it took us three times longer than usual to bathe, and then the water ran out completely. We turned all the faucets on but nothing came out. Exhausted from the days of activity, we turned in earlier than usual that evening. At around 2:00 a.m. I woke up. Thinking I must have heard the alarm go off, I soon realized it was the sound of water running throughout the townhouse. We had left all of the faucets turned on!

I quickly ran about turning off faucets, slopping through the water which had overflowed from the sinks and spread out all over the floor. I yelled out for Harold to wake up and soon he joined to help me mop up the water with whatever we could find. When every towel was used and the mop had soaked up the last of the water, we were exhausted. We had the situation under control by the time Erik awoke and came down to find us sitting at the table. Thankfully the water had been confined to the kitchen and bathroom, and had not leaked onto any carpeted areas.

Time was flying and we needed to get ourselves moving so while Harold grabbed Erik and marched him upstairs to get dressed, I began preparing breakfast.

Somehow we managed to get out the door on time, bundled in our winter coats and boots. With the disaster safely over, we were able to laugh at ourselves—and we did, uncontrollably. Harold then headed off to work, while Erik and I were on our way to see the allergy doctor. We were early for the appointment so we stopped at a café for coffee and hot chocolate and then were on our way again.

Shortly after arriving we were ushered into an examination room, where we waited until the doctor poked in his head to tell us he had yet to receive the x-rays so was going to call down for them. When he returned, he again examined Erik. This time it was Erik's left nostril that was obstructed; and when the x-rays arrived they showed a remarkable level of mucosal thickening in the maxillary sinuses.

We were aware there had been no improvement in Erik's condition, as he was still having problems with his breathing.

257

This time we were given a prescription for Koteldrin, a stronger medication; but the doctor believed we would need to pay attention to more than just Erik's allergy if we were to help him. He therefore gave me the name of a nose, eye and throat surgeon that Erik should see.

Upon leaving the doctor's office we were told to make another appointment for Erik once he had been seen by the surgeon.

CHAPTER 12
1979

On February 13, 1979, I took Erik to see the ear, nose and throat surgeon, who reviewed the records sent over by Erik's allergy doctor concerning the treatments and the results. The surgeon had also contacted both Erik's pediatrician and Dr. Cotanch; and from these sources he had made a determination. Erik had what is medically termed a marked hypertrophy of the right inferior turbinate, meaning the turbinate had become enlarged. Turbinates, also called nasal conchae or turbinal bones, are thin, curled, leaf-like bones within the nose that serve to enlarge the surface area of the nasal cavity. Erik also had a depression of the nasal dorsum, which meant that the back part of his nose had sunk below its surroundings—the surgeon referred to this as a developmental phenomenon. Erik's obstruction was believed to be due to intermittent edema of the turbinates, which would account for the fact that the blockage alternated between the right and left nostril. Intermittent edema is the coming and going of the swelling of the turbinates. The shots and medication Erik had been on to eliminate his allergic reactions to animal danders, dust, kapok, June and Fall pollens, and numerous molds was to continue. If the medication didn't result in any further improvement, it might be necessary to actually remove parts of the inferior turbinates themselves.

On May 10, 1979, I took Erik back to the allergy doctor, who agreed with the surgeon's report. He then introduced us to the use of a steroid aerosol called Decadron turbinaire, and I was instructed to give Erik two sprays in each nostril twice a day for the next seven days. Erik was also to continue his bi-weekly hypo-sensitization shots, and his medication was changed to 8 mg of Teldrin twice a day.

This course of treatment was found to be ineffective, so as a last resort surgery was performed to relieve sinus blockage and increase the nasal airway. Erik was admitted as an inpatient at Strong Hospital, where the surgery was performed with scopes through the nose. It was scheduled at a time when I had recently undergone foot surgery, making it hard for me to get around, so I opted to spend the night at the hospital with Erik instead of trying to make it back and forth from home. Because the sinuses are fixed and the tissue operated on does not move, post-operative pain is usually minimal; but it was explained that the surgery was not without risks—injury to the eye and the lining of the brain could occur, but these structures could also be damaged if the sinus disease was left untreated. The removal of nasal polyps and the operation resulted in a marked improvement. However, the surgery only relieved the symptoms associated with the blocked sinus and did not improve the underlining allergy.

Later, to add to this, Erik underwent a surgical procedure to remove his adenoids. I had no idea what adenoids were, but they were described to me as a single clump of tissue in the back of the nose. The tonsils and the adenoids are mostly composed of lymphoid tissue, which is found throughout the gastrointestinal tract and on the base of the tongue. Tonsils and adenoids can become "dysfunctional" and are more of a liability than an asset. In Erik's case, removal of the adenoids was necessary because they were too big: they blocked the back of his nose and forced him to breath through his mouth. It was also likely that they played a role in Erik's chronic and recurring sinus infections, or rhinosinusitis.

For this surgery Erik would be given a general anesthetic, and with the assistance of a small mirror, adenoid tissue would be "shaved" from the back of the nose. The procedure took only 15 minutes to complete.

With the year barely underway, already we were rushing back and forth to doctors. But though the surgery might have seemed monumental to the average person, for us it was minor. These were minor operations performed to fix common ailments.

***

We purchased our first house after months of searching for just the right house and the right location. Moving day was November 20, 1979. It was in a wonderful neighborhood, just down the road from where we were then currently living and though it seemed quite large for just the three of us, it was what we wanted. The house was quite spacious, having six bedrooms, two bathrooms, a living room, a family room, a recreation room, an eat-in kitchen and a galley kitchen off the recreation room. Eventually we turned one bedroom into a dual purpose room for laundry and sewing, with one other bedroom claimed as an office.

***

The year of 1980 came and went with no major catastrophes— allowing us all time to rest and think. It was a wonderful year for all of us. Erik still went to school with the same children, only now he lived in the neighborhood of another group of his friends. For us, the difference between living in an apartment and a home meant that we now had the extra room for sleepovers and room for me to start a home business.

It was a wonderful time as we finally felt settled; but with that 'settled' existence came responsibility of a type we had not experienced before. I admit I like the lighter side of family life:

261

watching our son grow; watching television together with a bowl of popcorn between us. I like catching up with a sister or brother over the phone, to find out the latest family happenings. I like it when family life is good. Who would have known that finally achieving our dream to own a house would be the cause for problems.

I would often think back to the time when I had written a poem about the three of us, which I had given to Harold for our anniversary in 1975. The poem had been framed and hung on our wall, blessing our home and our life together. Now, each time I passed it, I tried to remember how I had felt and why I had written the poem.

There were conflicts, harsh words, and bitter feelings. There was little affection, and deep emotional alienation. There were seasons of confusion and unhappiness. Most of all there were arguments about money, or disputes over raising Erik.

I don't believe I was pessimistic about marriage. I believed in marriage and its eternal significance. I embraced its opportunities for happiness, love and fulfillment. But I knew it could be hard. And I often heard of disappointment turning into despair that could eventually lead to divorce.

We were changing, and these changes formed a wedge between Harold and me. Up until this point we hadn't had time to take a good look at our marriage, or even face the responsibilities beyond caring for our son. Now, as the year progressed, we learned that what we continued to have in common was Erik. Beyond that, we had lost something. For the first time, I began to notice that Harold drank quite a bit and quite often. With his schooling behind him and having a good job as an electrician, he now only had to work eight hours a day; only he wasn't at home that often.

I was sure I had changed too, but in order to solve whatever it was that had changed our marriage, we needed to sit down and talk. We tried a couple of times to discuss our marital problems, but it always ended up in a battle over money or the need for personal space—or something else that was not at the root of the problem. Eventually, to keep the peace, we pretended the problem didn't exist, since neither one of us wanted a divorce or believed that what had happened couldn't be fixed.

Besides, I had learned a long time ago that the kind of marital troubles that lead to divorce were indistinguishable from those that could be overcome. Many marriages of middling-quality end in divorce. Many marriages that experience serious problems survive and eventually prosper. Maybe in our case the trouble would right itself.

***

What is it about braces? Why were they made to immediately draw attention to the mouth. In March of 1979 Erik's dentist had mentioned that Erik would eventually need braces to correct his overbite, so it really didn't come as a surprise when in 1981, just before his twelfth birthday, Erik was fitted with braces.

Dr. King, his dentist, explained that the teeth could slowly be moved and shifted into the proper position by applying pressure in certain directions through the use of bands, wires and elastic placed on the teeth. He explained that the change would take place slowly and carefully over an extended period of time. When I asked how long, he said that shifting teeth back into a functional position can take months to years. But that wouldn't be the end of it, since once the braces were removed Erik would most likely need a retainer to hold the teeth in their new position until they were stable. So, my son's beautiful wide smile now had a flash of steel. Though it didn't discourage him from smiling as often as he used to, it did add a sizable amount of time to his bedtime and morning rituals.

Since the paralysis, and even after gaining some of the use of his left side, Erik had worked very hard at being self-sufficient, which meant that he took longer than most kids to get ready for bed or school each morning. Sometimes I would offer to help, but he wouldn't have it. He insisted he could manage on his own, and he did.

Braces collect food and dental plaque very easily, and if proper oral hygiene is neglected during orthodontic treatment, both tooth decay and periodontal disease can easily occur. So Erik had to keep the braces as well as his teeth clean. It took time but the whole process would eventually eliminate his overbite.

Erik experienced some initial discomfort from wearing the braces, but this soon passed. Though his specific need for braces could be traced back to his mouth-breathing and the medications for his seizure, Erik found that he wasn't alone. Most of the children in his class wore braces; so instead of making him feel different, the braces made him feel part of his group of peers.

***

During the latter part of 1982, Erik was able to stop wearing his glasses, as his eyes had been corrected. Around the same time, his braces were taken off; and before the middle of 1983, he no longer needed his retainer. He also no longer required allergy injections and, finding that he had outgrown his allergies, the oral medication was stopped as well. Then followed a slow weaning-off of his seizure medication, which he had stopped taking altogether by the time he was 15 years of age.

Life was good. We managed to deal with the normal problems associated with a child becoming a teenager. By now Erik's size and body proportions were quite obvious. He looked like a dwarf, I guess; or at least this was what I heard more often than not. He was handsome; his head was large, but not extremely or abnormally so. His hair was thick, covering the scar of surgery, and his facial features were in balance with that of most black children.

I loved him—I loved him just as he was, and with good reason. He was self-sufficient, had a wonderful personality and a good sense of humor. His clothes, made by me for so many years, now seemed better made than those in the store; plus they were an exact fit to his proportions.

There was so much good in him, and so many lessons to learn each day as he progressed and grew into a person whose friendship was valued by those who came to know him. What more could a parent ask for in their child?

At the age of fourteen Erik began working within the structure of mainstream classes. This was the first time that he began to show signs of needing extra assistance in his school studies. For me, agreeing with the process was now not enough. I needed to truly understand what mainstreaming was all about, so I began by serving as a member on the Education Placement Committee of the school system, and later on the Committee for the Handicapped, which required attendance at a special training session to learn more about the forms of disabilities. It was indeed the best way to learn and understand how the system would help my son.

During my term of four years I read reports of students in the mainstream class structure who experienced problems beyond the classroom. Two cases in particular stood out in my mind as being challenging, in that the child's appearance did not reveal the existence of any problem.

The first was dyslexia. Dyslexia is a learning disability that affects a person's ability to read; thus, a dyslexic learns at their own level and pace, and typically excels in one or more other areas. They tend to experience difficulties with concentration, perception, memory, verbal skills, abstract reasoning, hand-eye coordination, low self-esteem, poor grades, and underachievement. Often, people with dyslexia are considered to be lazy, rebellious, class clowns, unmotivated, misfits, or of low intelligence. These misconceptions fail to understand dyslexia's effect on the person's life, and can lead to rejection, isolation, feelings of inferiority, discouragement, and low self-esteem.

Right up there with dyslexia is Attention-Deficit/Hyperactivity Disorder (ADHD), which as the title implies, is characterized by inattention and hyperactivity-impulsivity. Generally, these characteristics occur together, but one may be present without the other. In most cases, inattention, or attention deficit, wasn't apparent until a child entered elementary school. Children with ADHD had difficulty paying attention to details and were easily distracted, were constantly fidgeting or squirming around when seated, and were frequently having to get up or walk around.

I found it difficult to distinguish children suffering these conditions from the rebellious individual or the child who just liked attention until I experienced what these children experienced in the training sessions. The three day session was held in Albany, New York. I can remember one demonstration in particular that helped us experience dyslexia. A mirror was placed between a piece of paper and my view of what the pen placed in my hand was to write. I could visually see the words on the paper that I was to copy. I wrote, or tried to write, but my pen moved in the opposite direction. The letters were in reverse of what my mind was instructing me to do on command. It was frustrating as I labored to try and perform the function correctly but couldn't. Afterwards we were informed that the feelings we had experienced in trying to perform a simple task such as writing was what the child with dyslexia experienced at all times.

***

By the time Erik was ready to enter his freshman year of high school, he was transferred into the regular classroom, with only a resource class carried over from the mainstreaming structure. A resource class is similar to a study hall, where the student receives assistance with homework or a review of anything taught in the class that they had difficulty understanding.

One other disability of Erik's that required him being given assistance had to do with his paralysis. Erik's left hand never regained full use, and this made it hard for him to write with his right hand while holding his paper still with his left. To compensate for the additional effort required for him to write, he was allowed extra time on testing. Otherwise, Erik was seeing success in the school environment.

In keeping with his effort to be treated as an equal by his peers and as an independent by his parents, Erik began to work during the summers. His first job was for the Marine Corps, where he performed clerical assistance to the officers stationed at the recruiting office. Here he had his first experience with holding down a job, and he performed it so well that when it was time for him to leave the Marine Corps personnel made him an Honorary Marine Corps member.

His next summer job was for the Rochester Institute of Technology, where he worked in the computer department, having successfully completed his computer course training in his sophomore year. Even using one hand, Erik was better on a computer than most children using both hands. From the time he was 10 years of age, we had a computer in the house. I purchased one of the first IBM personal computers for my home-based business and Erik used it when he needed to complete a written homework assignment. This hands-on practice, along with the dexterity developed in playing so many video games, gave him a head start with the technology. My home-based business provided computer assistance to other companies, and eventually it expanded to include computer program training at Bryant and Stratton business school. For Erik, it became a guiding light toward his future endeavors.

During the summer of Erik's junior year, he worked in the computer room of Eastman Kodak Company, and it was around this time that he decided to work towards attaining a degree in the computing field. While working during his high school years, Erik also managed to maintain a B average and continued to be well liked by his peers. He joined clubs, kept actively involved with classmates during and after school, and managed to squeeze in family time with us.

Since Erik was ten years of age we had had an in-ground pool that he and his friends swam in at every opportunity, and upon his graduation Erik had accumulated awards in swimming. Academically, Erik received a grade point average of 3.8 and was within the top percentile of his graduating class. At his school's awards ceremony he was honored for his physical fitness participation and accomplishments, and received the Bill Farrow Award for fitness excellence. To this was added his award as a Black Scholar by the Urban League of Rochester. This entitlement required the student to have maintained a B average throughout high school.

Erik was charming, witty and accomplished—according to any level of standards And because of his personality, he was able to take full advantage of the social offerings of our community and the school. He attended both his junior and senior dances, with a date, and was invited to many of the parties afterwards.

The highlight of our feelings of accomplishment came on that day when he walked across the stage with his class and received his high school diploma. Many of our friends and those of his classmates gave Erik a standing ovation because they knew how hard he had worked to reach that point in his life.

So many memories to cherish; so many experiences to recall over the years ahead. Our son had grown into a man who we could respect and love for the rest of our lives.

CHAPTER 13
1988

On June 26, 1988, Erik graduated from Rush-Henrietta High School, and he had two graduation gift requests. The first was a car. He had received his driver's license at seventeen and, with minor revisions made within the car, was a cautious and good driver. The second request was to go to California to visit his Aunt on his father's side. During spring recess, Erik had saved up his money to make his first trip to California to visit his Aunt Dot.

In the beginning of the month of June, many changes came into play. First, Harold, who had been a member of the electrical union local 86 since the later part of the 70s, found himself on the bench. When an offer for a job laying cable lines in New York City came his way, he took it, leaving right after Erik's graduation.

On June 26, 1988, Erik left for Mission Viejo, California, and at 4:00 a.m. the next day I received the call from Erik's Aunt in California, bringing the past back into full focus again.

***

Tests were being done to determine the cause of his seizures while Erik remained stabilized in the Intensive Care Unit. The first twenty-four hours were critical for Erik, and though I couldn't be there with him, I could provide my assistance through prayer and keeping the lines of communication open.

I felt sick: I couldn't eat or sleep, and when Dot wasn't calling me, I was calling her. It was our method of supporting each other through the trying period. We had learned early on to never think negatively if we wanted to keep ourselves in control. The unspoken rule became never to express negativity to family or friends who needed our assurance.

It is difficult to console someone close to you who is feeling hopeless despair, especially if you are also intimately involved. The physical, emotional and mental condition brought on by despair will eventually build into grief; and grief is our body's natural process for healing emotional injury. Grieving can be hard, and the lack of understanding makes it harder, but we have to allow ourselves to grieve.

I prayed during those first twenty-four hours. Erik was very sick and I was trying not to be sick with him as the hours ticked away. Harold had been reached and, unable to come home, kept calling for information; and I kept supplying it, trying to be positive, which became easier, as somewhere deep inside I was sure Erik would be all right.

In a neighborhood that you have become a part of, there are no secrets. Before long, Erik's friends started calling to find out if we had heard anything more. People were sending cards and letters to him in California, letting him know they were thinking of him. But from what I knew, he would not be able to read them. Erik was unconscious. I knew this, but I was also writing to him.

***

And then, on June 29, the situation changed. Erik regained consciousness, and word came that he was improving. Yet, still unable to identify what had caused this physical phenomenon, the doctors were cautious in reporting Erik to be out of danger. Seizures can be caused by many conditions, diseases, injuries, and other factors. Erik's medical history could have explained him having a seizure, but there could also have been other causes, such as abnormalities in the blood vessels of the brain, bleeding into the brain, a brain tumor, high blood pressure, or even a stroke. It could also have been an infection involving the brain, such as encephalitis, brain abscess, and bacterial meningitis. By the evening of the 29th, Erik was listed as in a satisfactory condition, and he was transferred to a regular hospital room when he began responding coherently to questions asked of him.

All signs pointed to Erik having had generalized convulsions, which was better known as the grand-mal seizure. In this type of seizure, the patient loses consciousness and usually collapses. The loss of consciousness is followed by a general stiffening of the body for 30 to 60 seconds, then by violent jerking for a further 30 to 60 seconds, after which the patient goes into a deep sleep.

As a result of the seizure, Erik suffered some memory loss, which was to be expected. The doctor explained that the memory process can be interfered with by epileptic seizures or an underlying disorder in the brain. Confusion often follows an episode and, during this foggy time, new memory traces are not being laid down in the brain. Tonic-clonic (grand mal) seizures, in which consciousness is lost, can interfere with normal brain processes and disrupt the registration phase of short-term memory. Sometimes longer-term memories, from the period prior to the seizure, are lost as well, as these memories may have not yet been fully integrated into the brain's memory system. If a seizure is very severe and prolonged, with the patient experiencing insufficient oxygen to the brain, this can cause secondary damage to their memory system. Dr. Peterson assured me that by taking the steps we did to contact emergency medical services right away, we had saved Erik's life .

Later, Dr. Cotanch informed me that a significant level of confusion following a brain trauma is so common that the primary medical inquiry is to establish if the patient is oriented. Not knowing the day, week, year, where they are or what happened might result in the patient asking searching questions. Trying to cope with this confusion is extremely frustrating and leads to more confusion. In Erik's case, Dr. Cotanch believed the memory loss to be temporary, but other impairments may surface later.

Erik suffered from fatigue, and staying alert and awake was difficult. All through that day, Erik continued to improve, until later in the afternoon I was able to talk with him on the phone. I could hear the exhaustion in his voice, but even that seemed to lift when he realized it was me. I asked if he would like me to come to California or if he wanted to come home. After a slight pause, he said, "No!" When I asked for an explanation, he told me that he was fine now and that I should stay home. He hadn't had a real visit with Dot, and that was why he came, so he would stay in California just like we had planned.

I missed Erik, and the feeling that whelmed in me was that my whole world was falling apart. I felt desperate, confused and isolated during the days prior to his recovery, and now felt that I should be with him to help or support him. I needed to see that he was safe; to touch him and let him know I would help him through it. I was bombarded by questions from friends and neighbors who also wanted to see him. At first I felt hurt by his decision to go on with his vacation. Erik didn't need me, I thought. Then I came to my senses and realized that it wasn't that he didn't want or need me: it was that he wanted to have his vacation.

After what Dot had been through and handled so masterly, I did not fight Erik on his decision. She wanted him with her for the month and she had more than earned the right.

***

There was no more that could be done for Erik. He was determined to be in good health and was ready to leave the hospital on June 30. Dr. Peterson gave Dot a prescription for 100 mg of Dilantin to prevent future seizures. He informed her that it would be important to keep an eye on Erik, and if she noticed any change, be it new or a worsening in his condition, to report to him immediately.

Dot did indeed watch Erik closely during the days that followed his release. She also made sure he took his medication. But most importantly, she was determined to change the course that his visit had initially taken.

To start out slow, Erik and Dot visited with family members in the California area. Dot took Erik home with her to Mission Viejo, a relaxed and scenic city, which they explored during his first week. When she felt he was ready, they began to enjoy the other sites that California had to offer. At each location, Dot provided a narrative to help her nephew see and remember their adventure.

They did the grand tour, leaving Mission Viejo and traveling out for a day to take in the places that Erik most wanted to visit. They began with Los Angeles, with its tall palm trees sweeping an azure sky, and saw the "Hollywood" sign gleaming huge and white against a hillside. They took in the Museum of Contemporary Art, the George C. Paige Museum, the Carol and Barry Kaye Museum of Miniatures, and the Wells Fargo History Museum. Then it was on to baseball at Dodger Stadium and checking out the Lakers basketball court at the LA Sports Arena. They finished their tour of Los Angeles with visits to the Los Angeles Zoo, Griffith Park, and its numerous sandy beaches

In Anaheim they stopped by Disney's California Adventure, and at Universal Studios Hollywood watched and listened to the cameras rolling. They enjoyed getting an inside look at the sets and uncovering the behind-the-scenes secrets of legendary films.

Knott's Berry Farm, located in Buena Park in Orange County, was also on the schedule. Here Dot and Erik strolled through the six themed areas: Ghost Town, Fiesta Village, The Boardwalk, Indian Trails, Wild Water Wilderness and Camp Snoopy, the official home of Snoopy and the Peanuts characters. They had time later to visit the Soak Water Park. Knott's Berry Farm is named after it creator, Walter Knott, who was also a farmer. As the story goes, sometime in 1920, Walter Knott was an unsuccessful farmer until he nursed several abandoned berry plants back to health. From that humble beginning, Knott's Berry Farm Theme park took shape.

Muscle Beach, which the city of Santa Monica essentially closed to bodybuilding and public expositions in 1959, still remained an attraction, with fitness areas, restrooms and a widened bike path. They squeezed in a trip to Malibu, which surpasses even Beverly Hills in the number of movie stars' homes located there. A drive up the Malibu coast, with its dramatic ocean views and rocky cliffs, proved a delightful experience.

Venice, which had been built to resemble the Italian city of the same name, was also a must-see. With its network of canals, a business district built in Venetian architectural style, and its two huge amusement piers, Venice has become one of the finest amusement resorts on the West coast. There are artists and street performers, and the funky atmosphere provides a carnival atmosphere all year round, with free admission.

In San Diego they explored the San Diego Zoo, which features the largest collection of animals in North America; SeaWorld, the world-famous home of Shamu; and Wild Animal Park, a showcase of animals in their natural environment. They visited the Presidio, site of the city's original Spanish settlement, and found time to explore the Japanese Friendship Garden, the Botanical Building and Lily Pond, and the rose and desert gardens

Days in between were spent in Mission Viejo, going to the pool or the weight room. Some evenings they would go for walks or talk with family members over the phone. By the time July 31st arrived, they had done almost everything that they had planned for their month together.

Each day I would call and leave a message letting Erik know I was thinking of him and was hoping he was having a wonderful time. Some evenings he would call me to talk, and let me know what they planned to do the following day. After the seizure, I had noticed that Erik's speech was slurred, and Dr. Peterson had mentioned he had bit his tongue and that might have something to do with it. I tended to agree, as his speech seemed to be clearer each time I spoke with him.

In our conversations I would forward messages from his friends and he would send one back. He also provided enough detail in his descriptions of the places he had been for me to almost be able to picture them. It was comforting to know that his memory was intact.

When I went to the airport to pick up my returning son on August 1, the same Erik I had seen on his way to California had come back home to me.

CHAPTER 14
THROUGH IT ALL

I read somewhere the following parable:

   In ancient times, a king had a boulder placed on a roadway. Then he hid himself and watched to see if anyone would remove the huge rock.

   Some of the king's wealthiest merchants and courtiers came by and simply walked around it. Many loudly blamed the king for not keeping the roads clear, but none did anything about getting the big stone out of the way.

   Then a peasant came along carrying a load of vegetables. On approaching the boulder, the peasant laid down his burden and tried to move the stone to the side of the road. After much pushing and straining, he finally succeeded.

   As the peasant picked up his load of vegetables, he noticed a purse lying in the road where the boulder had been. The purse contained many gold coins and a note from the king indicating that the gold was for the person who removed the boulder from the roadway.

   The peasant learned what many others never understand. Every obstacle presents an opportunity to improve one's condition.

   I look back over the years and this parable reminds me of Erik's strength and determination to not let anything stand in his way of his being who he wanted to be. Though the opportunity was there, Erik did not seek assistance from Harold or me; instead, more often than not, he provided the strength we needed to go on.

My son is the apple of my eye and has been so since the day of his birth. He has always been the focus of my life and at the center of my heart. I think with love of when he was young: how he first walked, then ran, and then there was no stopping him. Each new day brings back fond memories of all that he has been.

Then came time for school, making friends, having fun, studying, working and playing. There were hard times, but these only served to make him stronger and capable of outstanding kindness, love for his family and friends, consideration to all those around him, compassion for those who needed it—all the parts of his personality that I now admire. Erik developed strength and self-confidence early in his life, and now that he is a man I can only wonder at his accomplishments and how he became such an admirable human being.

Erik's mental development has been on a normal level and his disabilities have always been placed second to his desire of accomplishment. Even in relatively slight matters, if he wanted to achieve something he would find a way. I remember when he first learned how to sit up. This happened simultaneously with his first attempt to crawl. Because of the shortness of his arms and legs, Erik was unable to get into a crawling position from a sitting position without some thought. He had one thing going in his favor and that was his flexibility. He learned that by leaning forward and placing his hands between his legs, he could swing his legs back and around and thus master the feat. And though he crawled using his hands and feet instead of his hands and knees, he could go as fast as any other first crawler.

Then there came the time when he asked me how to hold a pencil. I showed him and watched carefully as he tried. He was unable to write holding the pencil the way I had shown him, because of his fingers being short and thick, so he continued to manipulate the pencil on his own until he was finally able to make the pencil work for him. As I watched the entire process, it was then that I realized the extent of concentration and effort involved for him to change a standard method of doing a task in order to tailor it for his individual needs. It was not easy.

Today, Erik still has that smile that can brighten a room and draw all the attention to him in a positive manner. He has never lost his determination to succeed, though there were many times when I would have understood him backing down. These days, I find myself wondering more what it is that keeps him going. What could it be that makes Erik be Erik?. All I can say is that if he does fail when attempting a new feat, he will not give up. He is too determined to "win" to give up. It doesn't really matter what it is that guides him through life, I am only glad for its existence. Determination is a wonderful trait and I hope it always stays with him.

***

Throughout the years, Erik remained our only child, and amazingly, considering all the extra attention he was given, he was unspoiled. He gets along with his peers, adults and young children even today. He has learned from everyone he has been in contact with and they have learned from him. I have found that the experience of having an increased responsibility in the care of Erik has made me more aware and appreciative of children in general. I have come to realize that the development of our children is something often overlooked, taken as "matter of fact" and not put in its proper prospective. There is so much that is just expected of our children. We expect them to learn instinctively how to sit, crawl, walk and finally to run. We expect them to gibber, form words and then master the sentences of speech. Yet, as a parent of a "special" child, I could not expect this as a matter of course. I learned how to marvel at it all.

***

In August of 1988 Erik began the "college" experience, attending Monroe Community College, where he focused his studies on Computer Science.

Parents who are raising a child with any sort of handicap—whether physical, mental, or emotional—know how hard it is to find the many services the child will require, including the right kind of educational and vocational training. The problems both the children and their parents will have to face, as well as the financial costs involved in rising a "special" child, will be a constant part of the process.

Then there are the legal rights to consider. But regardless of whether you are successful or not, it will indeed be a learning experience and an experience that will help you to develop in the best of ways. And there will always be times when you say, "I wish that my whole life could be lived in moments with no thought of future or past". But the realization will surface that you can do this and you will succeed. Today, more so than when I first began writing this book, there are resources open for you to find what you need to know on any subject. The Internet has more information than one person can digest and it can be easily obtained through the many search engines by entering a sentence, a phrase or just a word.

There is something that should be said, whether or not it makes up for the troubled times, the anxiety or even for the things that will be missed—there will always be time. There will be time to revel without worry, there will time when we find out something that had remained unanswered, and there will be time to continue to grow in all facets of our existence.

I have often heard people who have escaped death say that they are changed by the experience. Well, I am changed, Erik is changed, and Harold is changed. I have learned that pain, near-madness and the threat of the death of someone you love can be endured and can be overcome. Because of this fact I am positive that we have a rosy future in store for us; because look what we've already been through.

CHAPTER 15
FINAL CHAPTER

Harold was a hard-working electrician and I am a proud and dedicated home-based computer business operator. But first and foremost we are proud and dedicated parents, who have raised our baby boy into adolescence, through the teenage years and on to manhood..

Everyone saw Harold and I as a strange match when we were first married, but it was something we didn't realize ourselves until later, when we started running into problems in our relationship—problems that we just couldn't seem to overcome.

Like any couple, we had arguments about small things—and those arguments frequently exploded into major confrontations that left our heads throbbing with anger, without either of us knowing how (or why) it had happened.

We both kept pushing each other emotionally, stubbornly insisting that the other was wrong and that they needed to wake up and smell the coffee and make some changes.

What's worse is that along with whatever it was we happened to be fighting about at the time, we would also dig up old issues from the past just to try to make the other person feel bad (whether they realized it or not).

I was constantly upset, and felt isolated and alone because Harold wouldn't spend enough time with me or do family things together anymore. He just didn't seem to pay attention to my needs.

The problem got to the point where both Harold and I quietly realized that our marriage had become a train wreck waiting to happen ... that divorce was becoming more likely each day ... that all those years we'd been together had come to an end. In November of 1989, Harold and I were divorced.

When you make the decision to divorce, you hope that it will lead to a better life for you and your children. But during the actual process of divorce, your children are not likely to see it that way. They often feel upset, worried, angry and sad.

Though Erik had begun his steps away from us, looking to peers and other role models as he worked to construct new identities, the divorce changed his life too. Almost paradoxically, even as he was exploring away from us, he relied on us as a stable point of reference and support. The family was someplace to fall back to, temporarily, when things in the bigger world became too frightening. Divorce changed that for him and it manifested itself in his grades dropping.

Erik expressed a need to understand, so I tried to explain things in such a way that he would know he was in no way responsible for the separation of his parents. Later, I wished I had offered him a chance to talk with a professional—a doctor, psychologist, or social worker—even though he claimed he understood. When I learned how hard the separation had been on Erik, I felt it would have been easier on him if he had had an opportunity to feel supported and heard, even though he was twenty years old.

But Erik has a level head, so he managed to overcome the disappointment of not seeing his parents united for life, though the progress in his education slowed during this period of time and he seemed to be searching. At times, he also seemed lost, until finally he appeared to have let go of the pain. He told me that he had rationalized it by thinking that he would still have two parents and could still visit them both, only he would see them separately from now on.

From that point Erik began to concentrate on his future and his studies until he found what he wanted to do. He realized his dream was to be a computer-aided drafting architect. So he continued to build on his training in computer sciences by learning the latest drafting software packages and architectural design principles.

After completing two years at Monroe Community College, Erik moved to California, where he lived with his Aunt Dot and took AutoCAD classes. This also allowed him time to be with his father, who had moved to California after our divorce.

One thing I had not realized until friends and family mentioned it was that Erik had always tried to give Harold and I equal time. If he went to the grocery store with me, then he would spend the equal amount of time with his dad. At first I thought they were crazy, but it became clear when, after two years of college, he said he wanted to go to California for two years. When I asked him to explain this, he said that he owed his father two years too.

What a son we had raised. It was then that I sat him down and told him that his life was his own and he deserved to live it as he wanted and not for his parents.

***

It was in 1992, while on assignment at Kodak, that I met my husband Mark; and in July of 1995 we were married. Even though Mark would play the role of a stepfather, it would be to a twenty-six year old, and not a child. Because Erik was self-sufficient and living in California with his Aunt Dorothy, there was no obvious tension, only congratulations and well wishes from Erik when we informed him of the marriage.

From their first meeting I was confident that Mark and Erik would get along, and they seemed to cement a positive relationship, with no conflict in their personalities or their strengths and weaknesses. Mark's reaction to Erik was similar to that of his friends, who never seemed to make Erik's size or disability a problem; instead they related to Erik as they would any other person. Also like Erik's friends and family, Mark never once asked about Erik's disabilities, and when later he mentioned my son, it was that he seemed nice and he liked him.

It was Thanksgiving Day, November 2000, when I first met Heather. Erik had talked about her during phone conversations but I had yet to meet her. He had sent a picture but I knew I needed to find out more, as I understood that the relationship had already moved to the next level—they were engaged. In our everyday life, things such as love, anger, fear, dependence or similar interests frequently link us powerfully with another person. I have observed that when couples are in love they often start saying exactly what is on their partner's mind. This suggests they may be sharing a unity or togetherness at some level of their consciousness. Love links us with another person, and maybe even allows a blending of minds, because we want to experience that. This is what I wanted to witness between my son and his fiancé.

Erik arrived in Rochester to spend Thanksgiving with the family only a couple of hours ahead of his fiancé, Heather, who was flying in from Oklahoma. That gave us only a small window to get him back to the house to drop off his things then head back to the airport to meet her plane. To Erik this meant we would have to hurry, but to me it meant the amount of time I would have to wean out more details about Heather.

Even though it had been a year since I had last seen him, Erik looked the same. All 3 ½ feet of him hadn't changed a bit, well, except for the extra facial hair he was growing, but beyond that he was still the same. We had talked on the phone so I was pretty much up with what he had been doing, his interests and his despairs, so now there was only one topic that attracted my interest.

I can't say that I ever doubted he had picked the right person for himself. Erik was a level-headed thirty-two year old who had been on his own on several occasions. He had long since learned the value of a dollar; that hard work and determination was at the base of every success story: and that marriage was not to be taken lightly. He was also not the type of man who played around—even though he was a dwarf, he was attractive and had the personality to draw women to his side.

The issue here was only that I loved my son and wanted to love my future daughter-in-law. We had talked about their relationship, but now it came down to his outlook on marriage. I needed to hear his reasons for wanting to marry Heather, and what he wanted for their life together. I wanted to know how her family viewed the union and what Heather herself had expressed as her reasons for accepting his proposal.

So we talked as we unpacked his suitcase. We talked some more as we drove back to the airport. As I listened and watched, my heart became settled, at least from his side of the relationship. Each time he talked of her his face lit up as the words tumbled out, because there was so much he considered special about Heather. For Erik there was no doubt—Heather was his destiny. Now all I needed was to meet Heather and to see if she felt the same way.

The traffic was heavy as we made our way back to the Rochester Airport, so we arrived later than anticipated. We had hoped to meet Heather at the arrivals gate, but we were sure her plane would have already landed and that the passengers were most likely heading toward baggage claim. That was fine, too, since Erik had already assured Heather to meet us there if we weren't at the gate.

I was indeed surprised, but quite happy, when Erik suggested that it would be much easier if he sat in the car, so that we didn't have to go to the parking lot, while I went in to get Heather. Funny, I had no doubt I would know her; not because she was a dwarf but because I had seen the picture of her that Erik carried with him, and from his description of her.

***

She stood there looking around, unaware of my eyes upon her as she tried to find a familiar face in the crowd. I would guess her to be approximately the same height as Erik. Her hair was long and blonde,

285

her face round, and her figure quite full. She had an expressive face that just then showed a little anxiety as she continued to look about her until her eyes finally located me. Then, at that instance, as I stood there looking in her direction, she smiled; and that smile told me everything I needed to know.

I identify with facial expressions. I see a smile as the most universal expression of friendliness and approval, but it needs to be analyzed. People smile with a "social smile", which is a way of acknowledging others even if we do not feel warm to them. It's a smile of politeness; but a "true" smile, with heightened eyebrows, reflects genuine joy or fondness. Genuine smiles are generated by the unconscious brain, so are automatic. When people feel pleasure, signals pass through the part of the brain that processes emotion. As well as making the mouth muscles move, along with the muscles that raise the cheeks, there are signals that make the eyes crease up and the eyebrows dip slightly. Heather's smile was a true smile.

I approached her as she walked in my direction, our eyes fixated on each other, looking for approval. Then we were in front of each other, and without hesitation I leaned down and hugged her and felt her arms as they hugged back. She had passed the initial test with flying colors. Later, in the car as we drove back to my house, I could hear her and Erik talking and exchanging glances in the back seat and I knew the feelings were mutual between the two of them.

Love is the world's most powerful emotion, leading to the creation of fabulous works of art such as Rodin's *The Kiss*, inspiring poetry by poets such as Elizabeth Barrett-Browning, and moving lyrics by singers such as Diana Ross. When you first fall in love, the very thought of your partner makes your heart beat speed up. And just being near him or her is almost electric. Sadly, these feelings don't last forever, but it can get better. It was examples of compatibility between Erik and Heather that I was searching for. I wanted the lasting love for Erik.

As I watched Erik and Heather in the rearview mirror, it was as though I was alone in the car. Having been separated for some time, they were absorbed in their conversation. I liked the coziness of their relationship; they seemed to give of each other, and each one expressed a strength, joy and vitality about them.

Thanksgiving was indeed just that as I saw Heather for who she was and how much she meant to my son. I witnessed the ease with which she slipped into our family fold, and it made me very happy. When you love someone, you value that person highly—so highly that you have made a choice to offer your resources to nurture them. You have also chosen to place their well-being and development as your highest priority. This is what I came to know about my son's relationship with Heather.

By the time they left, I had witnessed several close moments between them and knew that my son had found the person that would make him happy. I felt that Heather and Erik were soul mates.

On May 25, 2001, when my son Erik was married to Heather Goodban, I felt as though the connection of these two individuals had been destined since their birth. I believe that there is a special bond between a child and his mother and that this bond provides an insight that cannot be explained. I believe that this bond is what reveals the inner soul of anyone connected to him, and is at the base of understanding his choices in life.

***

As I sit here finalizing this story, it is indeed amazing to realize all the advancements in medicine that were responsible for my child being able to grow into adulthood and experience the joy of expanding his horizons in all walks of his life. I know now that his birth introduced medical phenomena that were not yet fully understood, and that at any time he could have been taken away from me; but he was saved. I can't believe that it was just for me, but I can believe that he is destined to prove to the world that he has so much to offer to life and that it is worth being party to. All I can say is watch out world—Erik is here and he will be your equal!

ABOUT THE AUTHOR

Juanita Tischendorf was born in Philadelphia, spent her adolescence in New Jersey and graduated from Fulton High School in upstate New York. After graduation she pursued secretarial studies at Rochester (NY) Business Institute. Computers eventually attracted her interest, and she became qualified as an instructor, writing books and supporting computer systems. But there was another interest, first a whim and then a passion: serious writing.

Beyond computer books, Juanita has written several works of fiction and self-help books which are targeted for market. Meanwhile a writing course at the University of Washington, and membership in the Writers Guild of America, fueled her self-confidence and prompted completion of the first manuscript she had ever begun: "Who Says I'm Small".

Achievements and awards for Juanita include a career profile by Rochester's "About Time" Magazine, and an interview for "Successful Women in Upstate New York" by Syracuse cable TV. More recently came an interview for the "Shades of Gray" program on WOKR-TV in Rochester, and a 2003 Editor's Choice award for outstanding achievement in poetry. She is listed in the 1991 edition of "2000 Notable American Women".

Today Juanita runs a home-based computer business in Rochester, NY, where she lives with her husband, Mark.

Printed in the United States
31345LVS00004B/1-48

9 781420 828894